THE SECURITY GAMBLE

Maryland Studies in Public Philosophy

Series Editor: The Director of
The Center for Philosophy and Public Policy
University of Maryland, College Park

THE SECURITY GAMBLE

Deterrence Dilemmas
in the Nuclear Age

Edited by

Douglas MacLean

ROWMAN & ALLANHELD
PUBLISHERS

ROWMAN & ALLANHELD

Published in the United States of America in 1984
by Rowman & Allanheld, Publishers
(A division of Littlefield, Adams & Company)
81 Adams Drive, Totowa, New Jersey 07512

Library of Congress Cataloging in Publication Data
Main entry under title:

The Security gamble.

Includes index.
1. Deterrence (Strategy)–Addresses, essays,
lectures. 2. Atomic weapons–Addresses, essays,
lectures. 3. Military policy–Addresses, essays,
lectures. I. MacLean, Douglas, 1947-   .
U162.6.S33 1984   355'.0217   84-15080
ISBN 0-8476-7329-4
ISBN 0-8476-7337-5 (pbk.)

84 85 86 / 10 9 8 7 6 5 4 3 2 1

Printed in the United States of America

CONTENTS

PREFACE

The Center for Philosophy and Public Policy was established in 1976 at the University of Maryland in College Park to conduct research into the values and concepts that underlie public policy. Most other research into public policy is empirical: it assesses costs, describes constituencies, and makes predictions. The Center's research is conceptual and normative. It investigates the structure of arguments and the nature of values relevant to the formation, justification, and criticism of public policy. The results of its research are disseminated through workshops, conferences, teaching materials, the Center's newsletter, books published in the Maryland Studies in Public Philosophy series, and other publications.

The chapters published in this book grew out of papers and responses originally prepared for a conference on nuclear deterrence held at the University of Maryland, April 7–9, 1983. This project was supported with grants from the Rockefeller Foundation and from the Maryland Humanities Council. The views expressed by the authors are, of course, their own and not necessarily those of the foundations supporting this project, the Center, or the institutions or agencies for which the authors work.

For the successful management of the conference special credit should go to Rachel Sailer and Lorrine Owen. The preparation of this book owes much to the generous efforts of Carroll Linkins and Claudia Mills.

DM

INTRODUCTION

Deterrence, from the Latin *deterrere* (to frighten from), is a common strategy of human behavior. We have devised many methods for preventing people from doing what we would prefer they did not do, from shaking a finger at children to warn them of the possible spanking to come, to announcing that cars parked in certain places will be towed away at their owner's expense. In interdependent choice contexts – situations where outcomes are determined by the decisions of more than one agent – conflicts of interest will prompt actors to try to influence one another's decisions with promises, threats, bargains, and bluffs about what each will or will not do.

In the confrontation of nuclear superpowers, each is capable of totally destroying the other. This situation is, in some ways, a paradigm of deterrence; but because of the nature of nuclear weapons, it is also entirely unique and perhaps paradoxical. The theory of nuclear deterrence – how possessing nuclear weapons can deter both their use and other sorts of aggression – was fully developed some decades ago near the beginning of the nuclear age, at least in its basic principles. The technological developments and changes in strategic balance since then have not led to changes in deterrence theory. But the fact that the ideas remain the same over time has not led experts to a consensus about what weapons or policies will maximize our security; nor has it produced a general public understanding and acceptance of deterrence.

This impasse may be due in part to the great uncertainties surrounding forecasts and predictions about how nuclear weapons might be used and the effects of using them. It may also be due to the difficulties of translating theory into practice, of incorporating nuclear weapons into security policies and military strategy.

Secretary of Defense Caspar Weinberger, responding to the recent resurgence of public concern about nuclear weapons, tried to address these issues. "The policy of deterrence is difficult for some to grasp," he said, "because it is based on a paradox. But this is quite simple: to make the cost of

---

Unless otherwise indicated all references and quotations are from chapters in this book.

nuclear war much higher than any possible benefit."[1] Two things are puzzling about this statement. The first concerns the link between the essence of deterrence, so succinctly stated here, and deterrence policies, which include the likely development of MX missiles in the United States, cruise missiles in Europe, and the possible development of antimissile defense systems in outer space. These developments cost billions of dollars, and they are provoking debates about whether they add to or detract from our security or whether they stabilize or fuel an arms race. These new weapons are being proposed, moreover, as additions to an arsenal of thousands of missiles and warheads. Many people think we already have the means to guarantee that no nation can benefit from launching a nuclear attack against the United States; they wonder whether deterrence must involve more than this or whether our nuclear arms policies involve more than deterrence.

The second puzzle in Weinberger's remark is that his description of deterrence leaves its paradox a mystery. Our policy is to deter nuclear war by guaranteeing that the cost will be higher than any possible benefit. But a nuclear attack is different from a spanking or a whopping parking fine; it is a different *kind* of response, and not just different in degree of suffering. A nuclear strike, even a retaliatory nuclear strike, will surely – perhaps intentionally – kill many innocent people, and a full-scale nuclear attack or response against the Soviet Union would most likely result, in the end, in as great a destruction of our own country as of our adversary. Whether we consider our deterrence intentions from the point of view of morality, then, or even in terms of narrow self-interest, they are bound to be problematic. If we believe it is moral or rational to have a deterrence policy, this means we believe it is moral or rational to be prepared conditionally to act in ways that seem to be immoral or irrational. This makes nuclear deterrence different from most situations where we can discourage unwanted actions by making the costs greater than the benefits. What matters here is *how* we discourage such actions.

Beginning with the first puzzle, what is the connection between the nature or theory of deterrence and deterrence policies, which include strategies for procuring, developing, and deploying nuclear weapons? Many policies, including a never-ending arms race, make the costs of nuclear war much higher than any possible benefit; but not all of these policies automatically make the world safer. Some policies, in fact, could make a nuclear war both more costly and more likely, by destabilizing the balance of terror. McGeorge Bundy explains why more and deadlier weapons can fuel an arms race that makes us less, not more, secure. Each new development by either side, he claims, increases the other side's fears more than it adds to one's own sense of security. This is true even of weapons that are supposed to be deployed for defensive purposes or to shore up some strategic gap. Bundy thinks that what *could* be done by the other side has a much greater impact on future decisions than any calculations or declarations about what *will* be done. Deterrence policies are fraught with uncertainties about what will be done, especially if deterrence fails, and these uncertainties undermine strategic planning.

Bundy stresses the importance of uncertainty and fear in the nuclear age. They lead him to an understanding of how deterrence works that is different from Weinberger's. Uncertainty becomes the basis for what Bundy calls existential deterrence, which works because neither side can ever know what would happen if either one of them detonated a nuclear weapon. No stated intentions, no commitments or agreements, can be relied upon to predict the consequences and probabilities of actions after the first attack. This uncertainty, according to Bundy, is the strongest deterrent force working. It had an effect in the Cuban missile crisis, and it has strong effects in international politics today.

Existential deterrence has several implications for deterrence policies. One is that procurement decisions based on calculations of what would be needed to fight a nuclear war are pointless and wasteful. Uncertainty exists today and is likely to continue to exist and to deter through any new developments, unless the survivability of one side's arsenal was truly threatened. Uncertainty also conditions debates about parity between the superpowers. Since nuclear weapons are unique in that "they are more terrifying to adversaries than they are comforting to their possessors" (the fear principle), rough equivalence and survivability are all either side needs. Bundy thinks further that uncertainty and fear work together to limit the possibilities of nuclear blackmail. Since both sides share a healthy fear of the uncertain consequences of using nuclear weapons, and since they know they each share this fear, "threats to do something rash become unpersuasive: they simply lack credibility." This deters the superpowers not only from attacking each other but also from threatening nonnuclear states, such as Sweden, Austria, and Japan.

So uncertainty and fear, the components of existential nuclear deterrence, are a healthy sign of strength. But Bundy acknowledges that uncertainty and fear are both potentially dangerous, too, especially if the survivability of either side's forces becomes threatened or one side begins to doubt that the other side wants to avoid nuclear war. To avoid possible disastrous consequences, deterrence policies should also pursue "reassurance of friends and detente with adversaries." These measures could further reduce the risk of war and they are absolutely necessary, according to Bundy, to any hope of stopping an arms race that is fueled by unchecked fear.

If existential deterrence is indeed the bedrock reality of the nuclear condition, as Bundy maintains, then we must ask why it is not more prominently reflected in policies involving nuclear weapons. Why does uncertainty give way to strategic calculations and force comparisons, and why is the healthy fear of nuclear war so often overshadowed by discussions of how it might be fought and won and which new weapons will help to win it? An historical answer is suggested here in the chapters by Herken and Quester.

Nuclear strategy has been dominated by two competing strands of thought. One, following Bernard Brodie, emphasizes the awesome destructive power of the atomic bomb and maintains that nuclear weapons can have no other purpose but to deter their own use. To achieve this end the ability to destroy your adversary's cities and industries is sufficient. On this idea of deterrence, it is in your interest that your adversary also have an invulnerable ability to destroy you. Mutual assured destruction, as this policy has been called, decreases the likelihood that nuclear weapons will ever be used. This is simple deterrence of the sort Bundy would endorse. It relies on healthy fears of nuclear war and the right kind of cost-benefit ratio to make deterrence work.

The other equally venerable strand of thinking about deterrence policy is motivated by a concern that deterrence might fail. Following William Liscum Borden, a contemporary of Brodie, these thinkers treat maintaining an awesome destructive capacity as but one aspect of nuclear arms policy. They insist on thinking through the possible uses of nuclear weapons in ways familiar to traditional military strategy. This includes contemplating their use in response to conventional aggression against the United States or our allies and maintaining the capacity for a wide range of responses, should deterrence fail. At the heart of this way of thinking is the counterforce theory, which claims that if deterrence fails, then, as Borden wrote in 1946, "A full-scale atomic war will not be won by pulverizing cities and industry, but by destroying the enemy's military power of retaliation."[2] For these nuclear-use theorists, a retaliatory force is not enough to deter nuclear war. First, we cannot ensure that this force will survive all possible attacks; and furthermore, it might not deter an attack in any case. Should we have to fight with these weapons, we must be prepared to survive and prevail. In any event, as these theorists all point out, this has been Soviet policy from the start.

Nuclear-use theory is not implied by Weinberger's raise-the-cost definition of deterrence, but neither is it ruled out. Nuclear-use theory does seem to be incompatible with the conclusions Bundy draws about existential deterrence. It minimizes the importance of uncertainty about what will happen if deterrence fails, it suggests that war planners do not have a healthy fear of nuclear war, and it can lead to policies that create unhealthy fears if one side begins to believe its nuclear weapons might be lost in a counterforce first strike. The imperatives of a counterforce strategy also fuel an arms race in a way that simply maintaining a retaliatory force does not. These are among the objections most frequently heard against nuclear-use theory.

Herken traces this debate between the mutual assured destruction theorists and the nuclear-use theorists back to the beginning of the nuclear age, in the late 1940s. Quester traces its origins back even further, suggesting that the issue is a perennial one of military strategy, of offense vs. defense, or of war fighters vs. war avoiders.

Quester focuses particularly on the reasons and motives for a counterforce strategy. According to his account, these range from the thought that counterforce (doing battle with one's equivalent and defeating the enemy's military) is morally more acceptable than countervalue (preventing attack by threatening civilian and economic targets) to less noble bureaucratic imperatives having to do with winning bigger budgets and career advancement. The former motive refers implicitly to the paradoxical nature of deterrence, while the latter suggests influences that are perhaps even stronger if more intellectually depressing. According to Quester, "The bias of the military is that defensively oriented technology is noninnovative, 'sit-still,' status-quo-oriented, while offensive technology is very innovative, constantly on the move, constantly replacing old systems with new systems." Quester is suggesting that counterforce and the arms race are fueled in part by traditional military psychology.

It is interesting to notice that the origin of mutual assured destruction as the basis of a nuclear deterrence policy came not from the military but from civilian strategists, mostly economists like Thomas Schelling and Oskar Morgenstern, who began applying the new techniques of game theory to defense policy around 1950.[3] But the situation today is more mixed, with some military experts warning against counterforce and some civilian strategists defending it. In any event, according to Quester, every United States president since Truman, even those initially committed to mutual assured destruction, have moved toward counterforce once in office. Quester opposes this tendency, but he blames it on Soviet policies (also militarily dominated) as much as on the United States military.

The questions of which experts to follow, who the experts are, and the role of the public in determining nuclear policies are pursued further in essays by Christopher Lehman, a State Department official (although expressing his own views here, of course, and not those of the government) and by William Greider, a journalist and well-known critic of current government policymaking. Lehman claims that different branches of government and also nongovernment actors and experts all currently play important roles in shaping military strategy and policy. Many of these actors shape policy indirectly, because the direct responsibility for shaping national security rests squarely in the executive branch. This is as it should be, according to Lehman, because it has access to more information and because defense policies must remain consistent and not be subject to the constant fluctuations of public opinion. But other voices are heard, he points out, and the executive branch officials responsible for national defense are themselves drawn from the public. Lehman concludes that the system works more or less as well as one could expect.

Greider disagrees. He sees government in our technologically complex and diffuse society as increasingly based on the model of an expert elite isolated from "the raw and unruly pressures of public sentiment," rather than on the model of representative democracy. "I think we are witnessing today," he warns, "only the early stages of what could become a fundamental collision between citizens and their national government over the deepest moral questions."

This conflict is dramatically expressed in the nuclear freeze movement. Greider believes that government officials mistakenly dismiss the freeze movement as a sudden and quixotic reaction to the newly rekindled fear of nuclear war. It is Greider's view that defense policies have for 30 years been managed by an exclusive nuclear elite of "generals and professors, policy analysts and selected politicians." Congress during this period has been hopelessly timid, voting "for whatever the Pentagon lobbyists tell them is the program," and the major news media join the nuclear elite in dismissing the freeze movement as a "fad which is beneath their serious examination." But Greider sees the freeze movement as having deep historical and religious roots, and he agrees with Father Timothy Healy that it is a moral groundswell. "The worry is not 'Am I going to be killed?' but 'Am I going to do evil?' " Greider describes public attitudes as complex but rational, as showing both a suspicion of the Soviet Union and a strong desire to control the arms race. He sees the SALT negotiations as basically a hoax, spawning treaties that will never stop that race. The freeze movement expresses the public's insistence that the government attempt real negotiations. Greider believes the goals of the freeze movement are achievable, because the superpowers now are at parity in their forces. But he also believes this potential for real negotiation is threatened by the nuclear elite, lost in "the insane dynamics of its own bizarre logic," preparing to deploy a new generation of weapons systems which would make the freeze concept obsolete. The "soft" but real cost of the arms race, Greider concludes, is that it undermines the legitimacy of our government, by making it seem unresponsive to deep and pervasive public moral concerns, and thus increases political alienation and malaise about the future.

The remaining essays in this book focus explicitly on some moral issues in deterrence, all of them bearing more or less directly on the second puzzle in Secretary Weinberger's remarks, the paradoxical nature of deterrence. J. Bryan Hehir, who was closely involved in drafting the influential pastoral letter on deterrence for the National Conference of Catholic Bishops, here puts the argument of that letter in a broader perspective. He describes the wider context of the public debate on deterrence and discusses some of the responses to and criticisms of the bishops' argument.

The pastoral letter comes at a time that Hehir describes as a "New Moment" in the United States nuclear debate, when there is both renewed public concern about nuclear weapons and strategy and also dissent by several experts from what had been a relatively unexamined strategic consensus. This new moment provides an opportunity to shape the future of the nuclear debate. The purpose of the pastoral letter is to help individual members of the Catholic Church form views about "the use of force, participation in warfare, and the responsibilities of citizenship" that are compatible with Catholic teaching, and "to help set the proper terms of moral debate in society" about nuclear weapons policies. The bishops are not technical experts, of course, but Hehir is certainly correct in thinking that the rich Catholic tradition of moral teaching on war and peace gives them a valuable role to play in the debate.

The Catholic "just-war" ethic has as its fundamental premise that any legitimate use of force must be a limited use, as defined by two principles: noncombatant immunity and proportionality. The use of nuclear weapons is difficult to reconcile with these principles. Under a countervalue strategy, the death of civilians is directly intended, so using nuclear weapons in this way is morally unacceptable. But using nuclear weapons in a counterforce strategy also threatens to bring massive civilian casualties or "collateral damage," thus most likely violating the principle of proportionality and perhaps the principle of noncombatant immunity as well. A further principle of Catholic moral teaching says that if it is wrong to perform some act then it is also wrong to intend to perform it. This would seem to create moral problems for justifying not only the use of nuclear weapons, but nuclear deterrence as well.

The pastoral letter, as Hehir explains, approaches this problem by considering three cases of the use of nuclear weapons. First, the bishops argue that any retaliatory strike against civilian populations is unacceptable. Second, they cannot perceive any situation in which the first use of nuclear weapons could be justified, pointing out that this creates an imperative to develop nonnuclear defense strategies. Finally, they consider the prospects for waging a limited nuclear war, one that would not violate the principle of proportionality. Because this is an empirical question, they conclude only that, given the risks involved, the burden of proof remains with those who claim limited wars are possible.

What is perhaps most interesting and problematic about the pastoral letter is that in spite of these conclusions about the use of nuclear weapons, it goes on to argue for a "strictly conditioned" acceptance of the policy of nuclear deterrence. The bishops accept nuclear deterrence as the most realistic means currently available of preventing nuclear war. Hehir acknowledges that this confrontation with the paradox of deterrence puts Catholic justification of deterrence on rather delicate ground. The strict conditions constitute a response to this problem. The bishops claim, essentially, that nuclear deterrence can have no purpose other than preventing nuclear war, and that deterrence is acceptable only contingent upon the attempt to negotiate arms control agreements that will make nuclear deterrence unnecessary.

Does the argument in the pastoral letter deal successfully with the moral paradox? George Sher concludes that it does not. Sher's essay gives us further insight into how the bishops struggled with this issue, by calling our attention to some changes between the second and third drafts of the letter. In the second draft, the bishops seem to claim that any use of nuclear weapons would be wrong, but they accept deterrence as the most likely way of avoiding nuclear war. It is a lesser evil than the alternatives. But Sher points out that this conclusion cannot be accepted consistently with the bishops' other moral principles, for they explicitly say that "[a]ny *use* of nuclear weapons which would violate the principles of noncombatant immunity or proportionality cannot be *intended* in a strategy of deterrence." Since no use is justifiable, no deterrence policies would seem to be acceptable. This conformance between intention and act has deep roots in Catholic moral teaching, and it is at the heart of what makes deterrence seem morally paradoxical.

In the third draft of the pastoral letter, the bishops claim there is a centimeter of doubt about the justifiable use of nuclear weapons. This, according to Sher, allows them to conclude that deterrence is conditionally acceptable without having to try to justify it as a lesser evil. If *some* morally legitimate use is possible, then this opens a window, even if only by a centimeter, for morally justifiable intentions, and thus for deterrence. But Sher claims that this new justification can no longer provide the basis for the strict conditions on accepting deterrence. What Sher believes can be claimed, and what he endorses, is a commitment to make deterrence less unstable and less risky than it is today, a conclusion that would seem to imply the bishops' demand for arms control. But there is no reason, according to Sher, to reject deterrence as a permanent condition, if it has any moral acceptability at all and if it proves to be the best and most stable way to prevent nuclear war.

The final four chapters in this book take up the philosophical issues in the paradox of deterrence. The paradox may be stated as either a paradox of morality or a paradox of rationality. It is, simply, that in some deterrence situations, it may be rational or moral conditionally to intend to perform an action that would seem to be irrational or immoral actually to perform, the condition being governed by another party's behavior. The idea in these situations is to influence the other's behavior by communicating intentions which influence his expectations of how you will respond. These are, in a sense, self-stultifying intentions, because they are meant to prevent the conditions from arising that would lead to their fulfillment.

Not all deterrence situations are paradoxical, of course. We attempt to deter crime, for example, by threatening to imprison convicted criminals. We thus hope to make the expected costs of committing crimes greater than any possible benefit. There is nothing paradoxical about this case or about carrying out the punishment if deterrence fails. The punishment is justifiable, and it might also deter future crimes. Criminal laws keep us from violating moral standards like the protection of innocents or proportionality. We do not threaten to imprison the families of criminals, nor can we impose punishments deemed to be cruel or unusual.

For deterrence to be paradoxical, the threatened action must be immoral or irrational, and the threat or conditional intention must be sincere. In a well-known article, Gregory Kavka discusses this paradox.[4] He shows how the credibility of a deterrer might depend on his ability to convince an adversary that he is capable of performing irrational or immoral acts. In some circumstances, a successful deterrer might need to be someone with a known irrational or immoral character. If deterrence seems morally justifiable or required in such a situation, then our moral goals might be better served by an immoral person. Under some hypothetical scenarios nuclear deterrence would fulfill these conditions.

Kavka refers to this paradoxical possibility briefly in his reply to Gauthier and Lewis in the final chapter. Kavka's principal concern in his main chapter, however, is to examine the complications in forming a moral judgment about nuclear deterrence under realistic assumptions.

Kavka maintains that the moral perplexities result from "a tension between threatening innocent people and doing what is necessary for self-defense." We tend to subscribe to absolutist moral principles about the impermissibility of imposing risks of death on innocent civilians and about the permissibility of doing whatever is necessary for national self-defense; since most people believe that nuclear deterrence is necessary for self-defense but that it inevitably imposes risks on civilians, it thus appears to be both permissible and impermissible. Kavka argues, however, that neither of the absolutist principles is acceptable as it stands. Both of them involve degrees of risk and degrees of wrongdoing.

Nuclear deterrence imposes threats on civilians, but the threats are of a kind that do not necessarily interfere with their normal lives. If there is a sense in which United States and Soviet citizens are all hostages of the deterrence policies of their governments, we are at least hostages in place who are free to continue our daily activities. While this does not automatically make the risks acceptable, it does prevent us from concluding directly that they are morally forbidden. Civilians, moreover, are not completely absolved of all responsibility for their government's policies. The question of citizen innocence is itself a complicated one, and innocence probably comes in degrees. Likewise, self-defense is not an absolute right that legitimizes any effective action. What is necessary for self-defense must be assessed along with what is reasonable, and this will involve determining whether or not the risks imposed on others in the pursuit of self-defense are disproportionate.

In the end, therefore, Kavka thinks that a rigid application of absolutist principles for morally judging nuclear deterrence must give way to a more complicated utilitarian balancing of risks and benefits. Nevertheless, he acknowledges that there remain non-utilitarian aspects to the problem, and he emphasizes that the utilitarian assessment is itself difficult, requiring no less than "the development of ways of assessing, under uncertainty, the dangers and advantages, for all humanity, of the various alternative nuclear deterrence policies."

David Gauthier also believes, like Kavka, that deterrence decisions should be evaluated in the same way as other problems of rational choice. In determining the rational course of action, the consequences of the different possible outcomes under alternative policies must be combined with the probabilities that those outcomes will occur. But unlike Kavka, Gauthier uses this framework to argue that paradoxes of deterrence are not real, even in hypothetical situations.

Those who believe deterrence is paradoxical are moved by the following thought. If carrying out a deterrence threat would be irrational, then it cannot be fully rational to form a sincere intention conditionally to act in that way, regardless of the independent benefits of forming and communicating this intention. Gauthier stands this argument on its head. If it is rational to form an intention, he claims, then it must be rational to act on it, however bad the consequences turn out to be. Actions are made rational, according to Gauthier, by the rationality of their intentions, and these must be based on expected, not actual, outcomes. It can be rational to choose the alternative with the worst possible outcome, because when all the possible outcomes under that alternative are weighted by their probabilities and added together, the alternative may have the best expected outcome. The deterrence option may therefore be rational because it gives the best chance of preventing nuclear war, even though the policy of deterrence makes the consequences of war much worse if deterrence fails.

David Lewis insists on maintaining the distinction between the act of forming an effective deterrent intention, which has its own consequences, and the act of carrying out the intention if deterrence fails. He believes that it may be rational to form the intention, for the kinds of reasons Gauthier discusses. But he agrees with Kavka, against Gauthier, that in at least some hypothetical situations, it would be wrong to fulfill the intention by retaliating. Because the two acts are separate, however, Lewis claims that the evaluation of the acts should be kept separate as well. Though he acknowledges the hypothetical possibility that their evaluations would diverge, he regards these cases and the paradox of deterrence as bogus in two important respects.

First, the paradox is a bogus intellectual puzzle, because it arises only for those who insist on forming an overall moral judgment. Lewis thinks we needn't do this. He is content in these hypothetical cases of paradoxical nuclear deterrence to conclude that it is right to form the intention but wrong to act on it. A person or government that adopted a policy of nuclear retaliation and was forced to fulfill it would deserve both our praise and our condemnation. "In forming that intention . . . (these people) are great patriots, and benefactors of us all. And now that they have formed the intention, they are ready to commit massacres whose like has never been seen. . . . They are evil beyond imagining, fiends in human shape." Lewis is content to let the paradox stand.

More important, however, Lewis also thinks that this paradox has no place in serious discussions about nuclear deterrence policies, whatever its intellectual fascination. In the real world, deterrence seems to work, but we cannot now predict what the situation would be like if it failed and whether retaliatory attacks would or would not accomplish good ends. Lewis concludes that serious moral discussion about nuclear deterrence should move away from concentrating on the paradox. It should focus instead on more relevant philosophical issues, like decision under extreme uncertainty, problems of incommensurable values, and the complicity and innocence of civilians.

Despite Secretary Weinberger's disclaimer, our nuclear deterrence policies remain difficult to grasp. The issue is now before the public, however, and the profound effects of the existence of nuclear weapons on our present and future world make it important that we attempt to understand these policies. By exploring historical, political, moral, and philosophical aspects of deterrence, this collection of essays aims to contribute to that understanding in a humanistic way.

NOTES

1 Caspar Weinberger, letter of August 23, 1982, sent to seventy publications. The full text is reprinted in *The New York Review of Books*, November 4, 1982, p. 27.

2 William Liscum Borden, *There Will Be No Time: The Revolution in Strategy* (New York: Macmillan, 1946), p. 87, as quoted in Herken's chapter.

3 See Thomas Schelling, *The Strategy of Conflict* (London: Oxford University Press, 1960); and Oskar Morgenstern, *The Question of National Defense* (New York: Random House, 1959).

4 Gregory Kavka, "Some Paradoxes of Deterrence," *The Journal of Philosophy* 75 (June 1978): 285–302.

PART 1
An Examination of United States Nuclear Deterrence Policies and Options

1
EXISTENTIAL DETERRENCE AND ITS CONSEQUENCES

Mcgeorge Bundy

My effort will be to examine the underlying implications of our present situation. The United States and the Soviet Union, even if they were to reach agreement tomorrow on both a full-scale freeze and massive reductions, would still face each other with thousands of thermonuclear warheads so deployed that neither side could hope to make a large-scale nuclear attack on the other without a wholly unacceptable risk of receiving catastrophic damage in reply.

I believe that the habits of debate which have developed among those who see their domestic opponents as the real enemy – and this is a state of mind that one can find on both sides of the debate – may have distracted attention from this reality and from some others that grow out of it.

Our traditional debates over deterrence policy have one striking characteristic: each side frequently accuses the other of having profoundly immoral intentions *if deterrence fails*. One side has been ringing the changes for two decades on the moral infamy of what is described as a *doctrine* of mutual assured destruction, claiming that proponents of this doctrine are content to have no other option than the indiscriminate slaughter of millions of innocent civilians. Conversely there are many who argue that it is the hard-liners who are morally outrageous with their insistence on plans and preparations for prevailing in prolonged nuclear war. I think it is wrong for people on either side of these debates to accuse those on the other of planning a particularly vicious kind of nuclear war, because neither side is declaring what in fact it would do in the dreadful event of such a war. Rather, each is setting up a measuring stick for the kinds of capabilities it believes necessary for the self-confident deterrence of the other side. These are not, on either side, true theories of war-fighting; they are criteria for the procurement of deterrent forces.

To students on both sides of the argument it should by now be a commonplace that for more than 20 years it has been the policy of our strategic planners *not* to plan massive attacks on cities as such. At the same time, the policy of our civilian leaders of all persuasions has been to press those planners for options, ever more varied, precisely so that the deterrent would never seem incredible because our capabilities were so limited that only a suicidal massive response was possible. As Milton Leitenberg has tersely and persuasively demonstrated in his prompt and clear discussion of Presidential Directive 59, the noisy changes of 1973–74 and 1977–80 have affected procurement priorities much more than basic targeting.[1] This complex task has been in the hands of military men from the beginning—men who do not target cities as such, but who do target military and industrial assets even when they are in or near cities, unless explicitly instructed to do otherwise. Pronouncements on both sides are designed to yield criteria for the size and shape of forces that deter. They are not descriptions of preferred forms of nuclear war. The right way to question these pronouncements is to examine the nature of the objective. What is nuclear deterrence in this decade? What are the best safeguards against its failure? What is it good for? And not good for?

* * *

The first question we should ask is whether or not nuclear deterrence is a phenomenon we are forced to coexist with. Cannot this condition somehow be transcended?

The question is of fundamental importance because obviously the world would be better off if the threat of nuclear destruction did not exist. If we could truly "ban the bomb" most of us would wish to do so. But can we? So far the answer of history has been negative. But history alone cannot determine the matter. It may show only that we have not tried hard enough, and certainly there have been many moments when a better effort might have been made. Yet on the whole, the larger lesson of the historical record is that fear of the bomb has always been less powerful in the decisions of nations than fear of the *adversary's* bomb. To put it another way, the weapons each side has sought have been those its government found necessary in the light of what others had done or might do. Not one of the nuclear weapons states has ever been ready to surrender that judgment to any other government or to any international authority. Flora Lewis was right to remind us of the comment of Sobolev at the UN objecting to the Baruch Plan, "that the Soviet Union was not seeking equality, but, rather, freedom to pursue its own policies in complete freedom and without any interference or control from the outside."[2]

This situation is not likely to change soon. It rests on the continuing and deeply rooted power of the idea of national sovereignty. The reality that the nations of the nuclear world are inescapably interdependent—dependent on each other's behavior—has not changed the deeply entrenched determination of nearly all nations, and in particular all nuclear weapons states, to make their choices on such matters through the decision-making process of a sovereign government in which authority, interest, hope, and fear are all defined in primarily national terms.

If anything could have led them to abandon their nation-centered ways, it should have been the bomb. The logic is compelling from Hiroshima onward. From Norman Cousins to Jonathan Schell, men preoccupied by nuclear danger have fixed on national sovereignty as the basic obstacle to the exorcism of the specter. They are right, but the obstacle persists. While there may be a special intensity to the state-centered dedication of the Soviet leadership, the beam is in other eyes, too, including our own. It is safe to assume, therefore, that the sovereign state is not about to be transcended.

Another possible means of transcendence is technological. Hope on this front has been rekindled, at least for some, by Mr. Reagan's speech of March 23, 1983. But is that hope well founded? I think not. The difficulty here is not simply in the extraordinary cost and complexity of the new systems we do not yet know how to build. There is also the problem that thermonuclear weapons impose a radically new calculus of advantage on anyone seeking to neutralize them: they make it necessary to defeat them all. Anything less is not good enough for safety, but only good enough, at best, for deterrence. The object must still be not to fight the Star War, but only to make sure that it does not break out. In this sense, the promise held out by the president's address is deeply misleading. Even if all of his assumptions about technological promise were true, it is extremely hard to believe we shall ever have a perfect defense against ballistic missiles, including those at sea. It is harder still to suppose that we could have something equally perfect against aircraft and cruise missiles too. Have our newly hopeful hawks forgotten so soon their asserted fear of the assertedly intercontinental backfire?

I believe we have two bedrock realities: the units of political account are nation-states, and thermonuclear weapons are different from any others. These two realities, mixed together in different ways with different additional ingredients, underlie all assessments of nuclear deterrence. Even taken alone they require some notion of deterrence, of the way in which nation-states are to coexist, *with* nuclear weapons and *without* nuclear war. Even states without nuclear weapons (or nuclear umbrellas from friends) must have a concept of deterrence—a view of what is necessary to prevent the use of nuclear weapons against them. In this sense, Sweden has a view of deterrence; so does Yugoslavia; so do Canada and Mexico.

These four cases illustrate two other basic elements in any calculus of deterrence that are frequently neglected in the more abstract and seemingly rigorous calculations made by those who approach the problem through assessments of the technical capabilities of the nuclear arsenals of the superpowers. First, it makes a great difference who it is that must be deterred. There is much concern in Canada and Mexico that the United States might somehow stumble into a nuclear war, but there is no concern whatever that the United States might resort to nuclear war against these bordering neighbors. Second, nuclear attack can often be deterred by other than nuclear means. Sweden and Yugoslavia make a different estimate about a different neighbor, but they still rely for deterrence not on nuclear weapons of their own but on a combination of substantial conventional strength, solid political self-confidence, and a calculation that the costs of both conventional and nuclear attack on them, in the judgment of any sane Soviet leadership, would greatly outweigh any possible advantage.

To some degree, of course, deterrence in these countries is related to deterrence elsewhere. Swedish and Yugoslavian leaders do not habitually speak out about the problem they might face if they were alone in the world with the Soviet Union, but one doubts that the matter is absent from their thoughts.

Obviously the judgment that deterrence has worked is not a judgment that any particular form of deterrence was the best available – or even that it was necessary. Consider the familiar appeal to history in our current debates over the defense of Europe: "deterrence has worked for the last 35 years." So it has, if what we mean is that the Soviet Union, barring the quite special case of the blockade of Berlin (which actually preceded the Alliance and was lifted shortly after its signing), has never resorted to force in its relations with NATO. But it is only an assumption, and one not open to proof, that the nuclear weapon was indispensable to this result. People of luminous reputation, from Churchill onward, have certainly asserted this proposition. But were they right? And if they were right in the 1950s, are their followers still right in the 1980s? And if the proposition held in Churchill's time and holds now, does it hold in quite the same way? What, if any, is the difference in the process of deterrence when the relation of one side to the other in nuclear weaponry has moved from monopoly to massive superiority to essential equivalence to debatable parity?

Perhaps an even more important question is what other elements contribute to deterrence. Is there perhaps an absence of any strong motive for aggression? Do we too readily assume the worst intentions on the part of our adversary? It is too easy to say that this is what military men are trained to do and that they are professionally obliged to focus on capabilities rather than intentions. Certainly capabilities are relevant, but are they everything? Obviously not in the case of Sweden. Is it self-evident that deterrence of attack on the Federal Republic of Germany is totally different? If the Soviet Union could overrun the Federal Republic in a week by a blitzkrieg—conventional or nuclear—would it be happy with the resulting situation, or would it be deterred in advance by the prospect?

Nor is military deterrence the only proper objective of those who seek to keep the peace. In a brilliant contribution to the current debate on deterrence in Europe, Michael Howard has reminded us that along with deterrence the Alliance has a second mission of at least equal importance—reassurance.[3] Reassurance, to Howard, is the process by which the nations of the Alliance have sought a level of self-confidence and strength that would allow them to pursue their national lives without the fear, both of Soviet power and of internal turmoil, that marked more than one of them in the first years after World War II. This mission has so far been successfully executed, and while both conventional and nuclear strength have been contributing elements, there have been others as well. One of the most important is a record of conduct, by each of the major powers in the Alliance, that has been only intermittently and partially disquieting to its partners. A second has been readiness, on the part of most of the allies most of the time, for reasonable accommodation with the Soviet Union. The reassurance afforded by military strength would have been quite inadequate without the parallel pursuit of some form of detente. Detente has never been a bad word in Europe, and indeed it has been formally recognized, with deterrence itself, as a central purpose of the Alliance since the Harmel Report of 1967.

Let me press the point one step further, again to a question, not an answer. Can detente be conceived of as a reinforcement of deterrence? In the sense that clear agreements can be more stable, more reliable, more costly to challenge, and more reassuring than tension caused by open disagreement, this seems logical. Is not Austria such a case? And what about West Berlin? If there was a place in earlier years where nuclear deterrence was relevant—some would say controlling—it was West Berlin. Is this so today? The situation of Berlin, as we all know, was a central element in the critically important agreements of 1971—agreements which led to a reordering of relations between the two governments of Germany, to a new order of communication among the divided German people, and so to a settlement, accepted by both great powers, of a 25-year contest over the immediate future of that crucial city and country. Since then, and more strongly every passing year, the freedom of West Berlin has rested on the overall cost of destroying that settlement, not on the immediate risk of war—let alone nuclear war. I put the question then, is not this settlement a form of deterrence? And is it not also much more reassuring than the kinds of deterrence on which we were forced to rely in the fifties and sixties?

So I propose that deterrence, however it works, should always be considered in the context of two other interconnected objectives – reassurance of friends and detente with adversaries. Deterrence is part, but only part, of the politics of nations. Those politics in turn are part of its own strength or weakness. And politics being politics, such elements are subject to change.

* * *

The interconnection with politics is only one of the sources of inescapable uncertainty in nuclear deterrence. Another is intrinsic to the weapons systems themselves, which are now so powerful and varied on both sides that no one can hope to have any clear idea of what would in fact happen "if deterrence failed" – that is, if nuclear war began. This difficulty is not escaped by any theory, because no theory can predict with any confidence the behavior of any government, friend or foe, in such a situation. Most scenarios for nuclear warfare between the Soviet Union and the United States reflect nothing more than the state of mind of their authors. Estimates of the ease or difficulty of limiting such a conflict, for example, are just that – estimates. Moreover, they are estimates of interacting behavior under conditions of quite unprecedented stress and danger, possibly in the midst of already appalling destruction. No one can have any certainty, for example, that credible communication would be possible between the adversaries even hours after such a conflict began. Credible communication requires leadership that is mutually recognized, operationally effective, and continuous, on both sides; who can promise that? Yet without such communication who knows how to stop the horror?

Similar inescapable uncertainties apply to every other element of the situation. Which weapons would function, and with what efficiency? What intentions would be read into what actions? Can we tell how Soviet decision-makers would regard a missile launch that *could* be aimed at either missile fields or nearby Moscow? How would an adversary interpret a temporary absence of response, when it could reflect almost anything: careful restraint, a plan for later coordinated retaliation, or the absence of any governing mind at all? Would the impulse to stop the slaughter be stronger than the impulse to kill the killers, and would it be the same or opposite on the two sides? Who can tell?

These terrible and unavoidable uncertainties have great meaning for the theory of deterrence. They create what I will call *existential* deterrence. My aim in using this fancy adjective is to distinguish this kind of deterrence from the kind that is based on strategic theories or declaratory policies or even international commitments. As long as we assume that each side has very large numbers of thermonuclear weapons which *could* be used against the opponent, even after the strongest possible pre-emptive attack, existential deterrence is strong. It rests on uncertainty about what *could happen*, not in what has been asserted. Existential deterrence had a powerful day-to-day effect on both governments in the course of the Cuban missile crisis. Neither side had any desire to expose itself to the uncertainties I have noted; neither enjoyed its inescapable dependence on the sanity, and even the restraint, of the other. Nothing whatever in the succeeding 20 years has weakened the compelling power of existential deterrence over decision-makers on both sides. It is, for example, what makes nonsense of the notion that Moscow might suddenly attack the ICBM fields of the United States.

The uncertainties which make existential deterrence so powerful have the further consequence that what either government says it might do, or even believes it might do, in the event of open conflict cannot be relied on either by friends or by opponents as a certain predicter of what it would actually do. Neither promises of restraint (no-first-use may be the most conspicuous in current debates) nor threats of condign retribution (the countervailing strategy comes to mind) could be confidently relied on. No one knows when or how such a crisis would arise, or who would be in charge at the moment on either side. No one knows what would happen, or how big any first strike would be, or what would happen next. The limits placed by these uncertainties on all kinds of plans and all kinds of expectations are inescapably tight. To take one simple and revealing case: every sensible senior officer in NATO has known for decades that there is literally no way to be sure just when or how – or whether – the president of the United States would authorize nuclear release. If General Rogers cannot know – if the president himself cannot know – how can Soviet leaders know?

The third element of existential deterrence – and perhaps the most important for deterrence theory – grows out of the same inescapable uncertainties: its deterrent power is unaffected by most changes in the arsenals on both sides. Because no one can predict how these enormous and amply survivable arsenals might be used, because these uncertainties create an enormously powerful existential deterrent, and because this reality is essentially unaffected by any changes except those which might truly challenge the overall survivability of the forces on either side, it makes no sense to base procurement decisions on refined calculations of the specific kinds of force that would be needed for a wide variety of limited nuclear responses. All such responses would be full of unpredictables. All would be open to catastrophic misinterpretation. None could be confidently expected to lead to a good result. The decision to have options is sensible, if only because there is no need to lend even marginal credibility to the destructive and erroneous notion that our presidents in recent decades have had no choices between the extremes of surrender and all-out retaliation.

At the current levels of survivable strength, however, the maintenance of such options has no necessary implications for procurement costs, and to let the pursuit of options drive procurement is quite wrong.

Existential deterrence has still other qualities. It deters quite impersonally; no provocative threats are needed to support its power. It deters both sides at once, since the unpredictable risk of catastrophe is essentially symmetrical. It makes full and impartial use of one of the great realities of nuclear weapons: they are far more terrifying to adversaries than they are comforting to their possessors. When we review the record, looking at the motives for the decisions of major governments, we find that while motive is not always clear, and frequently somewhat mixed, the dominant theme, beginning with Franklin Roosevelt in 1941, is fear – if we don't get it first, he (Hitler) may. The theme has many variations. He's got it, so we must – Stalin in 1945; they are doing it, so must we – Britain and France; they have done it, and we will – Mao; they will try, so we will succeed – Israel. Less fearful motives do operate: we will win; we will catch up; we will be great; we will even, perhaps, be safe. But fear dominates.

In the age of overkill, it still does. We do not dwell on what we can do to them, but on what they can do to us. We talk about it more than they do, but it would be wrong to suppose that we care more. What country has a longer and deeper awareness of the need to preserve itself from external danger than Soviet Russia? But the point is not centrally one of national attitudes; it is rather a consequence of the realities of nuclear exchange. If I kill a million, and he kills a million, have I won or lost? No special national attitude is required for the right answer: I have lost, and lost overwhelmingly. It does not help me at all that *so has he.*

Consider the process as it arises much earlier in the chain of such decisions, back where we deal with development or procurement, not with what might happen in action. When my side MIRVs, I get marginal comfort. It is large enough to prevent me from deciding that I ought to weigh all the consequences of the decision, but not large enough to let me claim or even believe that I have in fact gone ahead. But when the other side MIRVs, I start to talk of Present Danger. Is it not the same over there? When he builds his SS-20 he is only modernizing; assertions that the resulting change in the balance is important do not come from him. But when we reply with smaller forces, and with the purpose only of strengthening deterrence, does he read it that way? Does he not read instead what *might* be meant and *could* be done, and react accordingly?

Thus fear is bad, when it leads to action and reaction in the procurement race. Fear fuels that race, and a race there is, though the shape of its interaction is indeed no simple matter, as Albert Wohlstetter thinks it important to emphasize.[4] (What Wohlstetter appears to resent is only that our side has not raced very hard; to me, as far as that is true, it is merely a sign of some good sense.)

But from the point of view of existential deterrence, fear is *not* bad. We are saying that nuclear weapons, by any measure, spread more fear of disaster than hope of safety. The point has been stated one way or another by every president since Truman, and most recently by Mr. Reagan in the repeated categorical statement: "A nuclear war cannot be won and must never be fought." Russian political leaders are just as categorical. Political leaders, as I am afraid I have said before, have no interest in going into history as the men who led their country into such a disaster. Eisenhower's words of 1953 may be particularly vivid: "Could anyone wish his name to be coupled by history with such human degradation and destruction?" I submit that this was the voice of a man who had gazed on the realities of existential deterrence. I think that no sane leader can reach a different conclusion – and against insanity, as Churchill noted long ago, no posture offers protection.

While these fears have helped to keep us away from nuclear war, we must recognize that they have also fueled the nuclear arms competition. If your new weapons give me more fear than they give you comfort, the incentive for me to get more of my own is bound to be strong, and the more so where the decision is strongly influenced, as it is on both sides, by the preferences of military commanders. This does not mean that the senior men in uniform are insensitive to nuclear reality. I have known many of them, over many years, and with occasional exceptions I have found them soberly aware of that reality. Still, it is not easy for military men to treat with equanimity any new system that an adversary may deploy, and to some degree the very fact that nuclear war itself is unacceptable may tend to drive the military competition back into the field of development and deployment. Perhaps you have heard, as I have, the argument made by many Air Force officers that we must not let Soviet heavy weapons "drive us out of the ground-based missile business." But this is *not* a contest of appearances, in spite of much loose talk about the importance of perceptions. What we really need is only what *we need*, not what others may happen to have. What we need is a large and varied force with assured overall survivability. We cannot at present do with less, and there is nothing we can confidently expect to do with more. Henry Kissinger was right in 1976 when he questioned the meaning of "strategic superiority" at the level already reached then. Fear of losing a numbers game is as foolish as fear of nuclear war is wise.

This wise fear has one other meaning for the nature of deterrence: as long as we are convinced that governments on both sides do share that fear, the threat of nuclear blackmail can be contained. Direct threats to use nuclear weapons have not been frequent in the nuclear age, and even indirect threats have become fewer as the realities of existential deterrence have been recognized more and more widely. I do not think this is an accident. When sanity requires care, and when even the most bitter adversaries perceive each other as sane, threats to do something rash become unpersuasive; they simply lack credibility. The coercive value of nuclear threats has never been as high as various temporary believers in "atomic diplomacy" have temporarily believed. They are certain to be ineffective for use between possessors of massive survivable forces unless one side has a foolish loss of nerve. Those who predicted in the late 1970s that there would be dire political effects from Minuteman's window of vulnerability in the early 1980s should look around them now to see if they were right. The window was supposed to be wide open by now. Do they feel coerced? Or do they now agree with the Scowcroft Commission that this particular window was never open?

Even against nonnuclear states, the coercive power of nuclear strength is low. That does not prevent insensitive governments from making explicit or implicit threats. It does, however, limit the value of such pressure and tend to make it politically damaging to the threat-maker. We have seen this result twice recently. Soviet warnings to the Germans before their elections certainly helped the coalition which was led by Kohl and disfavored by Moscow. A clear reference to the nuclear vulnerability of Japan seems to have similarly produced a healthy reaction of unfrightened anger; not one of fear.

A further reinforcement to this condition derives from what Thomas Schelling first called the *tradition* of non-use of nuclear weapons. I agree with Schelling in assigning great importance to that tradition, which has been followed for 25 years since he first called attention to it in *The Strategy of Conflict*. The distinction between use and non-use is very much sharper than any distinction of one class or use of nuclear weapons from another. But both peoples and governments value the tradition of non-use, and no government today would dare to flirt in public, as Dwight Eisenhower did in 1953, with the proposition that "atomic weapons have virtually achieved conventional status within our armed services."

Let me offer two other brief comments in conclusion–the first about the continuing need for attention to our nuclear arsenal, and the second about the need for many other things. I must not leave the impression that the maintenance of existential deterrence is automatic. Such deterrence arises from the existence of large forces whose overall survivability is assured. That survivability is unfortunately open to technological threat, and there is good reason for prudent modernization as a response to such threats. There is no need to overdo it, as the present administration has done, in developing four distinct programs for updating the strategic bombing force. Yet *some* degree of modernization is clearly needed over time. This requirement can apply to every element in the force. It may be that the most serious analytical problem that faces the freeze movement is this question of the relation between modernization and survivability.

I also recognize that in focusing on existential deterrence I have slighted the need to limit nuclear danger in other ways – by broader and stronger agreements for arms control, by measures aimed at limiting the risks from accidental or unauthorized action, by all that can be included in the politics of reassurance and of detente, and indeed by a wider understanding on both sides of what deterrence is and is not good for. I am not saying that existential deterrence is all we can have, only that for as far ahead as I can see it must be *part* of what we have.

NOTES

1 Milton Leitenberg, "Presidential Directive (P.D.) 59: United States Nuclear Weapon Targeting Policy," *Journal of Peace Research* 18, no. 4 (1981).

2 Sobolev's comment is reported in *Foreign Relations of the United States*, 1946, I, p. 957.

3 Michael Howard, "Deterrence and Reassurance," *Foreign Affairs* (Winter 1982-83).

4 Albert Wohlstetter, "Is There a Strategic Arms Race?" *Foreign Policy* 15 (Summer 1978); and Wohlstetter, "Rivals but no Race," *Foreign Policy* 16 (Fall 1978).

2

THE NUCLEAR GNOSTICS

Gregg Herken

The theory of deterrence in its modern sense might have been first put into practice at the height of the 1948 Berlin crisis, when President Truman ordered "atomic-capable" B-29 bombers to forward bases in England and Germany, within striking distance of Russia. The nature of the threat that Truman wished to convey to the Russians was unambiguous. But the threat itself – perhaps characteristically – remained a bit vague: The bombers sent overseas were indeed capable of carrying atomic bombs, but the bombs themselves and the people necessary to arm them stayed at home on the president's order. There was a similar disparity between act and intention in the nation's emergency war plan for that year, code-named "Fleetwood." Had the United States gone to war over Berlin in 1948, "Fleetwood" identified 70 cities in the Soviet Union as targets for atomic bombs. There were at the time, however, only 50 nuclear weapons in the entire American arsenal. Three years after Hiroshima, it still took several days to assemble a single atomic bomb; only a handful of people had been trained to do this, and there were in any case too few specially modified bombers to carry the weapons to their targets in a single raid.[1]

Thirty-five years after that first Berlin crisis, both the thinking and the planning for nuclear war have changed markedly. Today's linear descendant of "Fleetwood" – SIOP VB – reportedly identifies up to 40,000 potential targets in the Soviet Union and has assigned upwards of 25,000 nuclear weapons for their destruction. If the United States were to go to war today these bombs would be carried to their targets by a technological array of ready bombers and missiles; some would reach their destinations in as little as ten minutes.[2]

In theory, the current war plan represents only a shift in emphasis from its earliest predecessor – a change of degree, not of substance. But surely this seems a change of such magnitude that it actually represents a change in kind from the thinking and planning for nuclear war that existed when Truman sent the first atomic bombers overseas.

At the end of his recent book on the evolution of nuclear strategy – paraphrasing a famous comment on the Crimean war – British military historian Lawrence Freedman observes about the present state of thinking and planning for nuclear war: "*C'est magnifique, mais ce n'est pas la strategie.*" In light of what we now know concerning current and projected plans to fight and "prevail" in a possible nuclear war, we might wish to stretch Freedman's paraphrase a bit further to read: It is terrifying, but it is not deterrence.[3]

* * *

The subject of nuclear war has never, of course, been unthinkable. As *The Wizards of Armageddon* by Fred Kaplan points out, what was probably both the best and the earliest thinking on the subject was done at Yale almost literally in the shadow of the atomic bombs dropped on Japan.[4] The chief theorist on the bomb at that time was Bernard Brodie, a 35-year-old professor of international relations. Brodie certainly did not invent the theory of deterrence – George Quester has convincingly shown how that concept well predated Hiroshima – but he was one of the first to argue that the atomic bomb might be a weapon ideally suited to the purpose of deterring attack. Brodie popularized the concept of nuclear deterrence in his 1946 book, *The Absolute Weapon: The Atomic Bomb and World Order.* "[E]verything about the atomic bomb," he wrote, "is overshadowed by the twin facts that it exists and its destructive power is fantastically great." It was also Brodie who first contended that it might be possible – indeed, it was now necessary – "to develop the habit of living with the atomic bomb." *The Absolute Weapon* contained perhaps the most concise expression of the principle of nuclear deterrence, one that has gone unamended to the present day: "Thus far the chief purpose of our military establishment has been to win wars. From now on its chief purpose must be to avert them. It can have almost no other useful purpose."[5]

That "almost" in the last line would, of course, be the basis for the debate over nuclear strategy that has now gone on for nearly two generations. What may have been lost sight of in the present debate is the fact that deterrence wasn't the only concept connected with the atomic bomb at this time – or even at Yale. Across the street from Brodie's office in the Hall of Graduate Studies by late 1945, a law student by the name of William Liscum Borden was also completing a book on the significance of the atomic bomb that would come to a conclusion almost diametrically opposed to that of *The Absolute Weapon*. Borden was a 25-year-old veteran of the Second World War, during which he had served as a bomber pilot for the

AAF. It was while returning from a night raid over occupied Europe that Borden had glimpsed a German V-2 rocket hurtle past his bomber on its way to England. That event, together with the news of Hiroshima, made an indelible impression on Borden's mind and gave him the inspiration for his book, *There Will Be No Time: The Revolution in Strategy.*[6]

Borden's book–which appeared at the same time as Brodie's– proclaimed that what he termed the "mutual-deterrent thesis" was a fallacy. Borden predicted that unless world federalism intervened, nuclear war was "certain and inevitable," and he urged that the nation prepare to fight and win such a war. Borden's argument was that fear of retaliation would not necessarily deter an enemy attack, but might actually provoke one–in what would be a "rocket Pearl Harbor." "A full-scale atomic war will not be won by pulverizing cities and industry," he wrote, "but by destroying the enemy's military power of retaliation." Borden concluded, accordingly, that America's preparations for a future war "must now *surpass*–not merely equal–the dictator's preparations."[7]

During the course of the next 30 years there would be further refinements of these two very different ways of looking at nuclear strategy and war, and the number of nuclear weapons in the world would grow almost exponentially. But the writings of Brodie and Borden together had defined–within six months of Hiroshima–the two rival positions in what would be a continuing debate over nuclear strategy. This has been a debate between Brodie's strategy of deterrence and Borden's strategy of counterforce, or nuclear war-fighting. It is a debate complicated by the fact that the choice is not between one strategy or the other, but of where the emphasis should be in the thinking and planning that concern nuclear weapons. It is a debate that has grown increasingly polemical–pitting, for example, the "MADmen" (for mutual assured destruction) against the "NUTS" (nuclear-use theorists). This debate also accounts for the central and enduring paradox which has bedeviled American nuclear weapons policy since the time that the Russians, too, have had the bomb.

* * *

It is interesting that the subsequent careers of the earliest of nuclear theorists shed a revealing historical sidelight on the course of the nuclear debate. Borden's emphasis on ensuring military superiority over any prospective enemy made him one of the most vocal and effective early promoters of the next development in nuclear weapons–the "Super" or hydrogen bomb. As aide to the chairman of the Senate Atomic Energy Committee, he remained committed to the goal outlined in his book of achieving "nuclear plenty" for the United States. At the same time, Borden's obsession with girding the nation for war–he had written that a democracy was most likely "to have spies circulating in its midst," and warned of a need for "extreme care among those charged with research and weapons production" – as well as his frustration with the slow progress toward a Super prompted him to charge opponents of the H-bomb with willfully obstructing and even sabotaging its development. In 1953, when he was no longer in the government, Borden wrote a famous letter to FBI director Hoover alleging that atomic scientist J. Robert Oppenheimer – an initial opponent of the Super – was "more probably than not a Soviet agent." After thus initiating the hearing into Oppenheimer's loyalty, Borden retired from the nuclear debate believing that his 1946 prediction of certain nuclear war had not been mistaken, but was merely premature.[8]

Brodie's career was also radically changed by the advent of the hydrogen bomb. In *The Absolute Weapon*, he had predicted that atomic bombs, terrible as they might be, were still likely to remain limited both in number and destructiveness because of the difficulty and expense involved in making them. The H-bomb changed all that. Shortly after the successful test of an American hydrogen bomb, Brodie conceded that the premises on which he had based the thesis of *The Absolute Weapon* were now obsolete, since there was likely to be henceforth no limit upon either the number or the destructiveness of nuclear weapons. Brodie wrote to a friend in 1953 that it was now clear to him that " 'strategy' and 'unlimited war' [were] simply incompatible concepts in a world of H-bombs." The following year he published a magazine article revealingly titled "Strategy Hits a Dead End." Brodie's subsequent work for the Rand Corporation turned to a more limited notion of deterrence – that of using the threat of tactical nuclear weapons to prevent war in Europe. This was also an idea that had initially appealed to Oppenheimer, but one that had ceased to be in vogue by the end of the Eisenhower administration. Ridiculed by colleagues for his iconoclastic position on tactical nuclear war, Brodie left Rand and eventually turned his attention to a study of the psychological causes of war. Before Brodie's death in 1978, his former associates at Rand, such as Herman Kahn and Sam Cohen, claimed that the invention of nuclear weapons as destructive and as available as the H-bomb caused Brodie to lose interest in nuclear strategy and faith in deterrence. Herman Kahn, for example, said that the arrival of the hydrogen bomb "just kind of swamped Brodie. . . . He gave up on defending against H-bombs. He didn't give up right away; he gave up slowly. His final position was that he just didn't want to think about it."[9]

* * *

There is perhaps an instructive irony in this brief account of the fate of the nation's earliest nuclear theorists; one that may have some application to the current debate over nuclear strategy. The world today seems to bear a much closer resemblance to the future sketched by Borden in 1946 than to that outlined by Brodie. There is, thus, a remarkably contemporary quality to the futuristic vision of Borden's book, which predicted that both the United States and Russia would eventually base nuclear-tipped rockets in underground protective "hedgehogs" located away from cities and on "undersea platforms scattered throughout the world's oceans." Yet the "certain and inevitable" war forecast by Borden has not occurred, and the "mutual-deterrent thesis"–to the extent it has been tested–has not proved a fallacy. The irony is that though we have created Borden's world, we still live by Brodie's adage.

Three themes actually run throughout the history of deterrence since Hiroshima. One is the uneven but relentless inflation of the nuclear arsenals on both side. Another–perhaps not unrelated–is the consistency with which American presidents have declared that the principal purpose of United States nuclear weapons is to deter, rather than fight, a war. The third is the steadily increasing amount of thinking and planning since 1945 for the use of these weapons in a war. This contradiction, or disparity between intending to prevent a war and preparing to fight one, has grown more pronounced as the number and variety of nuclear weapons increases on each side. It has become a nuclear-age variant of the antique paradox "to have peace, prepare for war."

Few, if any, of the participants in the nuclear debate have been, strictly speaking, either deterrers or war-fighters; virtually no one has urged a commitment to one strategy at the exclusion of the other. Historically, the emphasis of those actually responsible for making American nuclear weapons policy has been overwhelmingly on the side of deterrence. The record of successive presidential administrations suggests that, like the prospect of being hanged upon the morrow, the experience of "looking nuclear war down the throat," as science advisor Herbert York has said, concentrates the thinking of those who would give the mobilization order upon the task of preventing–not winning–a nuclear war.[10]

Harry Truman was the first president to be confronted with this choice. Truman, of course, is the only leader to have ordered the dropping of atomic bombs, and there is some evidence that the consequences of his decision may have affected his later thinking on the subject. Truman's own personal journal, in any case, confirms that he twice considered using nuclear weapons after Hiroshima, once when the peace negotiations to end the Korean war were not yet underway, and again when those talks were stalled. On the latter occasion, Truman's journal records an almost Walter Mitty-like fantasy in which the president thought about confronting Stalin and Mao with a nuclear ultimatum: "Now do you want an end to hostilities in Korea or do you want China and Siberia destroyed? You may have one or the other which ever you want. . . . You either accept our fair and just proposal or you will be completely destroyed." A subsequent entry indicated that Truman thought about reading "Confucius on morals" to Stalin, along with "Buddah's code," the Declaration of Independence, the French Declaration on Liberty and Fraternity, the Bill of Rights, the fifth, sixth, and seventh chapters of St. Matthew, and St. John's prophecy on the Antichrist. The realism that was always one of Truman's strengths prevented him from making such a nuclear threat, of course, or from actually using the atomic bomb in Korea. But the temptation must have been great.[11]

A similar kind of conversion on the subject of nuclear weapons would appear to have come to Dwight Eisenhower. Eisenhower is on record for having said in 1955 that if nuclear weapons could be used on strictly military targets, he could see "no reason why they shouldn't be used just exactly as you would use a bullet or anything else." Moreover, the administration's "New Look" and its declared policy of massive retaliation were each founded on the credibility of making nuclear threats. But according to those around him, Eisenhower experienced a moment of epiphany concerning deterrence as a result of an expert study of the preparations necessary to survive a nuclear war. When he commissioned the Gaither Panel in the spring of 1957, Eisenhower instructed them that their charter was to answer the question: "If you assume there is going to be a nuclear war, what should I do?"[12]

After several months of study the experts on the Gaither Panel reported that the annual cost of preparing to fight a nuclear war might approach $50 billion, with $40 billion alone necessary for a nationwide system of fallout shelters. This would represent a tripling of the defense budget from the Truman years; but even more staggering than the economic costs, some of the experts predicted, might be the social costs of such preparations. Jerome Wiesner, later the president of MIT, thought that the distortion of American society required by the steps he and the other Gaither panelists recommended would be so great that the society – and democracy itself – might not survive, even if there was no war.[13]

The destruction that would be caused by such a war had meanwhile also grown proportionally greater – as Brodie predicted it would – because of the incorporation of hydrogen bombs in nuclear war planning. By 1955, the power of the largest nuclear weapons in the United States arsenal had increased a thousandfold in only ten years, from a yield equivalent of 20 thousand tons to 20 million tons of conventional explosives. Had the United States gone to war in that year, the Strategic Air Command had the bombs and bombers available for its plan to destroy 118 out of 134 Russian cities, in what could be a single raid. Official estimates predicted approximately 76 million Russian casualties immediately after such an attack, of whom 60 million would be fatalities. By the account of one nuclear strategist familiar with the war plan, "strategic targeting just got incredibly sloppy at this time" because of the hydrogen bomb. In some cases the aiming point for a particular Russian target had been shifted from a single industry in a city, to the city's center, and finally to a point midway between two or more cities – since one bomb would consume them all. A Navy officer briefed on the 1955 war plan described it as a proposal to turn all of Russia into a "smoking, radiating ruin at the end of two hours."[14]

The evident result of embracing all of these horrors was, for Eisenhower, a change of attitude toward the nuclear debate. At the end of the briefing he received in November 1957 from the members of the Gaither Panel on their report, the president reportedly told the assembly of experts that he now realized he had asked them the wrong question. "You can't have this kind of war," Eisenhower said. "There aren't enough bulldozers to scrape the bodies off the streets."[15]

While he was essentially unfamiliar with the issues involved in the nuclear debate when he became defense secretary in 1961, Robert McNamara has almost certainly had the greatest impact of any person upon American nuclear strategy. By McNamara's own account, one of the things that had the greatest effect upon his thinking on the subject of nuclear weapons and war was an accident that occurred while he had been at the Pentagon only four days. When a B-52 bomber carrying two 24-megaton hydrogen bombs disintegrated in flight over North Carolina, one of the bombs separated from the wreckage and fell to earth, breaking open upon impact. A subsequent investigation showed that five of the six safety devices designed to prevent the weapon from accidentally exploding in such cases had failed in the crash. "Only a single switch," one of the investigators testified, "prevented the bomb from detonating and spreading fire and destruction over a wide area."[16]

The fact that the bomber's crash was only one of 60 nuclear accidents since the start of the atomic age – and the occurrence of what McNamara characterized as a "massive false alarm on the early warning system of a Soviet attack" just a short time after this incident – created an urgent concern on his part with the problem of averting an accidental nuclear war. It was undoubtedly this concern that also prompted McNamara to urge that presidents Kennedy and Johnson adopt a policy of what he now calls "no-second-strike-until," whereby no United States retaliatory blow would be approved following a nuclear explosion upon American territory until the president was personally convinced that the nation was under a sustained enemy attack. The equal depth of McNamara's concern with the prospect of deliberate nuclear war at this time has been attested to, as well, by Eisenhower science advisor Herbert York, who accompanied McNamara to a briefing on the war plan early in his tenure. (York has vividly described McNamara's stunned reaction to the disclosure that the full-scale attack upon Russia envisioned by SIOP I would not only kill between 365 and 425 million Russians and Chinese, but could also cause clouds of lethal radioactivity to be carried into Scandinavia and Eastern Europe.) Following this inauguration into the realities of the nuclear age, it should perhaps come as little surprise that during his first few weeks in office NcNamara reportedly favored a nuclear strategy of minimum deterrence, believing that as few as 200 nuclear weapons aimed at Russian cities would be sufficient to deter any Soviet attack.[17]

Given McNamara's manifest abhorrence of the prospect of nuclear war it is all the more ironic that he would eventually be credited with introducing the concept of nuclear war-fighting into American strategy. Counterforce targeting had, in fact, always been a component of United States planning, as an initial stage in a nuclear war. But it was McNamara's hope and intention to limit the damage that might be caused in a nuclear war by restricting the targeting of each side to military objectives, and thereby avoiding the destruction of cities. Certainly McNamara himself did not believe in 1962 that his celebrated "no-cities" doctrine made nuclear war any more likely or acceptable, but critics of the time argued that his revision of the SIOP to conform to that doctrine had both those effects. Responding in part to those critics – but even more to the Air Force, whose budget requests now included a whole new variety of war-fighting nuclear weapons – McNamara gradually and progressively backed away from the "no-cities" doctrine. By 1964 he had all but abandoned as well the idea of "damage limitation" in a nuclear war, reportedly instructing the nation's military leaders to ignore his earlier statements on the concept in their future planning.[18]

McNamara's important departure from earlier planning had been to admit a war-fighting role for nuclear weapons. Despite his later disclaimers, the options that he incorporated into the revised SIOP envisioned a nuclear war that would not necessarily end in a world-destroying holocaust, but that might in some significant way be controlled, and thus either restrained or escalated depending upon circumstances. Having, in effect, let the camel's nose into the doctrinal tent, McNamara – and his successors – would find it increasingly difficult to keep a war-fighting strategy from insinuating itself further into the thinking and planning that concerned nuclear weapons.

* * *

It seems unlikely that the nation's five presidents since John Kennedy have been any less committed than their predecessors to the principle of deterrence, or any more inclined to risk a nuclear war on the hope that it might be kept under control and the casualties limited. At the same time, the sophistication and variety of the ways in which a nuclear war might be fought have kept pace with the steady increase in the number, if not the power, of the weapons deployed by each side. Most obvious among the reasons for the persistence and the growth of war-fighting scenarios has been the always frightful but plausible prospect that caused McNamara finally to reject the idea of targeting only Soviet cities – the possibility that in an irrational world deterrence might fail. But a number of other pressures influenced the shift from deterrence to war-fighting, some of which may have grown more compelling with time. These have included domestic pressures for a "stronger" defense, a technological imperative to build any new weapon that works (as well as a bureaucratic imperative to build some that don't), a moral argument against mutual assured destruction, and – not least of these – the plain fact that Russian nuclear strategy, too, seems to be characterized by a similar ambiguity between preventing or fighting and winning a nuclear war. This last fact, combined with an accompanying Soviet military buildup, has within the last decade become perhaps the dominant reason for the change in American nuclear strategy.

The majority of those United States nuclear strategists who might be characterized as war-fighters have argued that it is less important that *we* believe we can fight and win a nuclear war than that the Russians believe we have such faith. In a curious way, our actual intentions have become less important in this battle of wills than our military capabilities. James Schlesinger, defense secretary under presidents Nixon and Ford, was presumably a no greater enthusiast of nuclear war than Robert McNamara when he carried out another major revision of the SIOP in 1974. Schlesinger has conceded off the public record that a principal motive behind his reason for adding a new range of "limited nuclear options" to the war plan was his concern that United States nuclear strategy appeared still to be excessively wedded to the concept of deterrence. By his own account, Schlesinger's thinking about nuclear weapons distinguishes between "declaratory policy, war plans, and what you are actually able to do," considering each separable. It was under the premise that you do not tell the enemy what you are *not* going to do that he further refined the strategy of war-fighting to include more flexibility and thus credibility, adding new categories of targets that might be destroyed at various stages of a nuclear war.[19]

Neither Nixon nor Ford were reportedly any more optimistic than Schlesinger that a nuclear war could actually be fought and won, much less controlled. (The story – perhaps apocryphal – is told that when Ford was first briefed in 1975 on the new SIOP's five options for responding to a Soviet attack he listened politely till the end and then inquired, "So, what are my options?," believing any of the five would inevitably lead to the final holocaust.)[20]

By the time Jimmy Carter arrived in Washington the strategy of war-fighting was well established alongside that of deterrence in the nation's military planning. Indeed, the increasing emphasis upon the theoretical propsect of fighting and winning a nuclear war in such planning may account in part for Carter's inaugural dedication to work toward ridding the planet of nuclear weapons, and for his own brief infatuation with the concept of minimum deterrence that had also intrigued McNamara. Like the experience of McNamara, Carter's encounter with nuclear realities seems especially ironic, since by the end of his administration the strategy of war-fighting had achieved a new eminence. Inadvertently, the president who at the outset perhaps came closest to professing a brand of nuclear pacifism had, by the end of his term, approved a war plan that contained the first comprehensive theory of victory.

As had been the case with his predecessors, along Carter's circuitous route to war-fighting had been noble intentions and unforeseen consequences in equal measure. During the 1960s, development of the most powerful of the war-fighting weapons to be added to America's arsenal—multiple and independently targetable missle warheads—had been initially supported by arms control enthusiasts as a means of avoiding antiballistic missiles, which were thought to be a threat to the stability of deterrence. In this case, however, the danger that was known proved less threatening than that which was not; as MIRVs became progressively more accurate atop Soviet and American missiles, they increasingly threatened the survival of retaliatory forces on both sides. Similarly, a weapon perhaps ideally suited for war-fighting—the MX—was evidently approved by Carter as the political cost of support for arms control intended to preserve deterrence. In the wake of the Soviet invasion of Afghanistan, Carter failed to get SALT II but remained nonetheless committed to MX.[21]

While both Carter and Defense Secretary Harold Brown by the end of their tenure had publicly disavowed the notion that a nuclear war could be fought, won, or controlled, the administration ultimately seemed to acknowledge the paradox that had overtaken nuclear planning when it announced in 1980 a new directive—the celebrated PD-59—adding still more flexibility to the war plan and holding out the prospect of victory achieved by disarming Russian forces and decapitating the Soviet leadership. Physicist Richard Garwin, President Nixon's science advisor, has testified to the degree to which war-fighting had by this time come to dominate the thinking of military planners in the Pentagon. According to Garwin, when he began to explain his views on nuclear weapons to a former colleague there—"that they were only for deterrence and all this idea of flexible response and a protracted, closely managed war was nonsense"—the latter had looked at him "as [if] I were some kind of fossil."

"All the talk in the Pentagon was on these other aspects," Garwin notes. "People had long since gone away from the use of nuclear weapons as a deterrent."[22]

* * *

Whether the Reagan administration will represent an actual departure from the thinking and planning of its predecessors in the matter of nuclear war is still uncertain, since that administration has not yet passed into history. Thus far Reagan and Defense Secretary Caspar Weinberger have done more to consolidate the changes made by President Carter than to pioneer in the strategy of war-fighting, though they have evidently refined the premises of PD-59 and extended them further in a document now being called Reagan-13, which envisions the prospect of a nuclear war lasting up to five years. Possibly the most significant but little-noticed change to date has been the administration's decision to reinstate the aim of "prevailing" over the Soviet Union as the goal of the present defense guidance on nuclear war. This is a term that first appeared in Air Force planning and in the Basic National Security Policy of the Eisenhower administration, but that was purposefully stricken from military planning during the Kennedy administration on the ground that it represented "a word of art," according to one Kennedy aide, and guaranteed an open-ended series of budget requests from the military services. The earliest concept of "prevailing" had behind it a vague faith that the Soviet Union would collapse following an all-out atomic onslaught; the present notion appears to be based upon much more selective attacks meant to destroy the control of the Soviet Union over its forces and its people.[23]

However, the extent to which the Reagan administration really believes it can control and win a nuclear war with the Soviet Union, or simply professes such faith in order to deter the Russians, ultimately remains a matter of conjecture. Certainly for some in the administration – Deputy Under Secretary of Defense T. K. Jones, most notably – the strategy of fighting, surviving, and winning a nuclear war is an article of true faith. But others – including Andrew Marshall, head of the Pentagon's Office of Net Assessments and a principal author of Reagan-13 – have claimed off the public record that the appearance of a war-fighting strategy in United States planning may be more important than its reality.

What is unique about this approach to nuclear strategy is that the Reagan administration has become the first to publicly proclaim its faith that the limited, winnable nuclear "war-between-the-bases" Borden hypothesized 39 years ago is possible, and to establish a nuclear weapons policy on that belief. What is also new is that for the first time – after a generation of effort, and at the cost of many billions of dollars – the United

States is now acquiring the theoretical capability to fight such a war. The war-fighters – whose role in nuclear strategy has been increasingly prominent – would seem to be ascendant in the nuclear debate. Yet the ambiguity that characterized American strategy at the time of the Berlin crisis is no less today; and the paradox between preventing and fighting a nuclear war has never been more evident.

* * *

It may be that the great but unheralded effect of the present rethinking of the unthinkable has been to bring about a change not in nuclear strategy, but in the nature of the nuclear debate. The current ascendancy of the war-fighters is attributable less to their own accomplishments than to the fact that the deterrers have fled the field. Not since Brodie's proclamation that strategy had hit a dead end with the invention of the hydrogen bomb has such profound doubt and despair accompanied the subject of nuclear weapons; nor such an apparently fundamental loss of faith in deterrence. Though it might be said to have endured for more than 30 years, the concept of mutual assured destruction has found few champions recently. But the confounders of MAD – the war-fighters – have thus far offered no better hope than the tenuous and untested chance that a nuclear war might prove limited and controllable. At the same time, those who have opposed the war-fighters and the deployment of new counterforce weapons – experts like Richard Garwin – have offered as an alternative only the unenviable option of launching our retaliatory blow upon warning of an enemy attack. Critics of the policy of launch-on-warning have argued that to do so would be to surrender our fate to machines, and thus tempt the malfunction of the "handful of vacuum and transistors" – in our case, microchips – that expunged the world in Nevil Shute's novel, *On the Beach*.[24]

The result of this intellectual dead-end in the nuclear debate has been to create an unprecedented degree of gnosticism on the subject of nuclear weapons and war – "gnostic" being the Greek word for "knowledge" or "insight." The original gnostics were a group of renegade theologians who radically reinterpreted the holy scriptures following the death of Christ. Elaine Pagels, author of *The Gnostic Gospels*, writes that gnosticism as a religious movement began because "many people at the time felt profoundly alienated from the world in which they lived, and longed for salvation as an escape from the constraints of political and social existence."[25]

A similar kind of feeling seems to pervade the current public debate over nuclear weapons and nuclear strategy. The perception that there are no longer any good alternatives to be offered by the experts or the government has caused that debate to become truly public for the first time and has given rise to the nuclear freeze movement. The question being asked by the nuclear gnostics has brought the debate on nuclear weapons that began in 1946 full circuit. It is a question that would certainly be familiar to Bernard Brodie, for Brodie originally borrowed it from two other strategists – Clausewitz and Marshal Foch – and made it the theme of his last book, *War and Politics*. It is the question, *"De quoi s'agit-il?"* – literally, "What is it all about; what is it for?" Remarkably, it is a question seldom asked about nuclear strategy and nuclear weapons by the public during the past 39 years, and one that has never truly received an answer.[26]

NOTES

1 Gregg Herken, *The Winning Weapon: The Atomic Bomb in the Cold War* (New York: Knopf, 1980), pp. 266–76.

2 Jay Kelley and Desmond Ball, "Strategic Nuclear Targeting," Unpublished manuscript, International Institute for Strategic Studies, London, August 1981, pp. 41–55.

3 Lawrence Freedman, *The Evolution of Nuclear Strategy* (New York: St. Martin's Press, 1981), p. 400.

4 Fred Kaplan, *The Wizards of Armageddon* (New York: Simon and Schuster, 1983).

5 Bernard Brodie, ed., *The Absolute Weapon: Atomic Power and World Order* (New York: Harcourt, Brace and Company, 1946), pp. 28, 73, 101–3.

6 William Liscum Borden, *There Will Be No Time: The Revolution in Strategy* (New York: Macmillan, 1946), p. ix. Interview with William Borden, Washington, DC, November 30, 1981.

7 Ibid., pp. 63, 83, 87.

8 Ibid., p. 214. Concerning Borden's role in the Oppenheimer affair, see Philip Stern, *The Oppenheimer Case: Security on Trial* (New York: Harper and Row, 1969), pp. 21–23. Borden interview.

9 Brodie to S. Jones, February 25, 1955, Box 1, Bernard Brodie MSS, Special Collections, UCLA. Interview with Herman Kahn, Hudson, New York, May 13, 1981. Interview with Sam Cohen, Marina Del Ray, Calif., April 2, 1982.

10 Interview with Herbert York, San Francisco, Calif., June 10, 1981.

11 Robert Ferrell, ed., *Off the Record: The Private Papers of Harry S. Truman* (New York: Harper and Row, 1980), p. 251.

12 Eisenhower is cited in John Lewis Gaddis, *Strategies of Containment: A Critical Appraisal of Postwar American National Security Policy* (New York: Oxford University Press, 1982), p. 149. Interview with Jerome Wiesner, MIT, September 2, 1982.

13 U.S. Congress, Joint Committee on Defense Production, "Deterrence and Survival in the Nuclear Age" [*The Gaither Report*], (Washington, DC, G.P.O. 1976). Wiesner interview. Interview with Spurgeon Keeny, Washington DC, May 7, 1982.

14 David Alan Rosenberg, "A Smoking Radiating Ruin at the End of Two Hours," *International Security* 6, no. 3 (Winter 1981/82): 3–38.

15 Wiesner interview.

16 Interview with Robert McNamara, Washington, DC, May 7, 1982. Concerning this incident and other nuclear weapons accidents, see "U.S. Nuclear Weapons Accidents: Danger in Our Midst," *The Defense Monitor* 10, no. 5 (1981), Center for Defense Information, Washington, DC.

17 McNamara interview. York interview.

18 Desmond Ball, *Politics and Force Levels: The Strategic Missile Program of the Kennedy Administration* (Berkeley: University of California Press, 1980). McNamara interview. Fred Kaplan, *The Wizards of Armageddon*, pp. 313–24.

19 Interview with James Schlesinger, Washington, DC, December 15, 1982.

20 Schlesinger later believed that the simple growth of nuclear arsenals made the flexibility of war planning almost useless: "The selectivity has been drowned out by the number of weapons." Schlesinger interview.

21 Ted Greenwood, *Making the MIRV: A Study of Defense Decision Making* (Cambridge, Mass.: Ballinger Press, 1975), pp. 73–78; 129–37. John Edwards, *Super Weapon: The Making of MX* (New York: W. W. Norton, 1982), pp. 171–99.

22 Thomas Powers, "Choosing a Strategy for World War III," *Atlantic Monthly,* November 1982, pp. 82–110. Interview with Richard Garwin, Yale, November 2, 1982.

23 Ibid. Robert Scheer, *With Enough Shovels: Reagan, Bush, and Nuclear War* (New York: Random House, 1982), pp. 18–26. Interview with T. K. Jones, Pentagon, June 5, 1981. Interview with Andrew Marshall, Pentagon, December 15, 1982.

24 Garwin interview. Richard Garwin, "Launch Under Attack to Redress Minuteman Vulnerability", *International Security* 4, no. 3 (Winter 1979/80): 117–39.

25 Elaine Pagels, *The Gnostic Gospels* (New York: Vintage Books, 1981), p. 152.

26 Bernard Brodie, *War and Politics* (New York: Macmillan, 1973), p. 1.

3

TRADITIONAL AND SOVIET MILITARY DOCTRINE: TENDENCIES AND DANGERS

George H. Quester

The intent of this chapter is to discuss what is a very natural tendency in American and Soviet military analysis (perhaps in all military analysis), and yet is now a very misleading or dangerous one. Military officers, out of a simple pride in doing their duty and a sense of morality shared with their countrymen at large, may fasten too much importance on defeating their opponents in battle. This outlook threatens any political accommodations or detente and further poses the risk of "a war nobody wanted."

This chapter begins by describing the general sources and traditional justifications of this outlook and some instances where it has been overcome in the United States. I then discuss the Soviet failure to frankly acknowledge the need to override this tendency and the serious damage this does to the entire Soviet-American relationship.

THE TRADITIONAL COUNTERFORCE TENDENCY

The tendency to concentrate on one's opposite number as the prime target shows up in all the services, but it is displayed most clearly in the writings of Alfred Thayer Mahan on naval policy and of Giulio Douhet on air force operations.

Mahan believed that what had been natural for the Royal Navy in its best years, and what would have to be natural for the U.S. Navy as its successor, was securing dominance of the sea by driving other fleets from it. Alternative uses of naval power, for example, harassing the merchant operations of the dominant sea power, he viewed as insufficiently ambitious. Mahan saw this as attempting to apply naval power without having first consolidated a sufficient hold on it.

So far we have been viewing the effect of a purely cruising warfare, not based upon powerful squadrons, only upon that particular part of the enemy's strength against which it is theoretically directed – upon his commerce and general wealth; upon the sinews of war. The evidence seems to show that even for its own special ends such a mode of war is inconclusive, worrying but not deadly; it might almost be said that it causes needless suffering.

It is not the taking of individual ships or convoys, be they few or many, that strikes down the money power of a nation; it is the possession of that overbearing power on the sea which drives the enemy's flag from it, or allows it to appear only as a fugitive; and which, by controlling the great common, closes the highways by which commerce moves to and from the enemy's shores.[1]

Strategists of aerial combat have similarly been inclined to debunk any plans which do not place highest priority on sweeping an enemy's air force from the sky.

We today often view the overhead means of delivery, by airplane or by ballistic missile, as enshrining the countervalue capabilities of "mutual assured destruction" (MAD). This situation is one in which either side is capable of inflicting retaliatory destruction on the other, regardless of who wins the exchanges of combat. Such retaliatory threats theoretically deter either side from ever launching such combat. Nuclear weapons provide the means of such retaliatory destruction today, but analysts between the two world wars imputed similar levels of destructiveness to the use of poison gas or dynamite.

Consider the destructive capabilities assumed by Douhet in his classic, *The Command of the Air:*

In general, aerial offensives will be directed against such targets as peacetime industrial and commercial establishments; important buildings, private and public; transportation arteries and centers; and certain designated areas of civilian population as well. To destroy these targets three kinds of bombs are needed – explosive, incendiary, and poison gas – apportioned as the situation may require. The explosives will demolish the target, the incendiaries set fire to it, and the poison-gas bombs prevent fire fighters from extinguishing the fires.[2]

Or consider the similar assumptions of J. F. C. Fuller in his widely read 1923 book, *The Reformation of War:*

I believe that, in future warfare, great cities, such as London, will be attacked from the air, and that a fleet of 500 aeroplanes each carrying 500 ten-pound bombs of, let us suppose, mustard gas, might cause 200,000 minor casualties and throw the whole city into panic within half an hour of their arrival.[3]

Yet while the premises of assured destruction seemed (prematurely) to have been established, both Douhet and Fuller in their strategic advice drifted again toward the counterforce approach – destroying the enemy's air force and his ability to wage war – as opposed to the countervalue approach – inflicting painful destruction for its own sake, to dissuade the enemy from continuing the war (or to deter an enemy from ever beginning a war). For example, Douhet:

> To have command of the air means to be in a position to prevent the enemy from flying while retaining the ability to fly oneself. . . .
> A nation which has command of the air is in a position to protect its own territory from enemy aerial attack and even to put a halt to the enemy's auxiliary actions in support of his land and sea operations, leaving him powerless to do much of anything.[4]

Turning to ground weapons, Clausewitz's *On War* can be interpreted in numerous and conflicting ways. The debate continues over whether to view him as the apostle of total war, or whether this message is overshadowed by his basic premise that war is the continuation of politics by other means. The two could be reconciled, of course, by seeing Clausewitz as an interpreter of the French Revolution and the Napoleonic period. Since the impact of politics on daily existence is more extensive and "total" now, war, as the continuation of politics, also has a more pervasively significant meaning for individual lives.

Clausewitz at one point translates this specifically into an enjoinder that the aim in warfare is to disarm the enemy. One could hardly phrase the counterforce self-image more clearly than this, and Clausewitz's words will ring true for the majority of military men.

THE AIM IS TO DISARM THE ENEMY

> I have already said that the aim of warfare is to disarm the enemy and it is time to show that, at least in theory, this is bound to be so.
> So long as I have not overthrown my opponent I am bound to fear he may overthrow me. Thus I am not in control: he dictates to me as much as I dictate to him.[5]

When all of Clausewitz's complications are taken into account, of course, the emphasis on total war is diminished, and with it the emphasis on disarming the forces of the other side. Clausewitz stresses the political object of war, which might stop short of a victory that had stripped the other side of its armed forces. He notes the importance of the defense as a periodic explainer of lulls in warfare. Yet Clausewitz's reader is ultimately left without a clear sign that one should renounce the disarmament of one's enemy. Here (and perhaps only here) could one achieve something meaningful and lasting by the energies invested in a war.

To see how far this emphasis on disarming the opposition goes back in history, we can turn to the writings of Sun Tzu, generally believed to have put his thoughts on paper between 400 and 300 BC, well before any of the writings of military strategists in the West.

> 5. Invincibility lies in the defence; the possibility of victory in the attack.
> 6. One defends when his strength is inadequate; he attacks when it is abundant.[6]

Why does one have to go to the offense, once one's strength is again adequate? Why is the attack necessary for any meaningful sense of victory? It is because victory entails getting rid of the enemy's menace, by disarming him.

How would such a stress in strategic purpose affect operational distinctions? At sea, it has been connected to the maxim of "never divide the fleet." If the object of our navy is to sink the other navy, then it makes sense to keep the fleet together. The mathematics of fire-exchange ratios, as theorized by F. W. Lanchester in the "Lanchester Square Law," suggest that the greatest counterforce impact will be achieved this way. If other functions are given greater priority, such as supporting landing forces ashore, protecting one's coast, or harassing an enemy's coasts, then very different deployment patterns are called for, and even differing ship designs.

In air warfare, a stress on winning control of the air presumably suggests assigning more resources to air-superiority fighters (such as the F-15), while a commitment to earlier use of air platforms would dictate a greater investment in fighter-bombers, planes sacrificing some potential for air-to-air combat in order to have a greater potential for air-to-ground combat (such as the F-16).

As an illustration of how such a bias toward counterforce affects procurement decisions, the accuracy of intercontinental ballistic missiles (ICBM) or various forms of ground-launched, sea-launched, or air-launched cruise missiles (GLCM, SLCM, ALCM) is hardly essential if the target is mainly the other side's urban population concentrations. Accuracy becomes much more desirable when the target is the other side's missile forces or some other portion of the enemy's military potential.

It is just as natural for the strategic nuclear forces of either side to aim at the strategic nuclear forces of the opponent as it was natural earlier for navies or for air forces to aim at each other. It has correspondingly seemed unnatural for missiles to be aimed at innocent civilians. Yet, bizarre as it may seem, peace may now depend on civilians being the target, and on the military's natural inclination toward counterforce targeting being overcome and renounced.

SOURCES OF THE COUNTERFORCE TENDENCY

I shall now outline some possible explanations for this bias of the professional military toward the counterforce role. A few of the explanations offered may portray the military officer as self-serving, much as the "bureaucratic politics" literature paints all government workers as selfish. But a larger part of the problem stems from the officer's deeper desire to render service for the public, for the ultimate consumer of whatever a military force produces.

The tendency toward counterforce operations, toward trying to win "command of the sea" or "command of the air" on "full control over the ground," will be recognizable and understandable, upon reflection, to all who have ever been afflicted with the "Protestant ethic" or similar goads toward hard work and success. It is natural to put first things first, to capitalize before consuming, to take care of the means to happiness first and then apply these means to consumption needs.

A navy therefore feels virtuous in first sinking the opposing navy and only then attending to other tasks, such as assisting sister services, harassing enemy merchant shipping, convoying its own merchant shipping, or attacking enemy coastlines and defending its own coastlines. An air force should first eliminate the opposition's air force and then (having established the capital position of air dominance) turn to secondary missions.

"Erst die arbeit, und dann das spiel" is an old German saying which drums diligence into young children. "First the work, and then the play." "First earn yourself a million dollars or two, and then buy yourself a yacht."

Military force is of course related to political and civilian uses. Clausewitz's aphorism about war being a continuation of politics is nowhere denied here, for every commander realizes that the ultimate justification of the domination of seas, air, or ground lies in the political uses of that domination. Yet the distinction between preparation and use which stems from the world of ordinary civilian endeavor implants a substantive psychological block here. One feels more virtuous in postponing considerations of use, in accumulating politically usable military power without yet having used it. Thinking about how one will spend one's income can get in the way of earning it. Becoming diverted by other uses of naval power can get in the way of acquiring that naval power. Even assisting the army is something that a navy feels justified in sliding back on the schedule, as compared with sinking the opposing navy.

We are not arguing that the ultimate uses of military power are ever fully forgotten. Rather, this is to contend that a more subtle bias is generated toward overemphasizing the counterforce role of military power. Just as some businessmen become so intent on acquiring money that they become incapable of enjoying spending it, so the stress on defeating the enemy in combat is given too much weight.

The dominant motive behind the bias we have outlined here may thus come in this sense of capitalization, the puritan feeling that it is noble to husband capability and round out capability, after which, in due time, capability will be used. When there are no more enemy ships to be sunk, no more enemy aircraft to be shot down, then one can with no trepidation turn to applying sea power or air power to more "applied" uses.

A second reason for the stress on counterforce appeals to traditional standards of nobility and morality. To attack the enemy of the same cut of uniform is fair game. To bomb civilians is not. For navies to attempt anything beyond attacking opposing navies is thus a dubious endeavor, because noncombatants are then the target. The most honorable note of military training anywhere is that the only legitimate target will be people in uniform on the other side.

Many American academics, specializing in the study of international relations since the introduction of nuclear weapons, believe it is necessary that civilians be the target of retaliatory forces on each side. This is part of what Donald Brennan meant to criticize when he labeled it MAD. These academics usually have no difficulty in persuading their students, in any semester-length course, that there is no practical alternative to the mutual targeting of non-military countervalue targets, since aiming at counterforce military targets would be very destabilizing and threatening to peace.

Yet, these academics and their students, and a fair number of policymakers in United States administrations in the 1960s, amount to a very small community, as opposed to the vast bulk of Americans who may still be appalled at the idea of deliberate targeting of civilians. Sunday sermons and newspaper editorials would be very quick to attack this as the height of immorality. This reinforces a signal which the military has received all along from its civilian constituency; it is more noble to go counterforce than countervalue, more noble to attack ships and airplanes and soldiers than to attack civilians.

No one has ever been tried for war crimes for shooting at or bombing military targets. If the German U-boat campaign of World War I had been directed only at British warships, rather than at civilian-registry merchantmen, the American public would never have become aroused to enter the war on Britain's side. All of the United States bombing raids in World War II, including even the nuclear bombing of Hiroshima, were rationalized as somehow directed at military targets.

The morality of counterforce efforts, and the immorality of countervalue campaigns, is thus part of the ambient public attitude in the United States and around the world, including the Soviet Union. Soviet military doctrine has always taken world opinion into account. They have tried to exploit such opinion, but have also somewhat internalized it. Soviet statements on possible nuclear war always declare that exclusively military targets will be bombed, a message as frightening as it is moral, and one which creates important problems to which we shall return.

A third motive for the counterforce emphasis is less noble. By sounding the counterforce bugle each service tries to win out against competing services fighting for budgetary allocations. To stress the threat of the opposing navy helps to convince one's citizens – and taxpayers – of the value in general of having a navy – and of paying what it costs to have a fine one. To stress the threat of the enemy's tank forces boosts appropriations for one's own tank forces. To place high priority on the shooting down of the enemy air force promotes one's own air force within the domestic decision-making process.

A fourth kind of motive blends aspects of the first three. When a navy is able to go out onto the high seas to do battle against the opposing navy, rather than being held close to shore to support the infantry, it is freer to act independently, to carry through a project all of its own. This gives a higher feeling of purity and accomplishment similar to the Protestant ethic noted at the outset. There may also be more gratification in executing a campaign without having to coordinate with, or take instructions from, a sister service (which is closer to the assumption of parochial bureaucratic self-indulgence). The analogy with business life would come with the executive who enjoys running his own company, who derives gratification not only from capitalizing his firm into the millions of dollars, but from being allowed to stick to his own way of doing things, working within a field he knows best. Sailors all around the world respect other sailors. Sailors prefer to conduct their combat against other sailors.

This brings us to the fifth and last psychological reinforcement for the military's inclination toward the use of counterforce. Disarming an enemy entails taking the offensive, rather than waiting for the enemy to attack. The history of strategic analysis does display some enthusiasts for the defense, but very few. The most memorable writers have always discussed more ambitious strategic goals. Trusting in the defense entails forswearing a "command of the sea" or "command of the air," forswearing "disarming the enemy," and since 1940 it most typically gets labeled "Maginot mentality."

Can one aspire to rise to high rank being an expert on minefields, or pill boxes, or concrete fortifications? The bias of the military is that defensively oriented technology is noninnovative, "sit-still," status-quo-oriented, while offensive technology is very innovative, constantly on the move, constantly replacing old systems with new systems.

There are indeed some respectable alternatives to the goal of a counterforce disarming of the enemy. The highest calling of the Swiss Army (a very respectable fighting force, by all estimates) is not to disarm the enemy, but to repulse the enemy, to impose the lesson that he ought not to try again to conquer the Swiss. Cynics would say that this is all the Swiss can hope to do, because of their small size; a larger Switzerland could eliminate the Austrian, French, Italian, German, and Russian menaces once and for all, stripping away their arms.

Yet more than size is at work here. The Swiss attitude is "leave us alone and we'll leave you alone." Switzerland does not get invaded, but it does not stampede anyone else into useless wars either. If size limitations were all that have kept Swiss officers from taking Clausewitz too seriously (with classical geographic limitations keeping the Swiss from getting very fond of Mahan), there might still be some other good reasons to welcome the Swiss model, to pose it as an alternative role-model for the military profession.

Does one ever see signs of counterforce thinking on the civilian side of foreign policy decision-making and analysis? A correct approach to the strategic problem should include a combination of consumption and investment, rather than stress solely on investment. Mahan aside, navies often contribute more when they concentrate less on the sinking of the opposite navy. All counterforce and no derivative service, for the bulk of a war, may be less than optimal service of the national interest.

Among civilian analysts of foreign policy, too, one sometimes sees similarly misleading biases which stress "vital interests." Nations have interests; they have opinions as to which outcome is preferable to another. But what do we mean then by "vital" interests? This term presumably refers to certain results which have much higher priority than others, to certain accomplishments which should be assured first, before any attention is assigned to other matters.

Once again some activities look very much like responsible capitalization, while others are relegated to the status of self-indulgent consumption. The elevation of some attainments as "vital" can become a shorthand by which too much attention is assigned to them.

ALTERNATIVE MILITARY EMPHASES

There are exceptions to this military bias toward "doing battle with your opposite number." Certain weapons, and the vested interest of the people trained to use those weapons, sometimes preclude doing counterforce battle of this kind.

Until recently, submarine warfare was of this nature. Submarines have been useful in a variety of ways, but have not typically been very effective against other submarines. A broader counterforce action, generated by reasoning akin to Mahan's, would have directed the submarines against the surface fleet of the opposing navy. Some of the German U-boats of both world wars and some of the US submarines of World War II were deployed with this target in mind. Yet the primary target in all three of these submarine campaigns became much more of a *guerre de course*, an assault on the merchant shipping of the enemy. It came close to victory in the two German attempts and contributed very much to victory in the US assault on Japanese shipping. Is Mahan turning in his grave because the US submarines of World War II went mainly after merchantmen and did not concentrate on sinking the Japanese fleet? The rest of the US Navy, in particular the aircraft carriers, indeed concentrated on sinking the Japanese Navy, but the whole of the United States naval effort (submarines being a very significant part of this) broadened their range of targets. This widening of focus is what ultimately led to victory.

Other forms of military equipment are clearly earmarked to counter something other than their opposite number. Antiaircraft guns are aimed at enemy aircraft, not at the antiaircraft guns of the other side. Antisubmarine warfare (ASW) was until recently carried out mainly from surface vehicles and aircraft and was surely not pledged to sweep the enemy's ASW from the seas. Mine-sweepers try to undo the work of the enemy's mine-layers, while mine-layers try to undo the work of the enemy's mine-sweepers.

Where the target on the other side is military in any sense, the officers involved can still rally around the banner of counterforce. Mines may sink any enemy battleship as readily as a merchantman. Yet mines and submarines still undoubtedly find more merchant targets than warship targets. Effective utilization of these tools therefore means that Mahan is paid lip-service at best; that no particular concentration on the counterforce role is attempted. Submarines and mine-layers thus begin using naval power right from the beginning of the war, rather than being fixated on capitalizing and expanding upon naval power.

If the mere investment in such types of ships and equipment pulls officers away from an excessive fascination with the counterforce role, the obverse relationship is probably also in effect. Navies taking Mahan seriously have probably tended to underinvest in mine-layers and submarines.

At least three critical questions must now always be asked concerning this stress on defeating the opposite military force.

First, can it be done? Or will the attempts be prone to failure, as more of your own force is consumed in the counterforce attack than gets taken out of the enemy force?

Second, is the primary concern in a war that other functions should be postponed until the grand accumulation of capital in a counterforce campaign is finally accomplished? Shouldn't one divert energies earlier to helping sister services and to attacking or shielding civilian targets?

Third, might not a focus on the counterforce stripping of an enemy's ability to fight be threatening and destabilizing, making war more likely?

The premise that counterforce preparations are destabilizing is now accepted, though often with reluctance, by the professional military. When either side has the ability to disarm the other's military, it will be tempted to do so, lest it lose this ability later on, or the other side attain it. Wars will therefore happen which would not otherwise have occurred. If both sides have the ability to disarm their opponents, victory may simply go to whoever strikes first. This will result in each side racing to strike in crisis, shooting first and asking questions later, producing a war which neither side may have wanted. This is often thought to be the way that World War I began. This has also often been feared to be the way World War III might begin.

A reasonable strategist must consider whether his country will win a war, if it happens, and whether in that case the cost of war can be reduced. But he will also have to consider the impact of any deployments and strategies on the likelihood of war. To stampede an adversary into a war which neither side wants is not good strategy, even if the stampede is caused by what looked optimal as the way to fight a war once it had been begun.

The clearest deviation from our instinctive military inclination toward doing battle with opposite numbers thus comes in the nuclear age, with weapons which for a time looked like they could play almost no counterforce role, but would have to be countervalue in nature. The submarine-based missiles of the original Polaris force had to be aimed at civilians, and so did the land-based U.S. Air Force missiles, so deficient in accuracy that they could be aimed only at Soviet cities. Since Soviet military command posts have tended to remain in cities, and since Soviet industry is crucial to maintaining military force, such weapons could still be rationalized as counter-military rather than counter-civilian; but the bulk of strategic reasoning identified them as weapons of revenge, rather than as weapons for the attainment of dominance.

Yet the attitudes we have been describing here are shown by the low enthusiasm in both services for these roles, as compared with the rest of the Navy, and as compared with the manned bombers of the U.S. Air Force. Each of these services has enthusiastically received the enhancements of accuracy which have become possible in the 1970s and which once again allow generals and admirals, colonels and navy captains, to contemplate doing battle with their opposites, rather than with civilians. But the natural instinct toward counterforce here threatens the stability of the strategic balance.

To continue with the homely analogy, the tendency to seek to disarm the opposite military force is just as natural as the individual's desire to save for the future. The Keynesian paradox was that this virtue of prudential saving could be bad for the economy in the net, when not enough investment opportunities appeared to soak up all savings at full employment. The paradox of arms control is that too keen an interest in winning wars may make wars more likely.

It is no easier to deflate the pride military strategists take in the counterforce role than to eliminate the instincts of stewardship and productivity which are at the root of working and saving for the future. Sweeping the enemy from the seas or skies or battlefield presents the possibility of further exploitation and also of political rewards.

At best we can hope that military officers will become more aware of what motivates them, so that they can perhaps discount it. At other decision-making levels, it is necessary to counteract these tendencies because they threaten to engage the country in dangerous confrontations with adversaries afflicted with similar tendencies.

THE OBTUSENESS OF SOVIET STRATEGIC PRONOUNCEMENTS

Americans can certainly agree that detente is in trouble, even if they disagree about whose fault it is. Critics of the Reagan administration, and of the latter half of the Carter administration, argue that the United States has needlessly returned to Cold War rhetoric and chosen to direct substantial new investments into weaponry. The "hawks" are having their day with the election of Ronald Reagan, and the very term suggests that the United States is to blame for an aggressive new turn in foreign policy.

Yet would the hawks be nearly as persuasive if the Soviets had done all they could to ease tension, to prove the continued possibility and value of detente? I will now attempt to delineate important moves that the Soviets could have but never in fact made in this regard, some at the level of concrete weapons procurements, others at the even more important level of declaratory statements of military strategic planning.

The Soviets have indeed substantially modernized their military forces since 1970, in both strategic nuclear forces and in the forces configured for conventional war. Part of the problem stems simply from such force augmentations. Previously, the more dovish US arms analysts predicted that the USSR would only match the United States in totals of ICBMs and of submarine-launched ballistic missiles (SLBMs). Yet the Soviets produced large numbers of both kinds of strategic nuclear missiles in the 1970s, ultimately exceeding the United States in the totals frozen at a status quo in SALT I. The Soviets have also very much modernized and expanded their conventional ground force capability, thus increasing Western Europe's exposure to the possibility of ground invasion.

The picture of Soviet blame, in terms only of procurements, however, is far from clear. Comparisons of missile totals often omit the strategic nuclear bomber, a category in which the Russians did not match the United States. They also exclude the French and British strategic nuclear forces, and US theater nuclear forces based forward in Western Europe, all of which could inflict considerable damage on the Soviet Union.

The United States did not add to its total of missile launchers in the 1970s, but it did increase substantially the total of nuclear warheads that could be delivered to Soviet targets. This was done by developing multiple warheads for the missiles it already possessed. This came initially in reaction to Soviet preparations for an ABM antimissile defense, a population defense system which the Soviets abandoned around the time they signed a treaty with the United States forbidding ABM. The US then held the advantage for most of the 1970s because of its lead in multiple-warhead (MIRV) technology. New problems were slated to arise in the 1980s when the Soviets caught up with the United States in MIRV technology and could apply this to the larger numbers of missiles they had acquired, missiles, furthermore, which had generally been greater in size and carrying capacity than those of the United States.

Given this confusing picture of possible actions and reactions, some may object that it is not Soviet procurements that are most to blame for fueling renewed rounds of the arms race in the 1980s, but rather some aspects of Soviet pronouncements, aspects very much in the counterforce tradition we have been describing.

Soviet statements of strategic doctrine are provocative. They are still tied too much to the older moral tradition of what the military's purpose should be in war: to protect one's own homeland and civilians, by destroying the enemy's military forces.

One could easily enough write out the script of what we would like the Soviet leadership to admit about nuclear war, for it is the mirror of what some American strategists and arms controllers have been writing for more than two decades. The Soviets should admit that nuclear retaliation will be so horrible for both sides as to make victory immaterial, and they should, even before this, admit that they are better off if the United States has assured means of inflicting such retaliation.

Since the gross levels of destruction that would occur in a future nuclear war are generally clear and stark enough, there is every reason to believe that Soviet analysts see the picture just as Americans have seen it.[7] The problem is that Soviet statements of their perceptions have not sufficiently acknowledged these realities. As a result, it has been possible for American analysts of a hawkish persuasion to argue that the Soviet leaders are not aware of these realities, are not intimidated by them, and are not guided by the same general formulations about the natures and priorities of nuclear war and peace as we are.[8]

Two major concessions have not yet been made in the Soviet discussion of nuclear strategic reality. The Russian commentary is, however, now close enough so that a hope for this final accommodation should not be abandoned. First, as noted quite lucidly by the late Donald Brennan in a published exchange with Raymond Garthoff, the Russians have never described it as desirable that the United States have a second-strike retaliatory capability, while the West has expressed the parallel desire.[9]

The Soviet commentary often stipulates that such a capability now exists on both sides; it concedes that the best efforts of Soviet military forces, for the moment, could not ward off such destruction. But it implies that Soviet forces should continue trying to terminate this retaliatory threat against the Soviet population, achieving success at some time in the future.

What is most lacking is an expression of feeling that each side should *want* the other to develop and maintain this retaliatory countervalue capability and restrain its own counterforce capabilities to avoid threatening this capability. Such was the conclusion of Oskar Morgenstern in a book which was part of the US arms control literature at the end of the 1950s, *The Question of National Defense.*

> *In view of modern technology of speedy weapons delivery from any point on earth to any other, it is in the interest of the United States for Russia to have an invulnerable retaliatory force and vice versa. . . .*
>
> We recall the extraordinary and steadily increasing danger of misinterpreting natural phenomena of the most varied kind as signs of an attack. Again, if the enemy with a vulnerable force does conclude falsely, even if only once, that he is being attacked and if we are in the ballistic missile age of nonrecallable action, a world catastrophe cannot be avoided.
>
> We do not want to live under conditions so precarious. We want to protect ourselves against accidents and errors where these have consequences of the magnitude of an all-out thermonuclear war.[10]

The second still-awaited Soviet doctrinal concession is an acknowledgment that there is no point in trying to win a nuclear war even if the other side has begun the attack. Soviet statements forswearing an interest in victory all too often become an assurance that the Soviet Union would never begin such a war, thus shifting the discussion to the alleged likelihood that the West would be the aggressor. Left much too vague is whether the alleged guilt of the United States, as aggressor, would then justify a Soviet effort to rebut this attack.

A truly forthcoming Soviet statement (again echoing what many Americans have said) would be that, no matter who started a nuclear war, there would be no point in trying to snatch victory away from the enemy and bring it home. Victory is as meaningless for the innocent in such a war as it is for the guilty. The only point of nuclear weaponry would be purely and simply to inflict retaliation.

There was a time when Soviet statements on nuclear war worried foreigners much more, because they seemd to question even whether such war would be hazardous. If the Soviets did not anticipate the destructiveness of nuclear war, could they be deterred by its prospect? Could they be deterred from any conventional invasion of Western Europe, or from trying to conquer the world by a nuclear sneak attack? When Stalin (and later, Mao) made such statements, they were of course most probably engaged in a colossal bluff, pretending to be indifferent to the power of nuclear weaponry, when they had none themselves.

Fearful commentators on Soviet strategy still detect strains of this kind of Soviet bluff (are we even sure the Soviets are bluffing, that they are not seriously indifferent to the destruction of Moscow and other cities?). This is especially true when Communist leaders seem to be laying heavy stress on civil defense measures, including shelter for themselves and some evacuation or shelter for the more valuable elements of the working population. Skeptics question the utility of Soviet civil defense preparations since these have never been fully rehearsed and since a thermonuclear attack would in any event tax even the most carefully prepared civil defense arrangements.

In any event, there is no shortage now of published Soviet statements admitting that nuclear war would be a disaster.[11] These statements have been appearing ever since the death of Stalin, often illustrated and elaborated in great detail. The Soviets concede that they would suffer badly and would lose a great deal in any nuclear war. They concede realistically that there is assured destruction under present conditions, and that such assured destruction is indeed mutual.

The problem is no longer that Soviet statements do not admit the likelihood of such a countervalue impact. Rather it is that, like many other commentators around the globe, they will not bring themselves to admit the desirability of such countervalue impact.

Is it impossible for the Soviet leadership to make so sweeping an acknowledgment? Some would say that we are simply asking too much of the Russians here. How could the leaders of the Communist world ever state so baldly that it was desirable—not just inevitable, but desirable—that the sick and wicked capitalist world be able to rain retaliatory destruction down on the Soviet Bloc in the event of World War III? We in the capitalist world can barely bring ourselves to admit the desirability of Communist retaliatory capability, and we are much less constrained and ideologically uniform in what our theorists put forward.

An important point is that only a majority of American analysts have endorsed the full logical premises of MAD, by which we should favor retaliatory capabilities in the hands of our adversary and become totally indifferent to victory in nuclear war, while other Americans reject such premises. Another important point is that Americans are being pushed away from MAD again, precisely because none of the Soviet statements have as yet fully endorsed these premises.

If it were politically and ideologically impossible for the Soviet leadership to advocate American retaliatory capabilities, it might similarly be impossible for them to shrug off all considerations of victory and defeat if a nuclear war were to occur. Soviet leaders stress that their forces are not intended or designed to attack, but that they are designed to defend. Yet to prepare to defend one's people, by the curious logic of nuclear deterrence, is more menacing than to prepare to retaliate. The result again is a stopping short of a full acknowledgment of the pointlessness of defending, or of doing anything else to alter the outcome of a nuclear war.

Soviet spokesmen, with too many American military officers nodding their heads in agreement, would say that MAD might be unavoidable for the moment, but cannot be a deliberately chosen military strategy. No one can ask a Soviet officer to cease attempting to blunt the military power of an enemy – if war comes, to give up trying to shield the Soviet motherland against attack. Is this not what Soviet cadets (or the cadets of the US service academies) are taught to devote their lives to, from the very day of taking the oath? How can a Soviet leadership which touts so much the moral superiority of "socialism" over capitalism not pledge itself to the defense of socialism in the event of war? How can an American leadership avoid matching this, given its moral feelings about western democracy as compared with Communist dictatorship?

Yet East and West must compromise their ideology as part of facing the reality of the threat of nuclear war. The Soviets have retreated from other ideological tenets in the past, as part of a recognition of military realities and as part of an arms control dialogue with the United States. It should be possible for the Russians to affirm that they see the same grim realities we do, with all of their concomitant ramifications. Rather than being bound by ideology, it is likely that the Russians have been restrained by an insufficient awareness of the extent of the damage done within the United States strategic debate by adhering to formulas which the very nature of nuclear war makes obsolete.

Because the Soviets continue to show interest in defending their homeland, and in who would win "the war the capitalists had started," they strengthen the arguments of those Americans who accuse the Kremlin of being callous about nuclear war. The Soviets are then, rather convincingly, portrayed as having a "different picture" of nuclear war from that held in the West. Meanwhile, Americans who oppose plans for nuclear war-fighting are accused of naive ethnocentrism, of projecting on to the Soviets a resignation to deterrence which is a simple mirror-image of our own feelings. There is no documentary support for this resignation.

For the lack of a few key sentences or paragraphs of Soviet description of strategic reality, the western analysts who favor increased spending on preparations for nuclear war are thus given a substantial reinforcement for their arguments.

Defenders of Soviet clinging to outmoded concepts of strategy will note that this traditionalism is now being wholeheartedly endorsed in the Reagan administration and was even earlier in the Carter and Nixon administrations. Has not the United States repeatedly planned for counterforce war-fighting usage of nuclear weapons, aimed at "military targets" all over the Soviet Union, rather than (as the academic analysts supposed) merely targeting Soviet cities as a straightforward deterrent? From Sunday sermon to newspaper editorial to military planner, is there not a great deal of American feeling that nuclear weapons should be used (if war comes) to win victories, rather than to kill millions of innocent Russian people, to strike at military targets rather than Russian cities?

American military planners and strategic analysts have indeed never been unanimous in endorsing mutual assured destruction. Yet the important point is that MAD did win a significant following in the United States, a following which has now diminished, in large part because the Soviets did not sufficiently enunciate their acceptance of it.[12] Despite all our pretentions of accuracy in military targeting and counterforce intention in the past (a pretense required by the background of American and world moral feelings we have already described), the reality of US nuclear war planning for many of the years since 1950 has been more fully consistent with MAD.

The American strategists believing in MAD know that it is good to direct nuclear warheads at the enemy's people and good to leave one's own people exposed to enemy nuclear attack, and that it is bad to deviate into counterforce targeting and designing protection for one's own people. The press and the clergy, backed by centuries of tradition, preach just the opposite. Facing these conflicting injunctions, American military officers have had to pretend to be finding military targets, even when they were aiming to hurt civilians, a pattern of necessary hypocrisy which obtained already during World War II in the bombings of Dresden, Cologne, Tokyo, and Hiroshima. It would be a mistake to overrate the sincerity of the counterforce motive here, just as it would be a dangerous mistake in the future to underrate it. Today's hypocrisy could become tomorrow's sincere accomplishment, with a first-strike possibility then emerging to provoke the world into a war.

The closest to a full endorsement of MAD by the United States government probably came in the later years of Robert McNamara's term as Secretary of Defense. Some muting was still inevitable, for it would always have been politically awkward for a US official to state explicitly that we looked forward to an assured vulnerability of American cities to Soviet attack. Nonetheless, one heard statements of concern around the Pentagon even in the early 1960s that the Soviets were moving too slowly toward getting their land-based ICBM and submarine-based missile forces into the shape required for an assured second-strike deterrent, the kind of survivable second-strike force that would presumably eliminate all nervousness in Moscow about a US preventive-war attack.

It must be noted that Secretary McNamara in 1962 briefly advocated traditional counterforce emphasis. His celebrated Ann Arbor speech proposed the "no-cities" doctrine, by which (in the event of Soviet aggressions against Europe) the nuclear forces of the United States would be directed only at military targets around the Soviet Union. They would strike at population centers only if American population centers had been struck.

This stress on military targeting, like most recent ventures such as former President Carter's PD-59, might or might not have included attempts to strip the Soviets of strategic nuclear capability. One version of military targeting spares Soviet cities – but also spares Soviet capabilities for striking at United States cities, to avoid putting Moscow into a nervous "use them or lose them" situation. Another, of course, includes Soviet missile silos in the category of military targets.

McNamara's short-lived enthusiasm for this use of nuclear weapons was probably intended to maximize the continuing United States advantages in nuclear force strength at the beginning of the 1960s and thus to balance supposed continuing Soviet advantages in conventional strength deployable into Europe. Within a few years, however, McNamara proved much more willing to resign himself to an approach which acknowledged Soviet needs for an assured second-strike force, matching and balancing out the same kind of posture for the United States.

Considerations of elegant counterforce war, in the planning and procurement of United States strategic forces, receded to less ambitious considerations of damage limitation, and then receded entirely to a maintenance of assured destruction vis-a-vis the Soviet Union. McNamara's own collection of excerpts from his posture statements and other public papers, published in 1968 as *The Essence of Security*, contains no reference to a damage limitation counterforce role for US strategic forces (i.e., to the traditional role of all military forces). Instead, it spells out a doctrine of mutual assured destruction that is not subtantially different from the arguments earlier of Morgenstern:

> We do not possess first-strike capability against the Soviet Union for precisely the same reason that they do not possess it against us. Quite simply, we have both built up our second-strike capability – in effect, retaliatory power – to the point that a first-strike capability on either side has become unattainable.
> There is, of course, no way by which the United States could have prevented the Soviet Union from acquiring its present second-strike capability, short of a massive preemptive first strike in the 1950s. The fact is, then, that neither the Soviet Union nor the United States can attack the other without being destroyed in retaliation; nor can either of us attain a first-strike capability in the foreseeable future. Further, both the Soviet Union and the United States now possess an actual and credible second-strike capability against one another, and

it is precisely this mutual capability that provides us both with the strongest possible motive to avoid a nuclear war.[13]

When options of more traditional uses of nuclear weapons surfaced again with Defense Secretary James Schlesinger in Richard Nixon's presidency, Desmond Ball very aptly labeled the entire venture a case of deja vu. The explanation for what then transpired, from Schlesinger to the plans for the MX, to PD-59, to the Reagan views on protracted nuclear war, would amount to a long and complicated story. It would include the emergence of enhanced accuracies playing an important role (if we can choose so easily among targets, why not exploit the choice?), with the desire of some American defense managers for expanded projects playing another role. But Soviet doctrinal statements would also be terribly important, at least for giving argumentive ammunition to the hawkish American advocates of new strategies and weapons systems.

President Reagan's sudden endorsement in March, 1983, of hopes for a future space-based laser ABM system amounted to the most explicit capstone of the American government's drift away from commitment to mutual assured destruction. This drift is rationalized by arguments of very uneven persuasiveness, but is nonetheless substantially reinforced by the contention that Soviet strategic doctrine had never itself accepted MAD.

HOPES FOR SOVIET ACCOMMODATION

The Soviets are not so obtuse as to have missed much of what we so readily perceive about the nature of any nuclear war.

They must also be aware of the impact their facade of obtuseness has made on the American strategic debate, in the last years of the Carter administration and in the time since Ronald Reagan was elected president. This is the basis of any hope that the strategic dialogue necessary for a mutual recognition of mutual assured destruction might ultimately be attained.

As noted, the Soviets had only a few more crucial steps to take. Several of these steps have very recently been taken, footnoted with a frank acknowledgment that hawkish United States commentators had fastened on shortcomings in earlier Soviet doctrines.

Whether such a process of strategic convergence will continue in the changing Soviet regime cannot be ascertained immediately. There will be forces in the Soviet Union intent on retaining some of the obtuseness of the older postures, still touting the virtues of seeking victory, in case the capitalists begin World War III, still asserting that their highest duty is to strike the weapons from the hands of the capitalist enemy and to protect the motherland against destruction. Such strategies not only produce higher defense budgets in the West; they also increase Soviet defense spending, perhaps in response to the augmentations provoked in the West.

Several news releases from the Soviet side late in 1981 illustrated both a more hopeful trend and its limitations. The releases included a highly publicized press conference with questions posed by *Pravda* to Leonid Brezhnev as well as a widely distributed following booklet entitled *The Threat to Europe*.[14] Aware of the importance American and other western strategic analysts had been attributing to the Soviet failure to renounce all interest in war-fighting options or in the difference between victory and defeat in a nuclear war, the Soviet statements stress repeatedly that the USSR would never initiate a nuclear war, would never launch a preemptive or preventive type of attack.

> Soviet military doctrine is of a purely defensive nature. "We never had and never will have any strategic doctrine other than a defensive one," says the declaration of the Warsaw Treaty states of 15 May 1980. It does not admit of either a first or pre-emptive strike or of any "lightning" invasion of Western Europe. In so doing it follows definite political, ethical and military principles. There is no aggressive element in Soviet military doctrine because the Soviet Union has no political, economic, social or military aims in Europe or anywhere else that it intends to secure by armed force.[15]

While never unwelcome, this kind of Soviet pledge is also never fully satisfying, since aggressors in this century have rarely admitted that they had begun a war. Hitler's advance on Warsaw came allegedly after the Poles had attacked Germany, and Kim Il-sung's push toward Pusan in 1950 came after a Communist claim that South Korea had attacked North Korea. If the Soviets were ever to launch an attack on the United States during our alleged "window of vulnerability," Moscow would surely claim that the capitalist world had begun the war.

Much more necessary, much more forthcoming, would be Soviet statements suggesting that, even if the USSR were heroically defending itself against a capitalist American aggression, victory would be meaningless, i.e., that even if Moscow still claimed the legitimacy of self-defense, it would not translate this into the prerogative of looking for a victory. *The Threat to Europe* comes closer to this than have Soviet statements in the past, at least indirectly, as when quoting a retired American admiral of liberal persuasion who had (like many Americans) noted the same pointlessness of victory.

> In this sense, we see eye to eye with Rear Admiral Gene La Rocque, Director of the US Centre for Defense Information, who says neither side could eventually consider itself a victor in the event of a major nuclear war between the USSR and the USA. More than a hundred million people would perish on either side, and up to three-quarters of the two countries' economic potentials would be destroyed.[16]

Yet *The Threat to Europe* is then more forthcoming than the Soviet leader it quotes, again neatly displaying the tensions and gaps we have been discussing here.

The booklet, after conceding western dissatisfactions with Soviet doctrine, itself concedes that there will be no victor in a nuclear war:

QUESTION. *Can a nuclear war be considered winnable?*

ANSWER. Western political and military writers contend that Soviet military doctrine is based exclusively on the belief that a world nuclear war can be won. But that is a simplistic and distorted view of our approach. In fact, the Soviet Union holds that nuclear war would be a universal disaster, and that it would most probably mean the end of civilisation. It may lead to the destruction of all humankind. There may be no victor in such a war, and it can solve no political problems. As Leonid Brezhnev pointed out in his reply to a *Pravda* correspondent on 21 October 1981, "anyone who starts a nuclear war in the hope of winning it has thereby decided to commit suicide. Whatever strength the attacker may have and whatever method of starting a nuclear war he may choose, he will not achieve his aims. Retaliation is unavoidable. That is our essential point of view."[17]

But the Brezhnev quote cited immediately thereafter simply said that "anyone who starts a nuclear war" will have committed suicide. The Russian view of events and history has always been that the United States is the initiator of war. This, then, amounts to far less of a concession, because the USSR "defensively" would be imposing unavoidable retaliation. Yet such "retaliation" in the past has often enough amounted to a pursuit of victory.

It is interesting that these recent Soviet statements noted that adequate concessions have not always been offered in the past, i.e., that some change of the professed Soviet strategic doctrine indeed must be called for, if the arms race is to be controlled.

Q. Why then do Soviet theoretical works on military strategy of, say, the early 60's refer to offensive action, to building up a military advantage? Doesn't this prove that Soviet military strategy reposes on these principles even today?

A. No, it proves no such thing. Soviet military strategy is neither immutable nor everlasting. It changes with the changing world. The same happens in the United States, where the strategy of flexible response and thereupon that of realistic deterrence replaced a doctrine of massive retaliation. Soviet theoretical works of the early 60's reflected the views of their time. And it was a time when the United States commanded a considerable nuclear-missile advantage, when it threatened the Soviet Union with massive nuclear strikes and declared that a nuclear war against the U.S.S.R. was winnable.[18]

The fullest acknowledgment of mutual assured destruction is still missing. A statement has not been made that it is actually in the Soviet interest to have the United States assured of a capability of attacking and destroying Soviet cities. Will we ever see Soviet publication of an analysis like Morgenstern's or McNamara's? If we do, it will end the myth that Soviet leadership does not understand the perils of nuclear war, and also lay to rest the military tradition that the professional soldier's highest priority must first be to destroy his opposite number.

CONCLUSION

The following points can therefore be concluded. First, a counterforce emphasis on striking at the enemy's military forces rather than at civilian targets has a long history for Americans, Russians, and virtually all of the military forces of the world.

Second, this emphasis is both outmoded and dangerous, in light of the development of weapons of retaliatory mass destruction since 1945. These weapons have been largely depended upon for world peace since the 1950s. Their use, or abuse, in the event of a counterforce attack is a great hazard. What must be avoided in the future are any confrontations of weaponry, or of strategic philosophy, which put either side into a "use them or lose them" situation.

Third, the Soviets have done less than their share of acknowledging this change in strategic reality, causing some Americans to worry that Moscow does not see this reality, causing other Americans to question whether this is indeed reality. Americans have been ambivalent in accepting the need for both sides to have assured second-strike means of inflicting retaliatory destruction. The present trend is against this, stemming in part from a Soviet obtuseness which seems to impose on the West all burdens and disadvantages of confronting this new reality here. Any departure from the new reality, back toward the old traditional emphases on disarming the opposing air force or navy, is undesirable. Any failure to acknowledge the new reality is similarly undesirable.

Fourth, there is hope that the Soviets can be convinced to accept the reality and desirability of mutual assured destruction. If their failure to accept MAD in their public statements explains some of the recent United States commitments to weapons like the MX and Pershing II, Moscow is not paying the price of its own disingenuousness. One hopes that it will participate in a franker discussion of nuclear deterrence before this price becomes too high.

NOTES

1 Alfred Thayer Mahan, *The Influence of Sea Power Upon History: 1660–1783* (New York: Hill and Wang reprint, 1957; originally published 1890), pp. 119, 121.

2 Giulio Douhet, *The Command of the Air* (New York: Coward–McCann, 1942), p. 20.

3 J. F. C. Fuller, *The Reformation of War* (New York: E. P. Dutton, 1923), p. 150.

4 Douhet, *The Command of the Air*, pp. 24–25. Also see Fuller, *The Reformation of War*, pp. 184–85.

5 Carl von Clausewitz, *On War*, edited and translated by Michael Howard and Peter Paret (Princeton: Princeton University Press, 1976), p. 77.

6 Sun Tzu, *The Art of War*, translated by Samuel B. Griffith (London: Oxford University Press, 1963), p. 85.

7 For some very balanced views of Soviet thinking, see Dimitri K. Simes, "Deterrence and Coercion in Soviet Policy," *International Security* 5, no. 3 (Winter 1980-81): 80-103; Robert Jervis, "Deterrence and Perception," *International Security* 7, no. 3 (Winter 1982-83): 3-30; Donald W. Hanson, "Is Soviet Strategic Doctrine Superior?," *International Security* 7, no. 3 (Winter 1982/83: 61-83; Stanley Sienkiewicz, "SALT and Soviet Nuclear Doctrine," *International Security* 2, no. 4 (Spring 1978): 84-100; John Erickson, "The Soviet View of Deterrence: A General Survey," *Survival* 24, no. 6 (November/December 1982): 242-51; and Richard Ned Lebow, "Misconceptions in American Strategic Assessment," *Political Science Quarterly* 97, no. 2 (Summer 1982): 187-206.

8 For an illustration of this kind of interpretation of Soviet strategic thinking, see Richard B. Foster, "On Prolonged Nuclear War," *International Security Review* 6, no. 4 (Winter 1981-82): 497-518. See also Richard Pipes, "Why the Soviet Union Thinks It Could Fight and Win a Nuclear War," *Commentary* 64, no. 7 (July 1977): 21-24; Edward L. Rowny, "The Soviets Are Still Russians," *Survey* 25, no. 2 (Srping 1980): 1-9; and Francis P. Hoeber and Amoretta M. Hoeber, "The Soviet View of Deterrence: Who Whom?," *Survey* 25, no. 2 (Spring 1980): 17-24.

9 See Donald G. Brennan, "Commentary," *International Security* 3, no. 3 (Winter 1978-79): 193-98. Brennan was responding to Raymond L. Garthoff, "Mutual Deterrence and Strategic Arms Limitation in Soviet Policy," *International Security* 3, no. 1 (Summer 1978): 112-47, later version reprinted in *Strategic Review* 10, no. 4 (Fall 1982): 36-51. See also Richard Pipes, "Soviet Strategic Doctrine: Another View," *Strategic Review* 10, no. 4 (Fall 1982): 52-58.

10 Oskar Morgenstern, *The Question of National Defense* (New York: Random House, 1959), p. 76.

11 See Raymond L. Garthoff, "The Death of Stalin and the Birth of Mutual Deterrence," *Survey* 25, no. 2 (Spring 1980): 10-16.

12 An important American statement of the underlying logic of MAD can be found in Wolfgang Panofsky, "The Mutual Hostage Relationship Between America and Russia," *Foreign Affairs* 52, no. 1 (October 1973): 109-18. This was published in response to an important article questioning the moral tenability of mutual deterrence, Fred C. Ikle, "Can Nuclear Deterrence Last Out the Century," *Foreign Affairs* 51, no. 2 (January 1973): 267-85.

13 Robert McNamara, *The Essence of Security* (New York: Harper and Row, 1968), pp. 35-36.

14 As reported in *The New York Times*, November 4, 1981, p. A6.

15 Soviet Committee for European Security and Cooperation, and Scientific Research Council on Peace and Disarmament, *The Threat to Europe* (Moscow: Progress Publishers, 1981), pp. 10-11.

16 Ibid., p. 9.

17 Ibid.

18 Ibid., p. 11.

PART 2
Deterrence and Moral Justification

4

MORAL ISSUES IN DETERRENCE POLICY

Rev. J. Bryan Hehir

An editorial in *The New Republic* (December 20, 1982) commenting on the second draft of the pastoral letter of the National Conference of Catholic Bishops, opened with the following observation: "The ground is not steady beneath the nuclear forces of the United States. The problem is not modes of basing but modes of thinking. The traditional strategy for our nuclear arsenal is shaken by a war of ideas about its purpose, perhaps the most decisive war of ideas in its history."[1]

The purpose of this chapter is to locate the contribution of the final version of the pastoral letter, *The Challenge of Peace: God's Promise and Our Response*, in the wider debate underway in the United States concerning issues of war and peace.[2] The argument will proceed in three steps: (1) an examination of the character of the public debate; (2) a summary of the nature and contents of the pastoral letter; and (3) a synthesis of selected responses elicited by the pastoral letter.

I. THE PUBLIC DEBATE: ITS DIMENSIONS

The impact of the pastoral letter can be attributed to a combination of its contents and the wider context in which it appeared. A national debate on nuclear strategy is afoot; the pastoral is one element in the debate. While the response to it has exceeded the expectations of most of us, the letter should be seen as a piece of a larger mosaic.

Early in the pastoral, the bishops highlight the "New Moment" they discern thirty-eight years into the nuclear age: "A prominent 'sign of the times' today is a sharply increased awareness of the danger of the nuclear arms race. Such awareness has produced a public discussion about nuclear policy here and in other countries which is unprecedented in its scope and depth. What has been accepted for years with almost no question is now subjected to the sharpest criticism. What previously had been defined as a safe and stable system of deterrence is today viewed with political and moral skepticism."[3]

It is possible to distinguish two levels of the public debate, both of which are relevant to the message of the pastoral letter: the "popular" level and the "policy" level.

The popular level of the public debate involves a broad-based mass movement comprised by a number of groups with differing views on specific issues of foreign and defense policy, but with a delicately fashioned common position against the present direction of the nuclear arms race. The popular level is symbolized by the freeze movement and by the effectiveness of the physicians' movement in catalyzing the public concern about the arms race. The freeze movement needs to be understood both as an example of "symbolic politics" and as a specific substantive proposal. At the symbolic level the significance of the "freeze" is that it has mobilized the most local level of American political life (e.g., town meetings in Vermont and city council meetings in California) in the debate about United States strategic doctrine.

The physicians, with their concentration on the medical consequences of nuclear war, have found a way to give ordinary citizens a means of grasping the often cosmic dimensions of the nuclear debate. The effect of both of these movements, along with other activist groups, has been the "democratization" of the nuclear debate; this is one dimension of the "New Moment."

The second dimension is the policy debate; here one finds both continuity and change. The continuity resides in the fact that intensive discussion of nuclear strategy is not new in the policy debate. The examination of many of the issues now found in the popular debate has been going on in a small circle of elites for the past three decades. The record is to be found voluminously in libraries and the locus of the debate is well known—inside the government, in think tanks, and in a few universities. What constitutes the "New Moment" at this level of discussion is the pressure on the conventional consensus which has pervaded this elite debate. While each administration has had its version of American nuclear strategy (e.g., massive retaliation, flexible response, selective options, countervailing strategy), a few premises have remained almost untouchable during the nuclear age. The change in the policy debate—the pressure on the consensus—is represented by voices of dissent or opposition to these untouchable premises, often by individuals who had either formulated them or defended them in the past.

Several striking examples of distinct pressures on the consensus can be found. First, the proposal made by McGeorge Bundy, George Kennan, Robert McNamara, and Gerard Smith in 1982 that a central premise of NATO strategy, the willingness to use nuclear weapons first if necessary to stop a conventional attack in Central Europe, should be changed.[4] The proposal that the Western Alliance should make a "no first use" pledge had been advanced previously in the policy debate, but the advocacy of it by individuals of this stature and experience signified a sea-change in the policy arena. Similarly, the extended discussion in the United States about the role of land-based ballistic missiles (ICBMs) in United States defense posture has illustrated much less than unanimity in the policy community. The problem of missile vulnerability has elicited quite different responses.

General Maxwell Taylor, former Chairman of the Joint Chiefs of Staff, has used the vulnerability issue to challenge the concept that the United States should continue to structure its strategic forces on the basis of a Triad (i.e., land- and sea-based missiles as well as bombers). In Taylor's view the debate about strategic forces has been bedeviled by a fascination with numbers and an obsession with matching Soviet deployments. The need, in his view, is for a substantial shift of perspective:

> We can refuse henceforth to race with the Soviets and instead base force requirements on sufficiency of destruction potential. We can abjure the outmoded Triad doctrine and select our future weapons not on the basis of their launch mode but on the basis of their reliability, survivability, and contribution to approved destruction tasks. More specifically we can cancel the MX program, progressively phase out all land-based ICBMs and transfer their targets to air- and sea-launched missiles.[5]

Here again, the content of the Taylor proposal is not original, but its association with Taylor provides a new impetus to a set of suggestions quite at variance with prevailing official policy.

Even at the official level, however, ideas are abroad which, even five years ago, would have been read out of court. The Scowcroft Commission, called together by President Reagan to review United States strategic force requirements, produced its report in April 1983. While it rather predictably supported a limited MX deployment, it did so in tandem with a proposal to move away from ICBMs with multiple independently targetable warheads (MIRVs).[6] The technology of "mirving" missiles has been the dominant note of United States strategic weapons deployment in the 1970s. Many outside analysts protested the trend, but a call by a presidential commission to reverse the "mirving" policy shows the fluidity of the present debate.

From the freeze through no-first-use to the Scowcroft Commission, the evidence of a "New Moment" in the United States nuclear debate is vividly apparent. The relevance of all this to the pastoral letter is twofold.

First, the "New Moment" is an "open moment"; the dissent from prevailing doctrine at the mass and elite levels of the public debate provides an opportunity. At certain turning points in the nuclear age key concepts have entered the discussion and shaped the direction of policy. When an "open moment" occurs, there is a time of opportunity – someone will shape the debate. The pastoral letter, appearing at a time of flux in the public discussion, has an opportunity to carve out space for the moral factor in the policy process. The letter appears at a propitious time; the danger is substantial but so are the opportunities.

Second, when the public debate is viewed in terms of its popular and policy dimensions, a striking parallel with the purposes of the pastoral letter is evident. In Part One of the pastoral, the bishops explain the dual function which Catholic teaching on warfare has had. Its first purpose has been "pastoral," i.e., to help each member of the Church form his or her conscience regarding the use of force, participation in warfare, and the responsibilities of citizenship. The second purpose of the moral teaching has been "policy-oriented," i.e., designed to help set the proper terms of moral debate in society about issues of war and peace.

The United States bishops' letter is expressly written to fulfill these two functions of conscience-formation and policy analysis. The bishops, in a section entitled "Religious Leadership and the Public Debate," set their objectives:

> The "New Moment" which exists in the public debate about nuclear weapons provides a creative opportunity and a moral imperative to examine the relationship between public opinion and public policy. We believe it necessary, for the sake of prevention, to build a barrier against the concept of nuclear war as a viable strategy for defense. . . . We believe religious leaders have a task, in concert with public officials, analysts, private organizations and the media to set the limits beyond which our military policy should not move in word or action.[7]

In light of this intention we can now examine how the bishops framed their contribution to the public debate.

II. THE PASTORAL LETTER: ITS DESIGN

The pastoral letter is a moral-religious analysis of some of the principal political and strategic questions of the nuclear age. The bishops do not think that they will provide new political, strategic, or technical insights, but they are convinced that they have an indispensable role to play in scrutinizing the political-strategic choices from the perspective of Catholic moral teaching on war and peace. In Part One of the letter, the bishops set forth the component elements of the Catholic vision – its biblical foundations, ecclesiological framework, and, most significantly, its moral principles. In light of this complex fabric of moral-religious criteria, the letter then moves to policy analysis in Parts Two and Three.

The policy perspective of the letter is shaped by two dimensions of the international system today: we live in a nuclear world which is also an increasingly interdependent world. Resolving the nuclear dilemma would still leave many of the interdependence issues untouched; concentrating on the interdependence questions, without confronting the nuclear challenge, leaves our future at substantial risk. The pastoral addresses two questions, therefore: building the peace in conditions of interdependence and keeping the peace in the nuclear age.

A. Building the Peace in an Interdependent World

The classical Catholic conception of peace is rooted in the biblical vision of *shalom*, articulated principally by St. Augustine in *The City of God* and elaborated in more detail in the papal teaching of this century. It describes peace in positive terms. The bishops use a typical quote, this one from Pope Paul VI: "Peace cannot be limited to a mere absence of war, the result of an ever precarious balance of forces. No, peace is something built up day after day, in the pursuit of an order intended by God, which implies a more perfect form of justice among men and women."[8]

Synthetically stated here is the classical tradition: peace is rooted in a conception of political order which must pervade every level of human society. The clearest statement of the classical view in recent Catholic teaching, Pope John XXIII's encyclical *Peace on Earth* (1963), argued that the "order" needed for peace must be informed by the values of truth, justice, freedom, and love. Building peace requires more than avoiding war. The pastoral letter, drawing on John XXIII, describes the structural defect in the international system: we are materially interdependent, faced with transnational problems but governed by wholly independent sovereign states. In the absence of a political structure adequate to meet the needs of the existing "international common good," meeting the challenge of interdependence (trade, monetary questions, human rights and, principally, the range of issues subsumed under the North-South agenda) will require vision, wisdom, and an acute sense of political and moral solidarity. In a section which has received little public attention ("Interdependence: From Fact to Policy") the pastoral seeks to highlight the meaning of this challenge for US foreign policy:

> The moral challenge of interdependence concerns shaping the relationships and rules of practice which will support our common need for security, welfare and safety. The challenge tests our idea of human community, our policy analysis and our political will. The need to prevent nuclear war is absolutely crucial, but even if this is achieved, there is much more to be done.[9]

B. Keeping the Peace in a Nuclear World

The section which has received substantial public attention is Part Two, "War and Peace in the Modern World." Here the pastoral, using principally the classical "just-war ethic," addresses three major questions: (1) the logic and language of the nuclear age; (2) strategy in the nuclear age; and (3) politics in the nuclear age.

1. The Logic and Language of the Nuclear Age

The controlling moral vision of the policy section acknowledges that in a sinful, still decentralized world of states, some use of force may be politically necessary and morally justifiable. This "just/limited war" moral doctrine is confronted with a revolutionary challenge by the nuclear age. The destructive capability of nuclear weapons forces the adherents of the just-war war ethic to declare themselves on the relationship of just-war moral criteria and the logic of nuclear war.

Before confronting the specific dimensions of this challenge, the bishops seek to make clear their view that nuclear weapons present a qualitatively new moral problem for the traditional conceptions of both politics and morals. The essence of the challenge was masterfully captured by Pope John Paul II in his address at Hiroshima in 1981: "In the past it was possible to destroy a village, a town, a region, even a country. Now it is the whole planet that has come under threat."[10]

Faced with this threat, the bishops seek to make clear that they are opposed to conceptions and descriptions of the nuclear question which fail to convey the radically new issues posed by nuclear weapons and nuclear strategy. The coming of the nuclear age has transformed the doctrine of Clausewitz that war is a rational extension of politics. The nuclear threat is such that to resort to these instruments of war places at risk the very values the use of force is supposed to protect. As the pastoral phrases the problem: "We live today, therefore, in the midst of a cosmic drama; we possess a power which should never be used, but which might be used if we do not reverse our direction. We live with nuclear weapons knowing we cannot afford to make one serious mistake. This fact dramatizes the precariousness of our position politically, morally and spiritually."[11]

The key aspect of the challenge for the moral doctrine concerns the possibility of controlling the use of nuclear weapons. The fundamental premise of the just-war ethic is that a *legitimate* use of force must always be a *limited* use of force. Limitation is conceived in terms of two moral principles: noncombatant immunity and proportionality.[12] The issue of control was a major theme in the preparation of the several drafts of the pastoral letter, in the literature consulted by the drafting committee, and in the extensive dialogues the Bernardin Committee had with the Reagan administration.

The result of this detailed process of research and reflection produced an attitude in the letter which is radically skeptical about the possibilities of controlling nuclear war. While not taking an apodictic position on such a complex empirical issue, the bishops express severe doubts about control and set themselves against careless rhetoric concerning "winnable nuclear wars." The pastoral letter is designed to help build a political-moral barrier against the concept of nuclear war as a viable strategy of defense and to resist rhetoric which fails to convey the moral and political threat posed by the nuclear age.

2. Strategy in the Nuclear Age

There are certain parallels between the technical strategic debate in the nuclear age and the discussion of the ethics of nuclear strategy. In his book *The Necessity for Choice,* Henry Kissinger held that the problem facing strategists was how to relate the *use* of nuclear weapons to the strategy of deterrence.[13] The extensive literature on the ethical issues of the nuclear age reflects this problem, and the pastoral letter divides its treatment of keeping the peace into a discussion of use and deterrence.

The letter comments on three cases of use of nuclear weapons. First, directly intended attacks on civilian populations or "counter-population warfare"; this case is considered for two reasons: (1) the moral principle at stake, noncombatant immunity, is central to the just-war ethic; and (2) at various times in the nuclear age the direct targeting of civilian centers has been considered or planned. The pastoral letter's analysis contains three significant characteristics. The basic judgment of the letter is to rule out, absolutely, direct attacks on civilian populations. The judgment is based upon the just-war tradition which found forceful expression in the Second Vatican Council's statement against "destruction of entire cities or of extensive areas along with their population. . . . It merits unequivocal and unhesitating condemnation."[14] The American bishops provide an application of this principle with direct relevance for nuclear strategy: they rule out retaliatory action against civilian populations even if our cities have been hit first.

The second case concerns the first use of nuclear weapons. The significance of this issue is twofold; the possibility of first use is still a central piece of NATO strategy, and a renewed debate about the strategy is now underway.[15] The bishops do not address the political debate as such; their purpose is to isolate the moral question in it. Briefly stated, is there a specific moral issue involved in the willingness to be the first party to move warfare from the conventional level to the nuclear level?

The pastoral finds a specific moral responsibility here. Its judgment is one of the more controversial sections of the letter. The bishops say: "We do not perceive any situation in which the deliberate initiation of nuclear warfare, on however restricted a scale, can be morally justified. Nonnuclear attacks by another state must be resisted by other than nuclear means. Therefore, a serious moral obligation exists to develop non-nuclear defensive strategies as rapidly as possible."[16]

It should be noted that different levels of moral authority are invoked in these two cases. In the judgment ruling out attacks on civilians, the American bishops simply reiterate a principle held throughout the Catholic Church. In the judgment against first use, they are applying a series of moral principles to a number of contingent political and strategic judgments. The bishops make clear this specific prohibition of first use is open to debate and indeed to contrary conclusions based on a different reading of the empirical data.[17]

The rationale of the pastoral's prohibition of first use should be seen in light of a general theme of the letter. In a series of judgments the bishops seek to build a multi-dimensional barrier against resort to nuclear weapons, to insulate them, as much as possible, from quick, early, or easy use. The specific support the bishops give to a no-first-use position should be seen as a dimension of this larger theme in the letter.

The third case is limited nuclear war. Here again, the bishops enter a much disputed technical question with a long history. They are aware that they cannot "settle" the empirical debate of whether a limited nuclear exchange can be kept "limited." Their approach in the pastoral is to raise a series of questions which express their radical skepticism about controlling such an exchange. Having pressed the question of what "limited" really means, they make the following assessment: "One of the criteria of the just-war tradition is a reasonable hope of success in bringing about justice and peace. We must ask whether such a reasonable hope can exist once nuclear weapons have been exchanged. The burden of proof remains on those who assert that meaningful limitation is possible."[18]

To summarize the pastoral letter's position on the use of nuclear weapons:

-the letter raises and responds to three distinct cases of use;

-the letter sets forth moral principles of limitation (noncombatant immunity, proportion, and reasonable hope of success) by which *any* case of use should be judged;

-the letter does not consider *every* case of use;

-the letter does not conclude that the use of nuclear weapons is intrinsically evil;

-there exists, therefore, a centimeter of ambiguity regarding the general question of the use of nuclear weapons.

It is in light of this purposeful ambiguity that the pastoral letter moves to evaluate the strategy of deterrence. It begins with a brief discussion of the meaning of deterrence in the nuclear age; this is needed because the moral problem emerges from the nature of the empirical problem. The paradox of deterrence was captured by a phrase used by the Second Vatican Council: "the stockpiling of arms which grows from year to year serves, in a way hitherto unthought of, as a deterrent to potential attackers. Many people look upon this as the most effective way known at the present time for maintaining some sort of peace among nations."[19]

Embedded in this cryptic description is an acknowledgment of the new reality which nuclear deterrence has brought to the perennial problems of warfare, politically and ethically. The result of deterrence, "some sort of peace," is described here in language meant to convey the unsatisfactory basis of our present security. The difficult political and moral issue is whether any other available means would even preserve a "sort of peace." Not highlighted in Vatican II's early and brief analysis of the problem of deterrence are the following questions which have structured the post-conciliar analysis of deterrence:

-does effective deterrence involve a "formed intention" to do evil?

-how should the relationship of threat, intention, and possible use be understood?

-how do we weigh morally the argument that deterrence has served the function of preventing any use of nuclear weapons?

-would less reliance on nuclear deterrence, its moral delegitimation, have the effect of "making the world safe for conventional war"?

The literature on these questions has grown remarkably during the period of the drafting of the pastoral.[20] A central contribution to the framing of the American bishops' position was Pope John Paul II's statement on deterrence in his Message to the Second Special Session of the United Nations on disarmament (1982):

> In current conditions "deterrence" based on balance, certainly not as an end in it-self but as a step on the way toward a progressive disarmament, may still be judged morally acceptablé. Nonetheless in order to ensure peace, it is indispensable not to be satisfied with this minimum which is always susceptible to the real danger of explosion.[21]

The pastoral letter cites the papal text, summarizes a commentary on it provided for the American bishops by Cardinal Casaroli,[22] the Vatican Secretary of State, and then proceeds to use the Holy Father's carefully circumscribed approval of deterrence in its assessment of US strategic policy. Since deterrence was perhaps the most complex and controversial topic of the entire pastoral the bishops went to some length to understand the nature of US deterrence policy.

Discussions with the United States government centered on questions of both strategic doctrine and targeting policy. Since the bishops had staked out such a clear and firm position against targeting civilian centers, the Reagan administration, in a series of letters to Cardinal Bernardin, went on record saying, "For moral, political and military reasons, the United States does not target the Soviet civilian population as such."[23] The bishops received this statement (and others like it) and acknowledged that it responded to their concerns about the *intent* of US policy regarding civilians, but did not settle the question of the morality of US deterrence policy as a whole.

The next issue involved what kind of "indirect" or "unintended" damage would follow from striking the urban-industrial targets which every US administration has openly said we target. In one of the more important sentences of the entire pastoral the bishops say: "A narrow adherence exclusively to the principle of noncombatant immunity as a criterion for policy is an inadequate moral posture for it ignores some evil and unacceptable consequences. Hence, we cannot be satisfied that the assertion of an intention not to strike civilians directly, or even the most honest effort to implement that intention, by itself constitutes a 'moral policy' for the use of nuclear weapons."[24]

These considerations plus a further discussion of the moral issues raised by even a well-intended counterforce strategy brought the American bishops to their judgment on the strategy of deterrence:

> These considerations of concrete elements of nuclear deterrence policy, made in light of John Paul II's evaluation, but applying it through our own prudential judgments, lead us to a strictly conditioned moral acceptance of nuclear deterrence. We cannot consider it adequate as a long-term basis for peace.[25]

Devoid of all modifiers, the judgment on deterrence is acceptance not condemnation. But the acceptance is "strictly conditioned." This phrase places two kinds of restraint on the strategy of deterrence. The first is temporal in nature; both John Paul II and the American bishops tie the justification for deterrence to an understanding that it be used as a framework for moving to a different basis of security among nations. This temporal assessment means that the "direction" of deterrence policy has moral significance – are steps being taken to move away from this fragile, paradoxical basis for interstate relations or is the direction of policy simply reinforcing the present state of affairs?

The second restraint concerns the character of the deterrent. The strictly conditioned justification of the deterrent rests upon its role of "preventing the use of nuclear weapons or other actions which could lead directly to a nuclear exchange."[26] The point here is to limit the role of nuclear deterrence to a very specific function in world affairs; the posture of deterrence is not to be used to pursue other goals than preventing nuclear war. To give specific content to this limited conception of deterrence the bishops make a series of concrete proposals:

They oppose: (1) extending deterrence to a variety of war-fighting strategies; (2) a quest for strategic superiority; (3) any blurring of the distinction between nuclear and conventional weapons; and (4) the deployment of weapons with "hard-target kill" capability.

They support: (1) immediate, bilateral, verifiable agreements to halt the testing, production, and deployment of new nuclear systems; (2) negotiating strategies aimed at deep cuts in superpower arsenals; (3) conclusion of a comprehensive test ban treaty; and (4) strengthening of command and control systems for nuclear weapons.

These last comments on strategies for arms control lead logically to a discussion of the political perspective of the pastoral letter.

3. Politics in the Nuclear Age

The strategic dilemma posed by nuclear deterrence admits of no facile solution. Three responses to the dilemma are visible today. One, "the technological fix," looks to the building of new nuclear systems, with defensive capabilities which would protect a nation from nuclear attack and also offset the moral problem of having a strategy of targeting civilian centers. A second, which may be described as "total moral dissent," based on a judgment that no morally acceptable policy can be fashioned from the present deterrent, calls for opposition to the concept of nuclear deterrence and withdrawal of all forms of cooperation with it. A third, the "political option," is the response espoused by the pastoral letter. Essentially the political option acknowledges that deterrence is not adequate "as a long-term basis for peace," but it can serve as a framework for moving toward a more satisfactory foundation for international relations.

The political option envisioned by the pastoral is principally concerned with United States-Soviet relations. The pastoral's perspective on superpower relations is described in one phrase as "cold realism."[27] The phrase conveys the fact that the pastoral takes full cognizance of the need to address the strategic dilemma of deterrence in a politically divided world. The division of the world is two-dimensional: first, it remains a world composed of sovereign nation-states; second, two of the states are superpowers divided, as the pastoral says, "by philosophy, ideology and competing interests."[28] These divisions, each of which could be placed in historical perspective and elaborated at some length, lie at the root of the dilemma of deterrence. In the words of the pastoral: "Deterrence reflects the radical distrust which marks international politics. . . ."[29]

The "realism" of the pastoral begins with an assessment of the division of East and West. It does not assume, however, that realism compels us to transform this division into a description of the world as good vs. evil (with the former conveniently wedded to our side), nor to conclude that no common interest exists between the superpowers. On the contrary, the political response of the pastoral is based on the conviction that the United States and the Soviet Union share at least one objective demonstrable common interest—that nuclear weapons never be used. Such a view is hardly euphoric or pervaded by facile optimism. It does not presume that either superpower is saintly, only that they are governed by people who recognize that in the nuclear age war is more likely to be the destruction of politics rather than its extension.

It is on the basis of this narrow but crucial common interest that the pastoral proposes a series of diplomatic measures and arms control initiatives. While the focus is on controlling nuclear forces, the pastoral extends its concern to various measures of conventional arms control as well.[30] In addition to these standard diplomatic concerns, the pastoral letter proposes efforts to make nonviolent means of defense and conflict resolution more applicable to personal activity and public policy.[31]

Finally, the political option for superpower relations needs to be related to the interdependence agenda described above as building the peace.

III. RESPONSE TO THE PASTORAL: OUTLINING THE DEBATE

In the opening pages of the pastoral the bishops say the letter is to speak "both to Catholics in a specific way and to the wider political community regarding public policy."[32] The dialogue which the bishops initiated has already generated a broad-based response. In addition to the extensive coverage in the national media and the discussions now proceeding in dioceses, parishes, schools, and colleges around the country, the pastoral has elicited thoughtful written commentary inside the Church and in the wider society.

This section of the chapter will outline examples of the criticism and commentary generated by the pastoral, then conclude with reflections on the future of the debate.

A. The Commentary

I will use four articles, two from within the Catholic community, two from experienced analysts in the strategic debate. Doing justice to any of these positions would require a separate essay for each.

1. Germain Grisez: Dissent on Deterrence

Professor Germain Grisez, a philosopher from Mount St. Mary's College in Emmitsburg, Maryland, has been one of the most prolific commentators on the various drafts of the pastoral. Grisez's position represents not only a significant dissent from the approach of the pastoral, it also reflects one school of Catholic authors who have written on deterrence for the last two decades.[33]

The essence of the position is that a factual analysis of existing deterrence policy, made in light of the principle of noncombatant immunity, leads to a condemnation of deterrence. Grisez focuses particularly on the *intention* required to make the deterrent credible to adversaries. In his judgment the intention which supports prevailing deterrence policy involves a willingness to target and strike civilian centers. As he puts the case, "Deterrence requires not only assured capability but manifest will. Therefore, our public policy must remain a firm commitment to kill millions of innocent persons if the deterrent fails."[34]

This definition of the problem leads Grisez to recommend dissent from deterrence and active resistance to its implementation as policy.

Relating this position to that taken in the pastoral, three points can be made. First, the bishops and Grisez agree on the centrality of the principle of noncombatant immunity and the corollary that "it is not morally acceptable to intend to kill the innocent as part of a strategy of deterring nuclear war."[35] Second, while Grisez is convinced that it is not possible "to will effective deterrence without choosing the death of civilians,"[36] the bishops do not come to such a definite conclusion on this factual judgment. They are concerned about this question, but after intensive discussions with representatives of the United States government, the bishops did not indict US policy on the grounds that it was designed to strike civilian centers directly. The letter did raise very serious doubts about the possibilities of a proportionate use of nuclear weapons even when not directly targeted on civilian centers:

> The location of industrial or militarily significant economic targets within heavily populated areas or in those areas affected by radioactive fallout could well involve such massive civilian casualties that, in our judgment, such a strike would be deemed morally disproportionate even though not intentionally indiscriminate.[37]

Third, the bishops' letter more readily acknowledges the "paradox of deterrence" of which many strategic analysts speak; this description concedes that every resolution of the deterrence question is less than satisfactory. Professor Grisez is of the view that admission of paradox involves either a failure of intelligence or moral courage or both. In his words, "a competent moral advisor always can find a morally upright solution to every problem."[38]

2. William O'Brien: Shaping a Usable Deterrent

Professor William O'Brien, a political scientist from Georgetown University, has written extensively and incisively about the meaning of just-war ethics in the nuclear age.[39] He disagrees with the thrust of the pastoral letter while remaining supportive of the bishops' efforts to show the continuing relevance of the traditional moral teaching. In an article written on the basis of the first drafts of the pastoral letter, O'Brien outlined his position and his differences with the approach of the bishops' letter.[40]

O'Brien's position is an effort to shape a *use* and *deterrence* policy which can be contained within the principles of noncombatant immunity and proportionality, as he interprets these criteria. While he frankly expresses severe doubts about our ability to contain nuclear weapons within predetermined limits, his position is that, "given the just cause of protecting the United States from nuclear aggression, intimidation and subjugation by an enemy dedicated to the destruction of our society, our values and of the Church itself, it seems to me that we have no alternative but to attempt to find a deterrence strategy that will be both practically effective and morally permissible."[41]

In pursuit of this objective, O'Brien endorses a counterforce, flexible-response deterrent. This would require a significant restructuring of the present deterrent so that only military objectives would be targeted. In this effort, he frankly admits that, "it is problematic whether the thresholds and rules of conduct necessary to maintain such a counter-force strategy could survive a nuclear war."[42]

In developing his position, Professor O'Brien cites differences with the bishops on both the interpretation of the principles of a just-war ethic and their application to US nuclear strategy. At the level of principle, two particularly important points are made. First, he believes the bishops do not give sufficient attention to the role of just-cause in their assessment of deterrence. Concretely, this means failure to assess the Soviet threat to American and Western values; as he states the case, "Lacking such an evaluation, the debate on the morality of nuclear deterrence and war becomes an exercise in judging means without reference to their ends."[43] Second, O'Brien's understanding of the principle of noncombatant immunity seems more flexible than that found in the pastoral letter. As he puts it, "Discrimination is not an ironclad principle. It is a relative prescription that enjoins us to concentrate our attacks on military objectives and to minimize our destruction of noncombatants and civilian targets. . . ."[44] His solution seems to be the subordination of the principle of noncombatant immunity to a secondary role, to be governed by a judgment of proportionality. The bishops accord independent status to the two principles, thereby giving a more restrictive interpretation to noncombatant immunity.

At the level of application, O'Brien's position is probably closer to the final version of the pastoral than he expected, but is still not identical with it. The bishops acknowledge, more by implication than assertion, that if any use of nuclear weapons could ever be justified it would be a second-strike, counterforce attack. Professor O'Brien's attempt to design a usable counterforce posture is thus analogous to the bishops' position. He is more permissive about "collateral damage" and would not share the same degree of skepticism about controlling the use of nuclear weapons.

Finally, he does not give arms control the same priority the bishops accord it, nor does he tie the justification of deterrence to efforts designed to move beyond deterrence.

3. Albert Wohlstetter: The Counterforce Case

One of the most prominent commentators on the pastoral from outside the Catholic community is Professor Albert Wohlstetter, a pioneer in the discipline of strategic thinking in the nuclear age. Wohlstetter has taken the publication of the pastoral letter as an occasion to comment on the strategic debate over the last 30 years.[45]

Wohlstetter is severely critical of the pastoral letter. While his disagreements reach beyond the positions of the bishops to several major voices in the strategic debate (e.g., McGeorge Bundy, Robert S. McNamara, Michael Howard), he focuses on the letter in his critique. The link between the pastoral letter and the wider strategic debate is that, "By revising many times in public their pastoral letter on war and peace, American Catholic bishops have dramatized the moral issues which statesmen, using empty threats to end the world, neglect or evade."[46]

The long and complex argument made by Wohlstetter cannot be easily summarized, much less answered in the space available here. Wohlstetter criticizes the bishops on three counts: their moral logic, their technical assessments, and their political principles.

Morally, he criticizes them for not adhering more stringently to the protection of the noncombatant immunity principle, particularly as it applies to the *threat* to bomb civilians. Technically, the bishops are criticized for relying on advisers who overstate the danger of losing control of nuclear weapons; these advisers are the "technological determinists" who fail to recognize the new possibilities for discrimination and control of nuclear weapons which are now available. Politically, the bishops are mesmerized by arms control as a concept; hence they fail to pay attention to individual measures, apart from negotiated reductions, which will provide greater security for the United States and a more satisfactory moral position.

In response to the bishops' efforts to write a political-moral charter for nuclear strategy, Wohlstetter offers his proposals. The publication of the pastoral "offers a unique opportunity to examine the moral, political and military issues together, and to show that, as the President suggests, threatening to bomb innocents is not part of the nature of things."[47] Wohlstetter's argument is that it is possible to place noncombatant immunity at the center of strategic planning because it can be observed, and collateral damage can also be reduced by new technological improvements in weaponry. Moreover, observance of the moral principle will also improve the effectiveness of the deterrent since threats to strike Soviet military and industrial targets are more threatening to Soviet "values" than promises to strike civilian centers.

Two major differences separate the pastoral from the position outlined by Professor Wohlstetter. First, on a key point, he seems to misread the letter. He takes the bishops' objections to a war-fighting deterrent to mean that they have absolutely ruled out any use of nuclear weapons. As I have indicated above, while the bishops do not *endorse* use of any kind they have in fact left a sliver of ambiguity about use. Second, while being equally convinced about the necessity to observe the principle of noncombatant immunity, the bishops are less confident about the possibility of controlling nuclear weapons and much less willing to provide legitimatization for the range of nuclear weapons which Wohlstetter seems to envision. The differences emerge in light of the following quotes from the Wohlstetter article:

> The bishops, their defenders and the strategists on whom they rely all talk of the uncontrollability of nuclear weapons as a deplorable but unavoidable fact of life. . . . However, it would be naive or worse to suppose that we cannot impose controls over both initial and subsequent use of nuclear weapons.[48]

The bishops' position is more accurately stated as saying that control of nuclear weapons is highly unlikely. The following is a restatement of a quote with which Mr. Wohlstetter seems totally to disagree, but which the bishops use and which derives from individuals who rival his own substantial experience and expertise. "It is time to recognize that no one has ever succeeded in advancing any persuasive reason to believe that any use of nuclear weapons even on the smallest scale could reliably be expected to remain limited."[49] The bishops and Professor Wohlstetter share a commitment to a key principle but do not share a common view on how best to protect the principle.

4. McGeorge Bundy: Existential Deterrence

A very different assessment of the substance of the pastoral letter comes from Mr. McGeorge Bundy, currently Professor of History at New York University and previously National Security Advisor in the Kennedy-Johnson administrations. Bundy uses the occasion of the pastoral letter to support many of its themes and to extend them into a reflection on the meaning of deterrence today. First, the points of agreement: "The bishops have studied the question closely, and they know what they are against: nuclear war. They have no difficulty explaining their firm opposition both to strategies that would merely produce catastrophic loss of human life as an 'unintended' consequence of megatonnage aimed at military targets. . . . They know the extraordinary uncertainty attending any attempt to 'limit' any nuclear exchange and the inalienable risk in any first use of nuclear weapons."[50]

However helpful these distinct positions may be, they must form a policy which is not only morally consistent but strategically coherent. This leads Bundy to an assessment of the meaning of deterrence 39 years into the nuclear age. He finds the "strictly conditioned acceptance" of deterrence a precise evaluation of its moral status today. He then proceeds to describe what conception of deterrence would correspond to this ethical judgment. To use his terms, existential deterrence is "a deterrence essentially independent of any particular theory of war fighting, a deterrence inherent in the deployments already made and seen to exist for many years to come even under the most optimistic assumptions."[51]

Existential deterrence is the objective deterrent which exists so long as both sides have weapons which *could* be used after any attack. This form of deterrence rests on "uncertainty about what could happen." Here Bundy's description comes close to the reliance the pastoral places on "ambiguity" as a key element of deterrence.[52] Existential deterrence has the very limited function described in the pastoral; it deters impersonally (provocative threats are not needed); and it deters both sides (the risk of catastrophe is shared by both powers.)[53]

The point here is not to affirm congruence between Bundy's notion of existential deterrence and the pastoral letter, but to show one commentator who finds the moral argument of the pastoral pointing toward an understanding of deterrence which limits it to one basic role: the prevention of nuclear war long enough to provide an opportunity to move beyond deterrence.

B. The Continuing Conversation

The bishops produced the pastoral letter through a series of intense dialogues: among themselves, with a spectrum of experts, with critics and supporters. In closing the letter they offer an invitation to a continuing conversation, a process of reflection, exchange, and action in the Church and in the wider society.

Each of the commentators reviewed here represents a dimension of the future dialogue. Professor Grisez's concern, that the current notion of deterrence and Christian moral principles are fundamentally incompatible, is shared by a growing number of people. A significant constituency appealed to the bishops to condemn the concept of deterrence and call the Church to a posture of total opposition. These concerns will not be easily dissipated. If the framework of deterrence seems not at all to be a step toward disarmament, there will be ever greater opposition to the idea of deterrence.

Professor O'Brien highlights quite different concerns, the costs—moral and political—of delegitimizing deterrence, the difficulty of making a clear-cut case against it, but the equal difficulty of fitting it securely in a moral framework. The pastoral's conditional acceptance of deterrence is more than Grisez believes it deserves and less than O'Brien believes is necessary if key values are to be sustained in international life. The pastoral will have to be related to Grisez's moral critique and O'Brien's searching empirical questions.

The arguments of Wohlstetter and Bundy symbolize the degree of attention accorded the letter in circles professionally concerned with defense and arms control. This pastoral was designed to contribute to the wider public debate; these articles illustrate how the pastoral letter of the bishops has made its way into the policy discussion.

But this is the beginning of the argument, not its conclusion. Wohlstetter's critique and Bundy's support set the framework within which the pastoral's proposals will have to be defended, expanded, refined, and communicated to a public which finds the "challenge of peace" at times both frightening and forbidding. Publication of the pastoral was one step in a long journey.

NOTES

1 "In Defense of Deterrence," *The New Republic* (December 20, 1982), p. 7.

2 National Conference of Catholic Bishops, *The Challenge of Peace: God's Promise and Our Response* (Washington, DC, 1983), hereafter cited as *The Challenge* with paragraph number.

3 *The Challenge*, no. 125.

4 M. Bundy, G. F. Kennan, R. S. McNamara, G. Smith, "Nuclear Weapons and the Atlantic Alliance," *Foreign Affairs* 60 (1982).

5 M. D. Taylor, "Build Up the Forces We Really Need," *The Washington Post* (March 6, 1983), p. C-8.

6 *Report of the President's Commission on Strategic Forces* (Washington, DC, 1983), pp. 14–16.

7 *The Challenge*, no. 140.

8 Paul VI, *The Development of Peoples* (Rome: 1966), no. 76.

9 *The Challenge*, no. 273.

10 John Paul II, *Address to Scientists and Scholars* (Rome: 1981), no. 4.

11 *The Challenge*, no. 124.

12 For a discussion of these principles, see Paul Ramsey, *War and the Christian Conscience* (Durham, N.C.: Duke University Press, 1961); *The Just War: Force and Political Responsibility* (New York: Scribner, 1968); William O'Brien, *The Conduct of Just and Limited War* (New York: Praeger, 1981); R. B. Potter, "The Moral Logic of War," *McCormick Quarterly* 23 (1970): 203–33.

13 Henry A. Kissinger, *The Necessity for Choice: Prospects of American Foreign Policy* (New York: Harper, 1961), p. 27.

14 Vatican II, *The Pastoral Constitution on the Church in the Modern World* (Rome: 1965), no. 80.

15 Cf. Bundy et al., "Nuclear Weapons." In response, see K. Kaiser, G. Leber, A. Mertes, F. J. Schulze, "Nuclear Weapons and the Preservation of Peace," *Foreign Affairs* 60 (1982): 1157–70.

16 *The Challenge*, no. 150.

17 Ibid., footnote no. 69; cf. also "Summary."

18 Ibid., no. 159.

19 *The Pastoral Constitution*, no. 81.

20 Cf. F. Winters, "The Bow or the Cloud? American Bishops Challenge the Arms Race," *America* 145 (1981): 26–30; "Nuclear Deterrence Morality: Atlantic Community Bishops in Tension," *Theological Studies* 43 (1982): 428–46; J. Langan, "The American Hierarchy and Nuclear Weapons," *Theological Studies* 43 (1982): 447–67; David Hollenbach, *Nuclear Ethics: A Christian Moral Argument* (New York: Paulist Press, 1983). For a review of the literature, see R. McCormick, "Notes on Moral Theology: 1981," *Theological Studies* 43 (1982): 113–19; "Notes on Moral Theology: 1982," *Theological Studies* 44 (1983): 94–114.

21 John Paul II, *Message to the Second Special Session of the United Nations on Disarmament* (1982) no. 8; cited in *The Challenge*, no. 173.

22 Cf. Report on Meeting to Discuss War and Peace Pastoral, *ORIGINS* 12 (April 7, 1983): 694 (*ORIGINS* is the documentary service of the National Conference of Catholic Bishops, Washington, DC).

23 Letter of Mr. William Clark, national security advisor to President Reagan, to Cardinal Bernardin (January 15, 1983); cf. also Secretary Weinberger's *Annual Report to the Congress* (February 1, 1983), p. 5. Both are cited in *The Challenge*, footnote 81.

24 *The Challenge*, no. 181.

25 Ibid., no. 186.

26 Ibid., no. 185.

27 Ibid., no. 255.

28 Ibid., no. 245.

29 Ibid., no. 174.

30 Ibid., no. 202-19.

31 Ibid., no. 221-30.

32 Ibid., no. 19.

33 G. Grisez, "The Moral Implications of a Nuclear Deterrent," *The Center Journal* 2 (1982): 9-24; for earlier writings in this vein, see Walter Stein, ed. *Nuclear Weapons and Christian Conscience* (London: Merlin Press, 1961).

34 Grisez, "The Moral Implications," p. 14.

35 *The Challenge*, no. 178.

36 Grisez, "Moral Doctrine No Longer At Risk," *National Catholic Register* (April 24, 1983), p. 8.

37 *The Challenge*, no. 182.

38 Grisez, "The Moral Implications," p. 19 (in the footnote).

39 See William O'Brien, *War and/or Survival* (New York: Doubleday, 1969); *The Conduct of Just and Limited War*.

40 William O'Brien, "Just War Doctrine in a Nuclear Context," *Theological Studies* 44 (1983): 191-220.

41 Ibid., pp. 218-19.

42 Ibid., p. 216.

43 Ibid., p. 200.

44 Ibid., p. 211.

45 A. Wohlstetter, "Bishops, Statesmen and Other Strategists on the Bombing of Innocents," *Commentary* (June 1983), pp. 15-35.

46 Ibid., p. 15.

47 Ibid., p. 15.

48 Ibid., p. 26.

49 Bundy et al., "Nuclear Weapons," p. 757.

50 McGeorge Bundy, "The Bishops and The Bomb," *New York Review of Books* (June 16, 1983), p. 3.

51 Ibid., p. 4.

52 Ibid.

53 Ibid., pp. 4-5.

5

THE U.S. BISHOPS' POSITION ON NUCLEAR DETERRENCE: A MORAL ASSESSMENT

George Sher

A policy which is seriously thought necessary to maintain peace, yet which may end by extinguishing all human life, raises moral perplexities on an unprecedented scale. This is certainly true of the prevailing policy of maintaining vast arsenals of nuclear weapons to be used in case of attack. In the last few years, a committee of United States Catholic bishops has addressed the moral status of nuclear deterrence in a series of drafts of a proposed pastoral letter. More recently, a revised version of their third draft was adopted by a full conference of United States Catholic bishops. In this paper, I shall critically discuss some aspects of the bishops' moral position. Because their letter's second and third drafts display certain interesting differences in argument, I shall use the contrast between them as the vehicle for my discussion.

I. THE BISHOPS' ARGUMENTS

Let us begin by summarizing the position to be discussed. In their letter's second and third drafts, and also in its final version, the bishops' overall conclusion is that nuclear deterrence is morally acceptable, but only on a conditional basis. More specifically, they hold that nuclear deterrence currently does perform certain essential tasks, but that it has such serious shortcomings that we may accept it only if we simultaneously pursue serious efforts to eliminate all need for nuclear threats. To assess the merits of this position, we must first understand (a) the moral advantages and drawbacks which the bishops attribute to nuclear deterrence, and (b) the ways in which they combine these advantages and drawbacks to establish that nuclear deterrence is conditionally acceptable.

Generally speaking, the arguments for and against nuclear deterrence are quite similar in the two drafts. In each draft, the most important benefit of deterrent threats is said to be their prevention of the actual use of nuclear weapons. The contention that deterrence has preserved "peace of a sort" for 38 years is "not subject to conclusive proof or disproof," but one "cannot simply dismiss its implications."[1] In addition, the third draft, though not the second, briefly mentions what is often considered a further benefit of deterrence: its connection with "the independence and freedom of nations, including the need to protect smaller nations from threats to their independence and integrity."[2] Balanced against such advantages, the second draft provides a concise but inclusive list of reasons why nuclear deterrence cannot be considered morally satisfactory. These reasons include (1) the fact that it is wrong to intend any use of nuclear weapons which would violate the principles of discrimination and proportionality traditionally associated with the doctrine of "just war"; (2) the human consequences (presumably the suffering, disease, death, and destruction of civilized institutions) that would ensue if deterrence were to fail; (3) the mistrust among nations which deterrence embodies; (4) the likely surpassing of all reasonable limits on destruction if deterrence fails; and (5) the fact that deterrence diverts resources from other human needs. Although this list does not reappear intact in the third draft, each entry reappears there in some form. The only significant change is that the human needs from which deterrence is said to divert resources are more closely associated with the needs of the third world. In aggregate, the items on the list clearly continue to ground the bishops' condemnation of deterrence.

Although the main elements of the bishops' position do not change much between drafts, there is a shift in the way these elements are combined to establish that deterrence is conditionally acceptable. In the second draft, a policy of nuclear deterrence is said to be conditionally acceptable because it is less evil than its current alternatives. As Cardinal John Krol has put the point:

As long as there is hope [of negotiations toward reduction and eventual phasing out of nuclear deterrence] . . . , Catholic moral teaching is willing, while negotiations proceed, to tolerate the possession of nuclear weapons for deterrence as the lesser of two evils. If that hope were to disappear, the moral attitude of the Catholic Church would certainly have to shift to one of uncompromising condemnation of both the use and possession of such weapons.[3]

However, although the "lesser evil" approach is in many ways natural, many Catholic moral theologians reject in principle the claim that we may sometimes pursue a good end through evil means. Perhaps because of this, the third draft no longer contends that deterrence is conditionally acceptable as the lesser of two evils. Instead, it appears to argue for conditional acceptance on somewhat different grounds. In particular, it implies that although the indiscriminate and disproportionate destructiveness of nuclear weapons renders it extremely unlikely that their use would ever be legitimate, this possibility cannot be entirely ruled out. Because their use could conceivably be legitimate in some circumstances, there is also some legitimacy to the *threat* to use them. Hence, deterrent threats, while far from desirable, are not absolutely forbidden.

In both drafts, the bishops have tried to reconcile the demands of morality (and prudence) with the hard realities of international politics. With this aim I am thoroughly in sympathy. I am, moreover, also sympathetic to their substantive conclusion that we are morally permitted to practice deterrence if, but only if, we simultaneously engage in genuine and persistent negotiations toward its abolition. However, when we turn from the general outlines of this position to the bishops' arguments for it, problems emerge.

II. SOME COMPLICATIONS

To appreciate these problems, we must first distinguish two possible versions of the "conditional acceptance" thesis. In its stronger form, the thesis says that nuclear deterrence is inherently unacceptable, and that no deterrent arrangements may ever be countenanced except on a strictly interim basis. In its weaker form, the thesis says only that certain elements of our *present* deterrent posture are unacceptable, and that any continuation of that posture must be accompanied by efforts to reduce and eventually eliminate those elements. Given their overall tone, the bishops clearly wish to defend the stronger of these theses. However, for the most part, the considerations they cite tell only for the weaker.

Thus, consider items (2) and (4) on their list. It is indeed true that the surpassing of defensible limits on destruction and the human consequences of such destruction would be evils of incalculable magnitude. However, it is also true that these evils would ensue only if deterrence failed and nuclear war broke out despite our deterrent threats. Because of this, the consequences of nuclear war will count against deterrence only if that policy runs an appreciable risk of failure. It is, of course, precisely the substantial (and increasing) risk associated with the current arms race that has led to the present debate. Nevertheless, without further argument, the consequences of failure will tell not against deterrence per se, but only against those elements of it which generate the risk. Neither the likely surpassing of limits in conflict nor the human consequences of this provides any argument against permanently accepting a super-stable deterrent. The more difficult question of whether any nuclear deterrent could *be* stable enough to warrant permanent acceptance is not explicitly addressed by the bishops, but will be taken up below.

A similar point can be made about the argument that nuclear deterrence is morally unacceptable because it diverts scarce resources away from human needs (item [5] on the bishops' list). To tell against deterrence as such, this argument would have to assume that (a) any policy of nuclear deterrence must inevitably be extremely costly, and that (b) its cost must always cause pressing social needs to go unmet. However, although the cost of deterrence will remain high as long as we continue allocating large sums of money for new research and development, that cost would be much lower if money were spent only to maintain systems already in place. Under these conditions, deterrence might well consume only a small fraction of our defense budget. (It was, indeed, precisely the comparatively low cost of nuclear deterrence that originally led the United States to threaten the use of nuclear weapons in response to a successful nonnuclear attack on NATO forces.) Moreover, even if the cost of nuclear deterrence does remain significant, the link between that cost and the unmet needs of the poor seems tenuous. If the world's rich nations lack the political will to help the poor, then reductions in defense spending will do little good; while if the will to help is present, then much can be done even within current constraints. All in all, it again appears that the bishops' argument does not tell against permanently accepting any form of deterrence. Instead, it implies only that if deterrence is to be permanent then we should strive to change those conditions which currently make it extremely costly and unstable.

So far, we have considered only arguments grounded in factors extrinsic to deterrence itself. This is why the arguments tell only against certain forms of nuclear deterrence. But the same cannot be said about the bishops' appeal to the mistrust associated with nuclear deterrence (item [3] on the list); for a degree of mistrust is indeed implied by any deterrent threat. However, even if nuclear deterrence does institutionalize a certain mistrust among nations, it hardly follows that it is unacceptable as a permanent policy; for it is far from clear what is wrong with this degree of institutionalized mistrust. Mistrust certainly does not always rule out such cooperative activities as trade and cultural exchange. Indeed, because any effective legal system must rely on the deterrent threat of punishment, and because an effective legal system appears to be both morally permissible and necessary for the maintenance of social order, a degree of institutionalized mistrust within a society appears to be necessary for that society's orderly functioning. If the mistrust that is inherent in a stable nuclear deterrent has different effects, or a different moral status, this has yet to be shown. Of course, it is one thing to threaten someone with prison or a fine if he himself acts wrongly, and quite another to threaten to kill hundreds of millions of innocent people if their *government* acts wrongly. If we condemn nuclear deterrence on this basis, however, then we are appealing not to the mistrust that it embodies, but rather to the special nature of the nuclear threat. We are, in short, shifting from consideration (3) to consideration (1) on the bishops' list.

III. INTENDING AND DOING

Of all the arguments advanced to show that any acceptance of nuclear deterrence must be conditional, the strongest is clearly that such deterrence, by nature, involves morally impermissible intentions. Filled out, the version of this argument which is advanced in the bishops' second draft appears to run as follows:

P1: It would be morally wrong to use nuclear weapons in the way that deterrent threats require (because any such use would bring destruction that neither discriminates proper from improper targets nor is proportional to any good that might thereby be obtained).

P2: If it is morally wrong to do A under circumstance C, then it is also morally wrong to intend to do A should C arise.

P3: A nation cannot credibly maintain nuclear deterrence unless its leaders do intend to use nuclear weapons if attacked.

Therefore,

C: It is morally wrong to maintain nuclear deterrence.

There is, of course, much to be said about this argument's premises. In particular, it has been plausibly argued that deterrent intentions themselves provide a counterexample to P2.[4] Here, however, I shall contest neither the argument's premises nor its validity. Instead, I want to concentrate on a different question: assuming that some such argument does succeed, does it permit even the conditional acceptance of deterrence which the bishops favor? To answer this question, I shall take up first the "lesser evil" approach of the bishops' second draft, and then the modification of P1 that is implicit in their third draft.

On the "lesser evil" approach, nuclear deterrence is said to be conditionally justified despite its wrongness because any alternative policy would bring a greater risk of nuclear war, and so would be even more wrong. If the objection to deterrence were merely the risk of its failure, then the claim that other strategies are currently even more risky would, if true, be decisive. However, if the wrongness of deterrence resides not in its consequences, but rather in the intentions it requires, then the issue is more complicated. On this account, the conditional acceptability of nuclear deterrence must be said to follow not merely from the fact that it is currently less risky than its alternatives, but rather from the fact that entertaining deterrent intentions, though wrong, is not as wrong as raising by a certain amount the probability that others will use or coercively threaten to use nuclear weapons.

But can our conditional acceptance of nuclear deterrence really be justified on this basis? I doubt that it can. To see the problems with the attempt, note first that actually using nuclear weapons to kill millions of in-nocent people is surely far more wrong than merely raising the probability that others will use such weapons (or will coercively threaten to use them). Because of this, and because the bishops believe that raising the probabil-ity of nuclear use or coercion by others is itself more wrong than entertain-ing deterrent intentions, they must believe that actually using nuclear weapons is yet more wrong than merely entertaining deterrent intentions to use them. Given the structure of their argument, the bishops must hold that the moral difference between intending to use nuclear weapons and actually using them is very great. However, if they believe that the moral difference between using and intending to use nuclear weapons is this great, then their reason for saying that all intentions to use such weapons are wrong can hardly rest on the standard claim that intentions are the earliest elements of the intended actions, or that intentions are continuous with the actions that are intended. Where these familiar strategies are used to connect intention and action, intending a wrong action must be con-sidered to be just as wrong, or almost as wrong, as actually performing it.[5] And yet, if the continuity between intention and action is not the source of the bishops' crucial premise P2, then what is the source of that premise? Given the absence of any alternative rationale, the view that nuclear deter-rence is the least of the current evils seems, ironically, to be the one moral option which is *not* open to the bishops. If entertaining deterrent inten-tions is wrong at all, then it appears to be more wrong than even such ex hypothesi more risky alternatives as unilateral disarmament. On the other hand, if entertaining deterrent intentions is less wrong than such more risky alternatives, then it is unclear why we should consider it wrong at all.

In the bishops' third draft, these problems do not arise. There the bish-ops no longer assert either that deterrence is the least of the current evils, or that it is less wrong than any available alternative policy. Moreover, they flatly state at the outset that "[a]ny *use* of nuclear weapons which would violate the principles of non-combatant immunity or proportionality may not be *intended* in a strategy of deterrence" (emphasis theirs).[6] Given these changes, the bishops' continuing insistence that deterrence is condi-tionally acceptable appears to rest on some retreat from the premise that all use of nuclear weapons is wrong. Instead of P1, they appear to accept the weaker premise that the legitimacy of using such weapons, and so too of intending to use them, is extremely dubious, but cannot definitively be ruled out in every conceivable case. This modification of P1 is not made ex-plicit, but it is suggested by certain changes of wording between the two drafts. Thus, for example, the second draft flatly denies that it is ever permissible to initiate the use of nuclear weapons:

> We do not perceive any situation in which the deliberate initiation of nuclear warfare, on however restricted a scale, can be morally justified. Non-nuclear at-tacks by another state must be resisted by other than nuclear means (p. 314).

In the third draft, the condemnation of first use is considerably less strong:

> We abhor the concept of initiating nuclear war on however restricted a scale. Because of the probable effects, the deliberate initiation of nuclear war in our judgment would be an unjustifiable moral risk. Therefore, a serious moral obligation exists to develop defensive strategies as rapidly as possible to preclude any justification for using nuclear weapons in response to non-nuclear attacks (p. 711).[7]

In addition, the argument that the permissibility of deterrence hinges on a "centimeter of doubt" as to whether all use of nuclear weapons is wrong has been advanced in public forum by an authoritative spokesman for the bishops' position.[8]

Can such a revision of P1 rescue the view that nuclear deterrence is conditionally acceptable? Here again, there appear to be serious difficulties. First, even if the revision does establish that some intentions to use nuclear weapons are permissible, the range of legitimate deterrent intentions cannot exceed the range of cases in which use is legitimate. In addition, the magnitude of the use which may legitimately be intended can never exceed the magnitude of the use which is permitted. Given the extremely narrow range of cases in which use would be permitted, and given the minimal nature of the permitted use, it is extremely unclear that publicizing an intention to use nuclear weapons in precisely the cases in which it is permissible to use them would have much deterrent effect. It is of course possible for a nation to be less than fully explicit about the circumstances under which it would use nuclear weapons. However, if a nation can generate enough uncertainty to deter attack when it in fact maintains an intention to make only extremely minimal use of nuclear weapons, then it should also be able to generate sufficient uncertainty to deter attack if it intends no use at all. Hence, rather than telling for the utility of extremely circumscribed deterrent intentions, appeals to the deterrent effects of uncertainty actually suggest that such intentions are unnecessary.

IV. DURATION, DETERRENCE, AND RISK

I have thus far contended that the bishops' arguments prove either too little or too much. Of their five main lines of argument, four establish, at best, that it is morally impermissible to continue to practice nuclear deterrence without attempting to eliminate some of its currently objectionable features; while the fifth, if successful at all, appears to imply that no meaningful nuclear deterrent is permissible on even a conditional basis. There is, I think, no plausible way of rescuing the conditional acceptance thesis without relinquishing the view that it is always wrong to intend to do what it is wrong to do. However, if one is willing to relinquish this view – as I am – then there may indeed be something more to say.

For consider again the bishops' earlier observation that any breakdown of deterrence would be a catastrophe of unimaginable proportions. Above, I argued that in itself this fact tells only against accepting an unstable or ineffective deterrent system. If the risk of failure is negligible, then the consequences of failure become irrelevant. But although we can at least conceive of a nuclear deterrent that is safe and stable over the short run, the prospects of maintaining such a system over the longer run are far less bright. If the probability of failure under current conditions is small but finite, then the probability of failure must be greater over a long period than over a short one. Moreover, even if the probability of failure under current conditions is close to nil, the swift changeability of geopolitical realities strongly suggests that these conditions will not remain constant. Thus, any reasonable assumptions must imply that the risk of breakdown increases over time. Given our undeniable obligation to minimize the risks to future as well as present human beings, this itself may appear to imply that it is impermissible to accept deterrence without simultaneously making sincere and persistent efforts to eliminate all nuclear weapons.

Although the bishops do not explicitly mention the relationship between the risk of breakdown and the length of time during which deterrence is practiced, it is, I think, precisely this relationship that lends credence to their claim that we may not accept deterrence as a permanent policy. Unlike the bishops' own appeal to risk, this argument does seem sufficiently general to apply to all forms of deterrence. Unfortunately, as it stands, even the augmented argument from risk does not succeed in establishing the bishops' conclusion. The problem with it, put briefly, is that the long-term risks of deterrence are considered, but not the long-term risks of alternative policies. There is, of course, an obvious prima facie case for believing that the risk of nuclear war is greater if thousands of launch-ready nuclear weapons exist than if they do not. As inherently risky as this situation is, however, we cannot say, a priori, that it is more risky over the long haul than one in which neither side has nuclear weapons, but one side has both the capacity and motivation to build them before the other side can produce a deterrent force. We cannot even say a priori that a deterrent system poses more long-term risk than restructuring the world political system in a way which minimizes both international rivalries and the fear and selfishness which produce them; for there is no a priori reason why such restructuring could not degenerate into a new arms race that was less stable than a deterrent stand-off.

With these observations, we move decisively away from the bishops' attempt to find a principled moral reason for rejecting any future policy of deterrence. As repulsive and frightening as deterrence is, there is neither a moral nor a prudential case for thinking of the future as a time at which it is not even a permissible option. Instead, then as now, it seems that the morally appropriate stance will be a pragmatic openness to whatever policies seem most likely to prevent the use of nuclear weapons without sacrificing other extremely important values.[9] Under this rubric, the bishops' conditional acceptance of deterrence might even be reversed. It could conceivably transpire that a nation is morally permitted to refrain from developing a nuclear deterrent if and only if it simultaneously strives to create future conditions under which such a deterrent can more safely be developed. But if this reversal is a theoretical possibility, it is, for the foreseeable future, immensely unlikely. Given the dangers which deterrence now poses, our first obligation is surely to reduce the current level of risk. Moreover, although the point requires more argument than I can give it, I believe that, under current conditions, this end would be best served by a mutual and verifiable reduction, and if possible the eventual elimination, of nuclear weapons. I have argued that the bishops are wrong to hold that the permanent elimination of nuclear weapons is morally required if this means that their reintroduction will never be morally permitted. It hardly follows that it is also wrong to hold that, as things now stand, sincere and persistent negotiations are a moral precondition of the legitimate use of deterrent threats.[10]

NOTES

1 "New Draft of Pastoral Letter. The Challenge of Peace: God's Promise and Our Response," *Origins NC Documentary Service* 12, 20 (October 28, 1982), p. 317. (Henceforth, this document will be referred to as "Second Draft.")

2 "Third Draft of Pastoral Letter. The Challenge of Peace: God's Promise and Our Response," *Origins NC Documentary Service* 12, 44 (April 14, 1983), p. 713. (Henceforth, this document will be referred to as "Third Draft.")

3 Quoted in Second Draft, p. 316.

4 See Gregory Kavka, "Some Paradoxes of Deterrence," *The Journal of Philosophy* 75, no. 6 (June 1978): 285–302.

5 This argument may seem too quick; for even if intending to do A *is* an early element of doing A, or is continuous with doing A, there might still appear to be cases in which intending A is much less wrong than actually doing A. In particular, this might be said if (a) the intention is causally or temporally remote from the action, and so would permit the agent to change his mind at various points before he must act, or if (b) when the moment of crisis arises, the intention is followed not by action but by repentance. But whatever the general force of these objections, neither applies to the case at hand. The possibility of changing one's mind can hardly mitigate the wrongness of an intention when what is intended is an immediate response to a circumstance which may arise at any moment. Moreover, even if wrong intentions *are* rendered less objectionable when followed by repentance, this is no reason to believe that an intention to do wrong which is *not* (yet) followed by repentance is any less wrong than the intended act itself.

6 Third Draft, p. 698.

7 Again, the second draft registers straightforward opposition to the use of nuclear weapons on military targets near population centers:

Aware of the controverted nature of the issue, we nonetheless feel obligated as a matter of practical moral guidance to register our opposition to a policy of attacking targets which lie so close to concentrations of population that destruction of the target would devastate the nearby population centers (p. 314).

In the third draft, the issue is treated more delicately:

The Reagan administration's policy is that under no circumstances may such weapons be used deliberately for the purpose of destroying populations. . . . This statement does not address another very troublesome problem, namely, that an attack on military targets or militarily significant industrial targets could involve "indirect" (i.e., unintended) but massive civilian casualties (p. 714).

A narrow adherence exclusively to the principle of non-combatant immunity as a criterion for policy is an inadequate moral posture for it ignores some evil and unacceptable consequences. Hence, we cannot be satisfied that the assertion of an intention not to strike civilians directly or even the most honest effort to implement that intention by itself constitutes a "moral policy" for the use of nuclear weapons (p. 714).

In the final draft, adopted by the full conference of U.S. bishops, the stronger stance of the second draft prevails.

8 J. Bryan Hehir, U.S. Catholic Conference, in "Moral Issues in Deterrence Policy," this volume.

9 The obligation to adopt the safest policies consistent with the protection of our values will obtain no matter what our values are, and no matter how much weight we attach to them. However, in practice, the policies we choose will depend heavily on the exact nature and weight of these values. Although this issue is often formulated in terms of the competing slogans "Better dead than Red" and "Better Red than dead," these slogans are misleading in at least two ways. First, the real choice is not between being Red and being dead, but rather between being Red and raising the risk of being dead by a certain amount. Moreover, second, the risk in question is one that is run not only by those of us who make the decisions, but also by innocent third parties the world over and, most likely, by all the (possible) future generations of mankind. When the risk to these parties is taken into account, issues of ideology and national interest quickly pale into moral insignificance. Indeed, I believe there is a real (though unaddressed) question as to whether any temporally parochial values ought to count at all in the debate.

10 This paper has been improved by the helpful suggestions of Arthur Kuflik.

6

AVOIDING ARMAGEDDON: WHOSE RESPONSIBILITY?

Christopher M. Lehman

It has been said by pundits that military strategy is the art of looking for danger, finding it everywhere, diagnosing it inaccurately, and prescribing the wrong remedy. In the highly politicized environment of the past few years, where defense policy and nuclear strategy have been hotly contested, growing numbers of individuals think the pundits are right – that our military strategy is way off the mark. This is particularly true in the area of nuclear strategy where debates have raged for decades among a fairly small group of individuals in government, Congress, and academia. These people have for years argued among themselves, in person and in print, and have helped to mold decisions on policies that ultimately affect every man, woman, and child in this country.

Now, to a greater extent than ever before, people all across the country are demanding that they enter into that once private preserve of the nuclear strategist. A recent example is the literature of the "nuclear freeze movement" which claims that nuclear strategy is far too important to be left to the experts. The issues, it is argued, are clear-cut, and the man in the street is as competent to judge as any expert – and perhaps more so.

What is the proper role for experts in the arcane world of nuclear strategy? Should we decide strategic nuclear policy by plebiscite? These and other important questions are the subject of this paper.

STRATEGY AND PROCESS

In the post-war era, the process by which American defense policy or strategy is developed has been quite complex. Since those policies involve the most vital interests of our country, and their implementation requires a substantial commitment of resources, policy formulation has been a highly political process involving negotiation and compromise among a variety of actors. The most important of these can be divided into three categories: the executive, Congress, and nongovernmental actors.

The Executive Branch

Throughout the post-war period, policy formulation with respect to nuclear weapons has been primarily the province of the executive branch of the government. As a result of the reorganization of the national security structure of our government after World War II, policy formulation regarding nuclear weapons issues as well as broader defense issues was centralized under the National Security Council. Within this organizational structure, the Department of Defense was to have principal responsibility for the development of military strategy including nuclear strategy, with the Joint Chiefs of Staff playing an important role in that effort.

In addition to the Department of Defense, several other executive agencies have been instrumental in the development of strategic policy over the years, including the Department of State, the intelligence community, and the Office of Management and Budget. Other agencies have also had an impact, including the former Atomic Energy Commission and the Arms Control and Disarmament Agency. Government "think tanks" were an influential element of the process as well. Several civilian research organizations have been involved in the business of "thinking for the government" since the early post-war years, and much of the rationale for America's nuclear policies was originally developed at these institutions. The Rand Corporation is one of the most notable of these institutions.

Congress

Although the formulation of nuclear policy has been primarily the province of the executive branch over the years, Congress has had a fair measure of influence in its development. It is Congress that provides the funds for implementing strategic policies and thus, if sufficiently aroused, it can use the power of the purse to block initiatives of the executive in this area. The MX missile controversy illustrates how the power to withhold appropriations can directly influence strategic nuclear policy.

An additional means for Congress to exert its influence derives from its authority to investigate and to oversee the operations of the executive branch. The congressional oversight hearing has, in fact, been the primary source of congressional intervention into the development of strategic nuclear policy over the years. Beginning in 1949 with the House Armed Services Committee hearings on "The National Defense Program: Unification and Strategy," the congressional oversight hearing has become an established means of exposing to Congress and the public the plans and policies of the executive branch regarding strategic issues.

These hearings have also provided an opportunity for committees to put pressure on the executive to alter those plans and policies. Some of the more noteworthy hearings included: the Senate Armed Services Committee "Airpower" hearings in 1956; the same committee's hearings on "The Status of U.S. Strategic Power" in 1968; and the Senate Foreign Relations Committee 1974 hearings on "U.S. and USSR Strategic Policies." More recently, the numerous hearings and debates on the SALT II Treaty and the proposed deployment of the MX missile have provided a forum for considering strategic nuclear policy issues and a platform for espousing alternative strategic policies.

In addition, in the wake of the 1969 ABM debate, Congress began to develop expanded sources of specialized technical expertise and information independent of the executive. The Congressional Research Service, a part of the Library of Congress, was expanded. The Office of Technology Assessment was created and congressional committees strengthened their technical and professional expertise. In 1974, the Congressional Budget Office was established.

Nongovernmental Actors

A variety of other actors outside of the government can also affect the development of military strategy and policy. These fall generally into four categories: (1) the intellectual community; (2) interest groups; (3) the media; and (4) public opinion. Each of these groups can function only indirectly. They have no policy-making authority and must work through governmental actors such as Congress, the Department of Defense, and the president. But these nongovernmental actors often force decision-makers within the government into action, and they establish parameters within which those decision-makers must remain.

Without a doubt, the most significant nongovernmental influence in the post-war years has been the intellectual community. From the early writings of such seminal thinkers as Bernard Brodie and Thomas Schelling, to the more recent policy analysis of the private think tanks under government contract, the civilian intellectual community has exerted continuing influence on the formulation of strategic policy. The scientific community, too, has had a significant impact. Much of the early discussion and debate over nuclear weapons and their utility was carried on among US scientists, and it was the intellectual community that first developed the rudimentary concept of nuclear deterrence.

In more recent years, a number of interest groups have been founded with nuclear policy issues as one of their main concerns. Among them, the Arms Control Association, the Union of Concerned Scientists, the Center for Defense Information, and the Council for a Livable World stand out at one end of the spectrum, and the American Security Council, the National Strategy Information Center, and the Heritage Foundation, at the other. These and other groups have been quite active since the 1970s in working to influence government decisions on nuclear policy and have sought to achieve their policy preferences through a variety of means, including publications, testimony before Congress, and lobbying Congress directly and through grassroots efforts.

The media, including television, newspapers, and periodicals, have played an important and growing role in influencing the development of nuclear policies. The press serves as the primary link between the government and the public, providing information on government policies to the citizenry and providing feedback on those policies to the government. Media coverage of congressional hearings, leaks from the executive branch, and investigative reporting have all heightened awareness of strategic nuclear issues from time to time as well as exerting influence over the development of policy by stimulating governmental actors into action or reaction.

Certain articles in prominent journals have had catalytic effects on the nuclear policy debate. A 1983 article in *Foreign Affairs* recommending that the United States adopt a policy of "no first use" of nuclear weapons revived a lively debate both in Europe and the United States on this important doctrinal issue.

The final nongovernmental actor is that nebulous creature called "public opinion." The direct impact of public opinion is generally far weaker than that of interest groups, but there are exceptions. Normally the opinions of the American people are not specifically directed to nuclear policy issues, and the few times this has occurred, there has been little consensus about what should be done. The advent of Sputnik in the 1950s and the nuclear freeze movement today are examples, however, of cases in which public opinion can influence policy.

The nuclear freeze issue has generated a great deal of public activity over the past two years and is widely interpreted as having had a significant impact in Congress and even within the executive branch. The issue was on the ballot in ten states and hundreds of cities, counties, and towns. The overall vote nationwide was approximately 60 percent in favor and 40 percent against with substantial numbers of voters failing to vote either way on the referendum. At least partially as a response to public concern (partisan political considerations were not entirely absent), the House of Representatives debated a nuclear freeze resolution in 1982 and again in 1983. President Reagan responded as well, addressing in a number of speeches the issues of arms control and the nuclear freeze.

Each of these nongovernmental actors then–the intellectual community, the interest groups, the media, and public opinion–have in their own unique way affected the development of strategic nuclear policy within the government. The complex interaction among these groups and their interaction with the two branches of the government directly involved with policy formulation have had varying results over time. However, it is clear that their influence on official government policy has been significant.

THE SYSTEM WORKS

This very complicated system called the policy process has actually functioned quite well over the years. The executive branch has retained primacy but Congress and nongovernmental actors have had direct impact on the formulation of policy at frequent junctures.

In a very real sense, this is just one more manifestation of the system of checks and balances established by our Constitution. The Constitution itself is surprisingly brief in its treatment of foreign affairs and defense and in fact makes no specific mention of any foreign affairs or national security power. The Constitution instead assigns lesser powers to Congress, or the president, or both. Congress is accorded the greatest number of powers (including providing for the common defense); by contrast, the president is accorded few specific powers—among them that he "shall be Commander-in-Chief of the Army and Navy." For powers beyond that, the president has relied on the general "executive power" vested in the office by Section I of Article II.

In the years prior to World War II, the dominance of the executive branch in foreign and defense matters was kept within limits and there was substantial agreement between the two branches. An exception was the Senate's use of the treaty power to frustrate President Wilson's hopes for the League of Nations.

After World War II, however, a period of executive dominance developed and has remained to this day. Beginning with the increased power of the president during wartime and boosted by the substantial foreign policy and military responsibilities of the post-war period, the presidency has retained dominance in the struggle for power with Congress. In fact, Congress acquiesced in large part in the growth of presidential power in the post-war years, and only in the 1970s did Congress begin to reassert its authority over foreign and defense policy. In the 1950s and 1960s, there was general consensus over America's defense and foreign policies and thus the Congress could go along with the executive branch.

Coincident with this reassertion of congressional authority, the longstanding consensus on nuclear weapons policy began to erode and Congress began to assert its influence in that policy area. In 1969, a major congressional debate was held over the issue of antiballistic missile deployments, focused on the question of strategic doctrine and how best to maintain deterrence. Again in 1974, there was a great deal of dispute in Congress and in the press over the "Schlesinger doctrine," which called for a policy of flexible response or limited counterforce as the best means of preserving deterrence.

During the Carter administration, a major public and congressional debate was held over the nuclear doctrine contained in Presidential Directive 59 (P.D. 59). Now, in the 1980s, debates have taken place again in Congress and in the public over the nuclear policies of the Reagan administration. In each case, substantial elements in Congress, supported by elements of all the nongovernmental actors, have challenged the merits of United States nuclear strategy. In each case, however, when votes were taken on funding necessary to implement that strategy, the executive branch position was upheld. This debate has continued with the annual funding requests for the MX and Trident II missiles and has been a part of the nuclear freeze controversy as well. Despite the debates, the political lobbying, and the expert testimony, Congress has supported the nuclear policies put forward by the president. There have been numerous votes and each time the policy proposed by the president has prevailed.

CONCLUSION

The making of national security policy is clearly, and appropriately, dominated by the executive branch. Only the various agencies in the national security community, each playing its assigned role, have the resources, the time, and the access to critical information that are indispensable to the formulation and conduct of foreign and defense policy.

But two points must be made. First, although all executive branch agencies answer to the president, national security expertise is not embodied in a monolithic group. There are lively differences of personal and organizational views, which have been described by former executive branch "insiders" such as Graham Allison, Morton Halperin, and Leslie Gelb. Policy formulation benefits from the military and technical expertise of the Pentagon, the intelligence community's assessments of Soviet capabilities and intentions, the State Department's worldwide perspective of broader foreign policy objectives, and the arms control advocacy of the Arms Control and Disarmament Agency. Any public perception of a dichotomy of "hawks" and "doves" is overly simplistic, as there is a broad consensus on such basic points as the necessity of avoiding nuclear war and of maintaining sufficient strength to deter our potential enemies. But the debate within the executive branch on specific issues is comprehensive and often intense.

Second, the executive branch's "experts" are not soulless automatons, but people, too. They do not seek nuclear incineration any more than the butcher, baker, or candlestick maker. While the SAC general and the diplomat are required by their jobs to focus on aspects of national security policy which may appear arcane to the outsider, their ultimate objectives are no different from anyone else's.

The entire national security community, including the president, answers ultimately to the American public. The system is designed to respond to the views and concerns of the informed citizenry. But we must also recognize that the public's attention to these issues is unavoidably diffuse and subject to broad swings in opinion. While the polls and media interest today are focused on the horrors of nuclear war and the dangers of the arms race, we should not forget that only a few short years ago – during the SALT II debate – there was a broad public perception (fed by the media) of a growing imbalance in strategic power and the need to preserve peace by matching Soviet strength. Candidate Reagan's views on SALT II and strategic policy were no secret before the 1980 election, and he was elected by the public, not by national security "experts."

Congress provides the necessary nexus between the broad concerns of the American public and narrower – but more informed – focus of the executive branch experts. More than the general or the diplomat, Congress must be responsive to the dynamic concerns of the people. In addition, Congress has developed extensive expertise in the details of national security issues, embodied in leading members of Congress in both parties and particularly in the staffs of the major committees.

In summary, the system benefits from this interplay of forces. Rightly so, the "experts" clearly dominate the making of national security policy. But these experts are in no way isolated from the concerns of the body politic. Public and individual concerns are heard and can have major impact on the development of national security policy.

NOTES

1 Two excellent sources for a more detailed review of the role of Congress in strategic policy development are: Robert N. Ginsburgh, *U.S. Military Strategy in the Sixties* (New York: W. W. Norton, 1965) and Samuel P. Huntington, "Strategic Planning and the Political Process," in *Components of Defense Policy*, edited by Davis B. Bobrow (Chicago: Rand McNally, 1965).

2 Robert H. Trice, "The Policymaking Process: Actors and Their Impact," in *American Defense Policy*, edited by John F. Reichart and Steven R. Sturm (Baltimore: The Johns Hopkins University Press, 1982), p. 506 and Samuel P. Huntington, *The Common Defense* (New York: Columbia University Press, 1961), pp. 174–78.

3 For a detailed treatment of the role of the intellectual community in strategic policy formulation, see Gene M. Lyons and Louis Morton, *Schools for Strategy: Education and Research in National Security Affairs* (New York: Frederick Praeger, 1965).

4 Trice, "The Policymaking Process," p. 507.

5 A number of excellent studies of the separation of powers among Congress and the presidency have been written including Louis Fisher, *President and Congress* (New York: Free Press, 1972), Richard Neustadt, *Presidential Power* (New York: Wiley, 1960), and Edwin Corwin, *The President: Office and Powers* (New York: New York University Press, 1940).

7

THE PEOPLE
VERSUS THE EXPERTS

William Greider

The democratic dilemma inherent in the governance of nuclear arms is unique only in its seriousness. The same tension between popular opinion and technocratic expertise is expressed in other essential areas of modern government, from regulatory controls to management of the economy. The decision-making in each area is dominated by a core elite of sophisticated interests, usually insulated from the gross pressures of public opinion, sometimes isolated from them. The public often expresses frustration and suspicion, watching these remote experts make important public decisions affecting their lives. The governing elites are, likewise, suspicious of public opinion, which they regard as crude and ill-informed, unequipped to deal with the complexities of the decisions.

In some ways, this is the natural outcome of the "progressive" vision of government first articulated by early 20th-century reformers who wished for "good government." They wanted to insulate government management from the raw and unruly pressures of public sentiment, to make it clean and rational and safe from "dirty politics." As our society became complex and specialized, as the national government expanded its intervention in private enterprise, this management approach prevailed in one area after another. Most of the decision-makers at the higher reaches, including even elected politicians, believe in that vision. At its core, it is antidemocratic.

Walter Lippmann in *Public Opinion* accurately foreshadowed the governing ethos of technocratic expertise that would emerge. Lippmann thought "public opinion" was an unstable, even menacing influence on the great affairs of government. He wrote:

It is not possible to assume that a world, carried on by division of labor and distribution of authority, can be governed by universal opinions in the whole population. Unconsciously, the theory sets up the single reader as theoretically omnicompetent, and puts upon the press the burden of accomplishing whatever representative government, industrial organization, and diplomacy have failed to accomplish. Acting upon everybody for 30 minutes in 24 hours, the press is asked to create a mystical force called Public Opinion that will take up the slack in public institutions. The press has often mistakenly pretended that it could do just that. It has, at great moral cost to itself, encouraged a democracy, still bound to its original premises, to expect newspapers to supply spontaneously for every organ of government, for every social problem, the machinery of information which these do not normally supply themselves.

Lippmann proposed a solution to this "trouble," as he called it:

[It] lies in social organization based on a system of analysis and record and in all the corollaries of that principle, in the abandonment of the theory of the omnicompetent citizen, in the decentralization of decision, in the coordination of decision by comparable record and analysis. If at the centers of management there is a running audit, which makes work intelligible to those who do it, and those who superintend it, issues when they arise are not the mere collisions of the blind.

This smug vision of proper government has largely prevailed in our time, most dramatically in those areas that are most complex and esoteric, like national-security policy for nuclear arms. One need not believe in the "mystical" powers of public opinion in order to see that technocrats also fail. The "centers of management," as Lippmann called them, also produce irrational decisions and disastrous public policies. The last 20 years of our history have been a series of struggles, from the war in Vietnam to the environmental and civil rights movements to the current agitation over nuclear arms, in which unblessed public opinion has tried to intervene in the closed circles of public management and to impose new values or new strategies. Most commentaries focus on the disruption and inconvenience these popular movements have caused for government managers. But when political leaders and their cadres whine about the uninformed masses disrupting the affairs of state with their ill-tempered opinions, they are really complaining about the democratic ideal itself.

I would turn the question around 180 degrees and argue this: the real pathology of our political system is not the paralysis of experts but their irresponsibility and self-indulgent isolation. The real danger this democratic republic faces in the coming years – and I believe it is profoundly threatening – is that the elite group that devises our national-security policies will continue to ignore or misunderstand these popular discontents. We are witnessing today only the early stages of what could become a fundamental collision between citizens and their national government over the deepest moral questions.

Most politicians, I should add, do not really believe this is true of the nuclear freeze movement. They see it as another cranky outburst of sentiment, shallow and transitory. They will try to placate it with symbolic words and gestures. If that doesn't work, they will denounce it as un-American. Our president already has.

They are wrong, I believe, for several reasons. First, they see the freeze movement as a sudden event – a bizarre expression that sprang up willy-nilly in the last few years largely in response to the bellicose chatter from Reagan and his administration about fighting and winning a nuclear war. This movement has much deeper roots, which I shall explain later on. Second, they misunderstand the deeper messages of this popular agitation. They dismiss the public outcry about our incredible nuclear arsenal as simply an expression of fear, like fear of toxic wastes or fear of atomic power or other popular fears of life-threatening technology. Nobody wants to be incinerated.

That fear certainly is a potent element driving public opinion on nuclear arms, but ordinary people are posing a deeper and tougher question which most politicans do not yet grasp. It was best explained by Father Timothy Healy, the wise Jesuit scholar who is president of Georgetown University. We were talking about the new pastoral letter on war and peace which the American Catholic bishops have produced. Father Healy said, "There is a deep worry in the body of the church and it's a worry that expresses itself politically. The worry is not 'Am I going to be killed?' but 'Am I going to do evil?' "

Am I going to do evil? An intriguing question: do individual citizens in a democracy bear some moral responsibility for the evil their government may do in their name? It is the same moral question that haunts modern Germans. It explains, I think, what one Catholic bishop meant when he called a local Trident submarine base an American Auschwitz. If one believes that the United States government is equipped and poised to commit a terrible act against mankind, then what is the obligation of individual citizens? What should they do about it? What can they do?

Those questions have occurred to many Americans, not just Catholics and not just Christians, in the last decade. This perspective is more complicated than simple fear and potentially more powerful as a force for political action. Anyone familiar with American history and its great struggles for reform knows that the pursuit of self-interest was usually intertwined with higher moral purposes. Americans have always wanted, not simply to be free and prosperous and safe in their private lives, but also to be good – to be good, either in personal spiritual terms or in terms of our shared civil religion that tells us that America is uniquely creating a just society. In our lifetime, the civil rights movement led by black preachers and yeoman farmers, undertakers and school principals, triumphed because its leaders understood that. Martin Luther King, Jr., located the moral fulcrum of white America's guilt and applied leverage. I am not suggesting that the popular movement against nuclear war has yet attained a critical mass comparable to the civil rights movement, but I would point out this: many of the freeze activists, perhaps most of them, are white, middle-class, middle-aged church-going folks and many of them think of themselves as the "new abolitionists." Like those morally inspired 19th-century activists – also white and middle-class – who struggled to abolish the evil institution of slavery, these people think they are also engaged in an historic struggle. They want to abolish the evil presence of nuclear arms, and not just ours, but everyone's.

I am emphasizing the religious component of this popular groundswell against nuclear arms because it is not widely appreciated and because it distinguishes this movement from earlier ideological or political campaigns which surfaced in the past and then lost their steam. I do not think it is a coincidence that we are seeing this moral fervor in an era when America is undergoing what some have called the Third Great Awakening – a period of highly personalized spiritual ferment, the born-again experience and evangelical commitment to religious belief. Those who see this ferment as merely right-wing fundamentalism simply do not understand its breadth and complexity. The original abolitionists drew much of their moral energy from the Second Great Awakening. I would predict that, in the coming years, we will see much more of this personal expression of belief in terms of political issues – and not just on nuclear arms – as churches and individuals attempt to redefine themselves.

Practical-minded people may dismiss these new abolitionists as visionary, as idealists committed to a hopeless cause. I do not predict, for instance, that they will prevail in their ultimate goal of abolition. I am not even sure they can prevail in their limited first step – that is, actually stopping the arms race. As a political reporter, I am well familiar with the awesome political forces that maintain the status quo of the arms race: the economic interests of the military manufacturers, the Cold War hysteria, the timidity and ignorance of most elected representatives. As an aside: let me emphasize the ignorance of most senators and congressmen on these issues. It is especially ironic that critics of the freeze movement should complain that these citizens haven't studied the intricacies of nuclear weapons and defense strategies because most members of Congress haven't either. Year-in and year-out, most members of Congress take the safe vote – they vote for whatever the Pentagon lobbyists tell them is the program. If you don't believe that, I urge you to interview senators or representatives at random, test the depth of their knowledge, and discover how much they hide their ignorance behind simple-minded rhetoric. At the very least, the freeze movement – the barrage of letters, phone calls, and citizen confrontations back home – has already had this salutary effect on Congress: it has compelled the politicians to do a little homework so they can answer the questions.

Nobody outside Washington has ever asked these questions before – which brings us around to the original subject, the political management of the arms race. As we all know, that management has for 30 years been the exclusive preserve of what I call the nuclear elite – generals and professors, policy analysts and selected politicians. They devised the strategies, invented the new weapons, bargained among themselves over how many bombs we need, what kind, how we might use them someday, and what kind of so-called arms control deals we should make with the Soviet Union. If you are satisfied with where this elite has taken us and with the new generation of nuclear weapons it now intends to build, then you are right to be worried that gross public opinion may paralyze policy. I, however, think the nuclear elite is lost – literally lost – in the insane dynamics of its own bizarre logic. Our only hope of restoring rationality – a fragile hope at best – lies in the forceful intervention of public opinion.

In the public dialogue surrounding these questions, the nuclear elite is usually described as two camps, variously labeled as hawks versus doves, liberals versus conservatives, the arms controllers versus the arms promoters. These labels are grossly misleading because they imply more disagreement than actually exists. In general, the governing elite shares the same premises, the same definition of reality, the same ideals. Except for the B-1 bomber, all of the dangerous new nuclear weapons systems Ronald Reagan wants to build were already planned and approved by Jimmy Carter. The Reagan administration had the bad taste to talk publicly about actually fighting a nuclear war and this scared people, both in America and Europe. But the substance of those doctrines was not new or different from the nuclear strategies of the preceding administrations, Republican and Democratic.

The Reaganites were, in fact, a bit puzzled by the public reactions. It took them a full year to figure out that they were frightening people, not reassuring them. They decided belatedly to cool it. Now the president has discovered arms control and is trying to convince the public that he believes in it. People have a right to be skeptical: Ronald Reagan has personally opposed every arms-control agreement negotiated by previous presidents over the last 20 years, starting with the atmospheric test ban treaty of 1963.

To understand why the Reagan administration was so confused about public opinion, we need to look back a few years and examine the origins of the current attitudes. The president, after all, was elected in 1980 by an electorate that declared itself strongly in favor of building up our national defense. Ronald Reagan promised to do that. Now a fickle public seems frightened by the fact that he is keeping his promise. What's going on here? Are Americans ambivalent about national defense? The short answer is yes. But a more complicated history lies behind it, one that makes public opinion seem more rational.

The crucial starting point for our contemporary politics was April of 1975 – the fall of Saigon, a humiliating moment in our national history. This event was deeply traumatic, disturbing our self-confidence and righteous self-image. America, the most powerful nation on earth, had finally "lost" a war. I think it is obvious now that conservatives understood the emotional depth of this event more clearly than liberal adversaries. Ordinary Americans felt a sense of impotence, accompanied by suspicions of betrayal in high places. Why were our boys made to fight and yet not permitted to win? This was a reasonable question. Was America becoming weak? Was it a pitiful helpless giant, as Richard Nixon put it?

In the following years, two important events seemed to confirm that threatening message. President Carter completed the negotiations three predecessors had worked on to return the Panama Canal Zone to Panamanian sovereignty. The Panama Canal Treaty reinforced the insecurities of millions of Americans in a very tangible way. The government seemed to be meekly placating a banana republic instead of standing up for what was ours.

This image of American impotence was finally expressed in the most melodramatic terms by the hostage drama in Iran. The humiliation and frustration of that episode produced some ugly expressions of popular will: T-shirts that said, "Nuke the Ayatollah" and "Nuke Iran til it glows." Americans wanted to get tough with the rest of the world, wanted to restore the respect we had come to expect.

These sentiments, as it happened, were encouraged and manipulated during these years by some conservative members of the nuclear elite. Financed largely by defense contractors, a group called the Committee on the Present Danger organized to broadcast the alarm about what had happened to our position of strength in another area, the balance of nuclear terror. The Russians are pulling ahead, they warned. We are now vulnerable to Soviet attack. We must take countermeasures or perish. This propaganda campaign on nuclear arms dovetailed neatly with the public fears about America's strength in the world. Ronald Reagan was particularly vicious – and effective – in exploiting these fears and resentments. He attacked the Panama Canal Treaty as a betrayal of America, he denounced the SALT II treaty of 1979 as a formula for permanent inferiority, and he promised to be tough as president. A lot of former senators, most of them liberal Democrats, learned in 1980 how potent those themes were.

The essential point about Reagan's political behavior, however, is that he really violated the unwritten code of the nuclear elite. SALT II, after all, had been negotiated among the various interest groups of the elite. By attacking it, he was really declaring his independence from the status quo. In the short run, this was smart politics – speaking directly to that amorphous body of popular fear and resentment. In the long run, it created his present dilemma.

By 1983, the public seems to have turned on the president's idea of toughness. Whenever the Reagan administration talks up its involvement in Central America, the public opinion polls register alarm like a thermometer registering heat. The presumed consensus for increased defense spending has evaporated. When Ronald Reagan talks about nukes, people are frightened. They also do not believe him.

This is reflected in polling data from the Harris Poll, taken in January 1983. Despite the red-baiting by the president and the *Reader's Digest*, an overwhelming majority—76 percent—favor a bilateral freeze with the Soviet Union on the construction of new nuclear weapons. An even larger majority—90 percent—would like to see an end to the production, storage, and testing of all nuclear weapons everywhere. The public believes—by 66 (agree) to 31 percent (disagree)—that Reagan is doing an unsatisfactory job of negotiating arms agreements with the Russians. Indeed, by 57 to 39 percent, a majority fears that Reagan may well get us into a major nuclear war.

The president keeps telling us that the Soviets have gained nuclear superiority. This is an especially demagogic claim because—unless he is hopelessly uninformed—the president must know that his own military leaders disagree with him. He persists in saying it, trying to arouse our fears. Most Americans, I am happy to note, do not believe him. Harris found that by a substantial majority—64 (agree) to 27 percent (disagree)—Americans feel the United States is at least equally as strong as the Russians. What is most striking is that this confidence in nuclear parity has increased since 1980, when only 53 percent believed in it. I am sure there are complicated explanations for that shift in opinion, but I am also sure that one important factor is the emergence of an active and intelligent counterforce to the nuclear propaganda from Washington—namely, this grass roots movement.

The origins of these antinuclear sentiments actually lie in some of the events already described and involve some of the same themes. In ways that were not fully understood at the time, the tragedy in Vietnam profoundly undermined the legitimacy and authority of our policy. Ordinary citizens outside the circles of antiwar activists were appalled by those events and concluded that the government was lying to them, that the governing elite was capable of disastrous decisions, if left to its own reflexes, and that the United States of America was capable of endangering its own citizens while it claimed to protect them. Finally, Vietnam taught a lot of Americans that their government was capable of using its power in immoral ways. A lot of middle-aged, middle-class Americans were left with the question: am I responsible?

These perceptions fed directly into the creation and development of a number of scattered but similar study groups and other organizations which focused on the larger implications of war and peace in the nuclear age. I have already cited the importance of what was happening in churches. This political organizing in the 1970s was less visible and even feeble compared with the larger propaganda machine that was cranking up the pro-defense constituency. On the other hand, it was genuinely a grass roots movement in origin, not created and manipulated by Washington front groups. In early 1980, many of these groups coalesced around the new strategy invented by Randall Forsberg. The first test of the bilateral freeze approach was successful – three referendum victories in western Massachusetts in November, 1980, at the same time those three jurisdictions were voting for Ronald Reagan. Since then, organizations and campaigns have multiplied across the nation, collecting more than 11 million votes in the 1982 advisory referendums.

Thus, the last ten years have really produced two parallel streams of popular distrust of the national government's management of national security. And the general public remains somewhat uncertain on these questions. It wants America to be strong and respected; it also wants peace and an end to the arms race. The same polls that show overwhelming skepticism about Reagan's stewardship also reflect overwhelming suspicion of the Soviet Union.

The public resolves this conflict in what seems to me a most rational way: it recognizes the Soviets as a hostile enemy, but it wants our government to get serious about normalizing relations with this enemy power, and not simply in the area of arms control. A strong majority – 72 percent – favor agreement with the Soviets to guarantee free access to Middle East oil. A smaller majority – 56 percent – favor a treaty to exchange scientists and other technical missions. And, notwithstanding Reagan's ill-fated crusade against the Soviet gas pipeline, a substantial majority of Americans – 69 percent – want to expand trade between the United States and Russia. This seems to me a rather clear-eyed and sober view of present realities, much more rational than the tired Cold War rhetoric we hear from our president. Again, I believe the freeze movement can take a little credit for that. While it educates politicians, it is also educating citizens.

The intellectual premises for the freeze movement are still not widely understood by the politicians. The first one is that the SALT process is a failure. It does not really control the arms race; it merely ratifies and regulates the dimensions of each new round. The right wing's defeat of the SALT II treaty, therefore, was not a tragedy but an opportunity – a vacuum in which new thinking might be heard.

A few years back, those who denounced the SALT process as a hoax were dismissed as irresponsible cranks. The decade of SALT negotiations was based on the elegant theory that each treaty was supposed to be a building block toward an arch that would someday put a cap over the arms building. The reality was that this arch would never be closed. Each treaty required the political leaders to make a trade-off in order to secure the support of military leaders. Each trade-off guaranteed that the arms race would continue unabated. A similar bargaining process probably takes place in Moscow. In 1972, the trade-off was that the United States agreed not to build an ABM defense system, but to allow MIRVs, the multiple-warheads that increased the number of bombs dramatically through the 1970s. In 1979, the trade-off was the imposition of new ceilings on the number of nuclear launchers, for the permission to build the MX missile, a weapon that would give America the threatening potential of a first-strike. Meanwhile, thanks to cruise missiles and other systems, the number of warheads would double again in the coming decade.

The nuclear elite is lost in its own crazy theology, but the new public pressure is beginning to force the theoreticians to address their own contradictions. In a recent essay in *Time Magazine* (March 21, 1983), Henry Kissinger, of all people, concluded solemnly that the SALT process and its underlying theory are obsolete. Why? Because the original treaty he negotiated allowed the introduction of multiple warheads. "There can be no doubt that the age of MIRVs has doomed the SALT approach." Now Kissinger characteristically makes this sound like a new insight which he alone has discovered. In fact, that is exactly what critics of SALT said back in 1972 when Nixon and Kissinger announced their diplomatic triumph. In any case, it is progress for someone as respectable as Kissinger to begin to come to terms with reality. Of course, Kissinger does not want to freeze the arms race, to actually stop it, right now. That would be dangerous, he tells us. Kissinger's solution is to go ahead and build the MX and other weapons but meanwhile begin planning for the real solution – 500 or so new single-warhead missiles. Then in the 1990s, he assures us, we can start dismantling those MIRVs he authorized back in 1972. If Henry Kissinger's thinking is the finest flower of our nuclear elite, we are in deep, deep trouble.

Meanwhile, our president has also been responding to the popular agitation by the freeze campaign in his own way. He seems to have dropped the red-baiting – perhaps because the polls showed it was having no effect on popular support for a freeze. Instead, he is restyling himself as a champion of arms control. It is doubtful, however, that Reagan really believes in arms treaties. His so-called new idea is really reopening the theoretical arguments from the 1960s – the notion of a defensive system like the ABM. This would be dangerous, of course, for the very reasons that led Kissinger and Nixon to negotiate a ban on defensive systems in the original SALT treaty. If Reagan's vision prevails, SALT I will prove to be one of history's most hollow triumphs. We will have MIRVs and we will have nuclear defensive systems. One might even call it a hoax.

The conservatives are really pursuing a scheme more grandiose than even the ABM. They call it the "High Frontier" because it involves taking the nuclear arms race directly into space. They propose building a system of armed satellites that allegedly would destroy all of the Soviet missiles before they reach our shores. Rational people should look upon the "High Frontier" as a gigantic jobs program in which the principal beneficiaries will be companies like Boeing.

When the freeze movement first surfaced as a new national phenomenon, it was ironically the doves of the arms-control community who were most offended by it. They expressed open contempt, denouncing it as simplistic. These earnest people had devoted ten or 15 years of their lives to the SALT process and now a bunch of outsiders had come along to try to tell them SALT wasn't any good. In the initial stages, the arms-control community tried rather clumsily to co-opt the freeze movement, to claim this upsurge of popular sentiment was really an expression of unhappiness that SALT II had not been ratified. They tried to persuade the freeze leaders to settle for ratification as their goal. After many months of argument, the arms-controllers are beginning to grasp that this new movement really is different. Some of them have come to share the freeze movement's views, but many are adamant in their original opinions.

In 20 years of managing the arms race, these people did not devote much energy to educating the public or developing popular support for stronger arms-control strategies. They talked mostly to each other. Now that this popular support exists, they regard it as an intrusion on their good works. The major news media, incidentally, have taken the same position as the nuclear elite. If you read the *New York Times* or the *Washington Post* or the news magazines, you will note their hostility toward the freeze movement. They treat it as a fad which is beneath their serious examination. Periodically, as the movement has grown stronger and stronger, the major newspapers and magazines run analytical pieces reporting its imminent collapse. None of them, as far as I have seen, has tried to explain in serious terms what this movement is expressing.

The freeze movement has a second fundamental premise which is sound but is admittedly much more fragile. It is that the arms race has reached an historic moment of opportunity – after 15 years of extraordinary expenditures and sacrifice, the Soviets really have caught up with the US arsenal, just as they said they would do, just as US planners expected for many years. This approximate parity presents us with the chance – and it is only a chance – that both sides might now agree to stop, to not go forward with the inevitable next round. The Russians, obviously, have strong practical incentives for that sort of agreement, particularly the relief from the economic burdens of the arms race. But if the United States goes ahead and introduces the new generation of weapons systems, then the history of this competition tells us that the Soviets will follow. This is the logic that explains why freeze advocates feel that America holds the controlling cards.

If the freeze campaign can move political judgment enough to actually stop the deployment of new weapons systems and to offer a freeze proposal to the Russians, there is at least the possibility of an historic breakthrough.

Obviously, this strategy contains a tremendous gamble. What if the United States offered to negotiate a freeze and the Russians wouldn't play? If that occurs, the freeze movement is dead. At least that strategy would be dead, though I do not think this would necessarily dissipate the popular discontent with continuing the arms race.

In political terms, we are a long way from answering that question and it is doubtful whether it will ever be achieved. Aided by congressional timidity, Reagan may succeed in deploying the new weapons and rendering the freeze concept obsolete. The central objective of the freeze campaign has been to force the president to alter his negotiating stance, to propose a freeze. Failing that, the campaign hopes to elect a president in 1984 committed to this new approach. Those elitists believing it unseemly for citizens to undermine their president's negotiating position by attacking it should be reminded that this is precisely what Ronald Reagan did for 20 years before he became president.

Now we are witnessing a conspiracy in reverse—the nuclear establishment rallying around the president, trying to devise new arguments for deploying the MX missile, so that they can short-circuit the popular desire to stop. Having attacked the nuclear elite for betraying America, the president is now extending a hand to those discredited nuclear experts from the Carter administration, seeking their help in keeping these new weapons systems alive. And the nuclear elite is responding. In their different ways, all members of this elite have a powerful self-interest in retaining control over nuclear arms strategy. All of them will lose something if the public actually gets a handle on this subject.

Any clear-eyed student of practical politics would have to predict that the nuclear elite will probably win this struggle and that this country will go ahead with its new generation of weapons. The Soviets will then strive to match us and the arms race will continue for another decade or two until something happens—perhaps something dreadful—to shock the world out of the present dynamic.

In the meantime, however, moral philosophers and students of public policy should ponder the costs—what this arms race is doing to our democracy, right now, in the absence of a nuclear holocaust. If the arms proliferation continues, it will further undermine the very legitimacy of our government. It will convince millions more that their government is actually threatening their lives, not defending them. It will produce not only more alienation in electoral politics but a deeper malaise about the future itself. Anyone who has talked to children on this subject must sense that their perspective on the future, on their own lives, is damaged in a very direct way by their perceptions of nuclear disaster ahead, of an unheeding government racing toward mass destruction.

Now, these are the "soft" costs of the arms race—not measurable by megatons or throw-weight—but they are real. My fear is that the nuclear elite controlling the political decision-making will ignore the public distress and plunge on with its insane logic. We will all pay the price for that and so will our democratic institutions: decay and disrespect, a higher level of disenchantment and civil disobedience.

In sum, it is time that for once the experts listen more carefully to the people. If this paralyzes our defense experts and prevents them from rolling forward with the arms race, then I would say these unruly citizens have done a good day's work for the republic, not to mention the world.

8

DETERRENCE, MAXIMIZATION, AND RATIONALITY

David Gauthier

1. WHY DETERRENCE SEEMS IRRATIONAL

Is deterrence a fully rational policy? In our world deterrence works –
sometimes. But in a more perfect world, in which actors rationally related
their choices to their beliefs and preferences, and in which those beliefs
and preferences were matters of common knowledge, could deterrence
work? Some say "No."[1] Others hold a conception of rationality that would
commit them to saying "No," were they to consider the issue.[2] I say "Yes."
Deterrence can be part of a fully rational policy. I propose to demonstrate
this.

At the heart of a deterrent policy is the expression of a conditional intention. An actor A expresses the intention to perform an action x should another actor B perform an action y. If B would do y did A not express her
intention, then we may say that A's expression of intention deters B from
doing y. In expressing her intention as part of a deterrent policy, A seeks
to decrease the probability of B doing y by increasing his estimate of her
conditional probability of doing x should he do y.

We need better labels than x and y if our talk about deterrence is to be
perspicuous. In at least some situations, A's deterrent intention is *retaliatory; A* expresses the intention to retaliate should B do y. So let us call x
RETAL. And what A seeks to deter is an action that would give advantage
to B in relation to A; let us then call y ADVANT. We shall then say that an
actor A expresses the intention to RETAL should another actor B
ADVANT.

A seeks to affect B's estimate of her conditional probability of RETAL
should he ADVANT. Why does she expect her expression of conditional intention to have this effect? Let us suppose that A and B are rational; on the

received view of rationality, an actor seeks to maximize expected utility, the fulfillment of her preferences given her beliefs. If *A* expects to affect *B*'s estimate of what she will do, then she must expect to affect his beliefs about her preferences and/or beliefs. Or so it seems.

A wants to deter *B* from ADVANT. She believes that *B* is less likely to ADVANT if he expects her response to be RETAL than if he expects a different response, NON-RETAL. She therefore expresses the intention to RETAL should he ADVANT. For this to affect *B*, it would seem that he must take her expression of intention to indicate her preference for RETAL over NON-RETAL, given ADVANT. Perhaps *A* does have this preference, and so seeks to *inform B* that she prefers RETAL. Perhaps *A* does not have this preference, but seeks to *deceive B* into supposing that she prefers RETAL. But in either case the deterrent effect of her expression of intention would seem to require that *B* be initially uninformed, or at least uncertain, about her preference. Were he informed of her preference, then his estimate of her conditional probability of choosing RETAL should he ADVANT would be unaffected by any claim she might make about her intention.

But is this so? Must the actor to be deterred be initially uncertain about the preferences of the would-be deterrer? Let us consider the matter more closely. We suppose that *B* knows *A*'s preferences between RETAL and NON-RETAL, given ADVANT. If she prefers RETAL, then his knowledge should suffice to deter him from ADVANT, supposing that his preferences are such that he can be deterred at all. *A* needs no deterrent policy. If she prefers NON-RETAL, then how can her expression of the conditional intention to RETAL should he ADVANT be credible? How can it affect his estimate of what she will do?

First we might suppose that, although *A* prefers NON-RETAL to RETAL ceteris paribus, yet she also prefers being a woman of her word. She may value sincerity directly, or she may find it instrumentally useful to her. In expressing her intention to RETAL should *B* ADVANT, she stakes her reputation for being a woman of her word, and *B*, knowing or believing this, realizes that by expressing her intention she has transformed the situation. She prefers NON-RETAL to RETAL, but she also prefers honoring a commitment leading to RETAL, to dishonoring a commitment even if it brings about NON-RETAL. Her expression of conditional intention does not affect her preferences but brings a different set into play, and so affects *B*'s estimate of the utilities of the courses of action open to her should he ADVANT.

Second, *A* may be imperfectly rational, unable fully to control her behavior in terms of her considered preferences. If *B* ADVANTs, then her cool preference for NON-RETAL may be overcome by anger, or rage, or panic, so that she may RETAL. In this case we should no doubt say, not that *A* expresses a conditional intention to RETAL, but rather that she expresses a warning that she will, or may, find herself choosing RETAL should he ADVANT. Fortunately for *A*, her inability to control her behavior stands her in good stead, enabling her to deter, or at least to seek to deter, *B* from ADVANT by warning him of her probable folly should he do it. Such an inability may seem suspect, as altogether too convenient, making us hesitant to accept this apparent mode of deterrence at face value.

Third, *A*'s expression of intention may not stand alone, but may activate forces themselves beyond her control, which may make NON-RETAL less desirable, or RETAL more desirable, than would otherwise have been the case. Perhaps *A* has made a side bet which she loses should she fail to abide by her stated intention, or perhaps she has insured herself against the costs of having to carry out what otherwise would be an unprofitable course of action. And fourth, in expressing her intention, *A* may also delegate her power to choose; some other person, or some pre-programmed device, capable of ignoring her preferences, will ensure that if *B* ADVANTs, RETAL will ensue. These complicating cases will play no part in our discussion. My interest in this paper is in deterrent policies that do not call into play external factors no longer within the actor's control.

My interest is also in genuine expressions of intention, and not in warnings. No doubt we are not always in such control of our actions that our cool, long-term, considered preferences prevail. But as I have noted, there is something suspect about arranging to gain from this lack of control, about extracting rational advantage from seeming irrationality. I shall consider would-be deterrers who are able to carry out what they intend, and who form their intentions on a rational, utility-maximizing basis. *A* then does not warn *B*, but coolly informs him that she will deliberately RETAL should he ADVANT.

And last, my interest is not in the provision of deterrent information about preferences. Rather we shall examine situations in which there is no doubt, in the minds of those concerned, that, at least if other things are equal, the would-be deterrer *A* disprefers RETAL to NON-RETAL, should *B* ADVANT.

It would therefore seem that we are left with but one possibility for a deterrent policy among rational persons informed of each other's preferences and beliefs. We must suppose that the would-be deterrer prefers to be a person of her word. *A*, in expressing her conditional intention, must transform the situation, preferring to abide by her commitment even though, ceteris paribus, she would prefer the outcome of ignoring the commitment. She prefers NON-RETAL to RETAL, but having expressed the intention to RETAL given ADVANT, she prefers carrying out her intention to ignoring it, should her attempt to deter fail.

Although some deterrent policies may seem to invite this characterization, there are, in my view, insuperable difficulties with it, if we insist firmly on the full rationality of the actors. Of course since we impose no a priori constraints on the content of preferences, an actor may simply take satisfaction in making commitments which she then carries out. But why would a rational actor choose to make commitments to dispreferred courses of action? Perhaps she finds masochistic satisfaction in making and carrying out such commitments. But if deterrent policies are rational only for a peculiar variety of masochist, then most real-world examples of such policies survive only because of irrationality. Let us not be so hasty to judge them. I shall suppose that, in general, the actor's concern is with the instrumental and not the intrinsic benefits of adhering to an expressed intention. What are these benefits? What does A gain if she actually responds to ADVANT by RETAL, having expressed the intention so to respond?

If B ADVANTs, then A's attempt to deter him has failed. Any gain that would compensate for the cost of RETAL must then derive from further, future consequences of choosing RETAL that extend beyond the particular deterrent situation. Presumably these consequences are the effects of carrying out her expressed intention on the deterrent value of expressing similar intentions in other situations. If A RETALs, showing that her expression of intention was seriously meant, then in the future, similar expressions of intention should have a greater effect on others' expectations of what she will do than if she fails to RETAL.

But among fully rational persons is this effect possible? If A is rational, then B rationally expects her to do what she believes will maximize her expected utility. What she has done in the past may provide information about her preferences and beliefs, but we are supposing these to be common knowledge. How then can what A has done affect B's expectation of what she will do in the future? He expects her to maximize her expected utility; how can what she has done affect her expected utility? We are not concerned with behavior that alters the payoffs or outcomes *possible* for A. If in choosing RETAL A neither informs B about her preferences nor alters the possible outcomes of her future choices, then B has no reason to take what she has done into account in forming his expectations about what she will do in the future. A rational observer, informed of A's preferences, could only interpret her choice of RETAL as a lapse from rationality, in no way affecting expectations about her future choices on the supposition that they will be made rationally.

The only expectation one can rationally form about rational utility-maximizers is that they will seek to maximize expected utility. The only reputation they can rationally gain is the reputation for maximizing expected utility. If carrying out an expressed intention is not itself utility-maximizing, then it can have no effect on the expectations of rational and informed persons that would suffice to make it utility-maximizing.

To suppose otherwise is to fail to think through the forward-looking implications of maximizing rationality. A utilitarian, dedicated to collective maximization, cannot have reason to keep his promises in order to gain a reputation as a promise-keeper among a community of utilitarians, although he may have reason to act so among us non-utilitarians. Similarly, an individual utility-maximizer can have no reason to carry out her intentions, in order to gain a reputation as a woman of her word, among a community of informed individual utility-maximizers, although she may have reason to act so among less rational persons. We seem then to have exposed a deep irrationality at the core of deterrent policies. Leaving aside the provision of information about one's preferences, or the issuance of a warning about one's irrationality, or the invocation of factors beyond one's control that would determine one's response, we seem forced to conclude that A cannot expect B to alter his estimate of her conditional probability to RETAL should he ADVANT, on the basis of her expressed intention to RETAL, if ceteris paribus she would prefer NON-RETAL. And so A cannot expect to decrease the probability of B choosing ADVANT by her expression of conditional intention; she is not able to deter, or rationally to attempt to deter, B from ADVANT.

2. WHY NUCLEAR RETALIATION SEEMS IRRATIONAL

I shall show that it may be rational to adopt a deterrent policy committing one to the performance of a disadvantageous, non-utility-maximizing action should deterrence fail. But before turning to this demonstration, let us pause to entertain the possibility that my argument so far has been mistaken, and that A might have reason to carry out an otherwise disadvantageous expressed intention because of its effect on expectations about her future behavior. It is clear that this can be relevant to the rationality of a deterrent policy only if A is concerned about future deterrence.

Although our analysis of deterrence is intended to apply generally, I am particularly concerned with the rationality of deterrent policies in the context of relations among those nations possessing nuclear weapons. More precisely, I am concerned with a policy which has as its core the expressed intention to respond to a nuclear strike with a counterstrike. I shall call this the policy of nuclear retaliation.

To exemplify this policy and set it in the context of deterrence, let us suppose that one nation – call it the SU – is perceived by another nation – call it the US – to constitute a nuclear threat. The US fears that the SU will launch a nuclear strike, or, perhaps more plausibly, will credibly threaten to launch such a strike should the US refuse some demand or resist some initiative, or, perhaps more plausibly still, will act in some way inimical to the interests of the US that could be effectively countered only by markedly increasing the probability that the SU will launch a nuclear strike. The US seeks to deter the SU from a policy that would or might lead to a nuclear strike, whether unconditionally or as a result of US refusal to acquiesce in or endeavor to counter some SU initiative. To do this, the US announces the intention to resist any SU initiative even if resistance invites a nuclear strike, and should a strike occur, to retaliate even if this provokes full-scale nuclear combat. In talking about the strike policy of the SU, and the retaliatory policy of the US, I shall intend the policies just sketched. In particular, a strike policy may center on the threat to strike should some demand not be met, and a retaliatory policy may center on the refusal to submit to such a demand even though a nuclear exchange may result.

Now, it is possible that the US prefers suffering a nuclear strike to submitting to a demand by the SU. It is also possible that the US prefers retaliating against a nuclear strike, with the prospect then of fighting a nuclear war, to accepting passively a single strike and so, effectively, cutting its nuclear losses by capitulating. But suppose, plausibly, that the consequences of nuclear warfare are such that the US would always prefer less nuclear devastation to more; nevertheless it seeks to deter the SU from a strike policy by expressing the intention to choose its less preferred retaliatory response. It is then engaged in just the type of deterrent policy that we have put rationally in question. It seems clear that an appeal to future expectations would not here provide ground for altering US preferences in order to defend deterrence in terms of future effects. For the US to claim that, despite its preference for minimizing nuclear devastation, retaliation would be advantageous in the long run because it would make the future use of a retaliatory policy credible and so effective, would be to overlook the probable lack of a relevant long run. After a nuclear exchange, future expectations, if any, would likely have very little basis in the policies of the nations prior to the exchange. Thus, even if in some cases a deterrent policy could be rationalized by an appeal to future expectations, nuclear retaliation lacks such a rationale.

Retaliation would therefore seem to be an irrational policy. If submission is preferred to retaliation, as minimizing the expected nuclear devastation one suffers, then the expression of the conditional intention to retaliate would lack credibility. The US could not expect to affect the SU's expectations about US behavior by expressing such an intention, and so the US could not decrease the probability of the SU pursuing a strike policy by announcing its own policy of nuclear retaliation. Among sufficiently rational and informed nations, nuclear deterrence must fail. If it succeeds in the real world, then the expressed intention not to submit and to retaliate must serve, it seems, to inform the potential attacker of the would-be deterrer's real preferences, or to deceive the attacker about those preferences, or to warn the attacker to expect an irrational response to a strike policy.

But this conclusion is mistaken. We have reached it by focusing entirely on the benefits and costs of actually carrying out the conditional intention that is the core of a deterrent policy. We have failed to consider the benefits and costs of forming or adopting such a conditional intention. The argument against the rationality of nuclear retaliation, or more generally against a deterrent policy, has this structure: it is not utility-maximizing to carry out the nonsubmissive, retaliatory intention; therefore it is not rational so to act; therefore it is not rational to form the intention; therefore a rational person cannot sincerely express the intention; therefore another rational and informed person cannot be deterred by the expression of the intention. The structure of the argument that I shall present and defend is: it may be utility-maximizing to form the nonsubmissive, retaliatory intention; therefore it may be rational to form such an intention; if it is rational to form the intention it is rational to act on the intention; therefore a rational person can sincerely express the intention; therefore another rational and informed person can be deterred by the expression of the intention. We shall of course have to consider why this argument succeeds and the former argument fails.

I shall therefore defend the rationality of deterrent policies, and more particularly of nuclear retaliation. But my defense is a limited one. Indeed, among rational and informed actors, a policy of pure and simple deterrence is not rational, although it may be rational as part of a larger policy directed, among other things, at the obsolescence of deterrence. Putting my position into an historical context, I shall defend Hobbes's formulation of the first law of nature: "That every man, ought to endeavour Peace, as farre as he has hope of obtaining it; and when he cannot obtain it, that he may seek, and use, all helps, and advantages of Warre."[3] Deterrence is both an advantage of war and, among rational actors, a means to peace. Or rather, some deterrent policies may have these features. But as a means to peace, a deterrent policy looks to its own supersession. For recognition of the rationality of deterrence is inseparable from recognition of the rationality of moving, not unilaterally but mutually, beyond deterrence.

3. THE STRUCTURE OF DETERRENCE

To give precision to our analysis of deterrence, I shall focus on situations with a very simple structure. An actor who, consistently with our previous usage, we call B, has a choice between two alternatives, y and y', where y corresponds to ADVANT. If he chooses y, then another actor, A, knowing B's choice, has a choice between two alternatives, x and x', where x corresponds to RETAL and x' to NON-RETAL. If B chooses y', then A may or may not have a choice between x and x' or other alternatives; initially we need suppose only that some outcome is expected. There are, then, three possible outcomes relevant to our analysis: yx, or ADVANT followed by RETAL; yx', or ADVANT followed by NON-RETAL; and y' . . ., or B's choice of his alternative to ADVANT followed by a possible but unspecified choice by A. Each actor orders these possible outcomes; for simplicity we assume that neither is indifferent between any two. There are then six possible orderings for each actor, and so 36 different possible pairs of orderings.

Only one of these 36 pairs determines a deterrent situation. Consider first A's orderings. Since she seeks to deter B from ADVANT, she must prefer y' . . ., the expected outcome if B chooses his alternative action, to both yx and yx'. Since she seeks to deter B from ADVANT by expressing a conditional intention to RETAL contrary to her known preferences, she must prefer yx' to yx. Now consider B's orderings. Since A seeks to deter him from ADVANT by expressing her conditional intention to RETAL, he must prefer yx' to yx. If A has any need to seek to deter B from ADVANT, then he must prefer yx' to y' . . ., and if she is to have any hope of deterring him, then he must prefer y' . . . to yx. A's ordering is: y' . . . $> yx' > yx$; B's ordering is: $yx' > y'$ . . . $> yx$.

Let us take a brief, closer look at the outcome if B chooses y'. I shall not pursue the implications of this discussion in the present paper, although it raises issues of some interest and importance. If deterrence is to be possible, then, should B choose y', A must have a choice w (where this includes the limiting case in which she has no alternative to w) such that she prefers $y'w$ to yx' and he prefers $y'w$ to yx. If for every alternative w' such that A prefers $y'w'$ to yx', B prefers yx to $y'w'$, then, much as A might wish to deter B from choosing y she has no conditional intention sufficient. If for every alternative w'' such that B prefers $y'w''$ to yx, A prefers yx' to $y'w''$, then even though A may have a conditional intention sufficient to deter B she has no interest in using it.

Suppose then that A prefers $y'w$ to yx', and B prefers $y'w$ to yx. If B also prefers yx' to $y'w$, then A will seek to deter B from choosing y. But the expression of a conditional intention to choose x in response to y, even if fully credible, may be insufficient to deter B. For A may have an alternative w' to w such that A prefers $y'w'$ to $y'w$, but also such that B prefers yx to $y'w'$. Were B to choose y' in response to A's conditional intention to respond to y with x, then he would expect A to choose w' rather than w, so that he would be worse off than if he had ignored A's attempt to deter. However, were A to combine her expression of conditional intention to choose x in response to y, with the credible expression of a conditional intention to choose w in response to y', then B, preferring $y'w$ to *yx*, would choose *y'*. In this case *A* is able to deter *B* only if she is able to combine her *threat* with an *offer*—an offer to refrain from her utility-maximizing choice in order to leave *B* open to her threat. Note that although *A*'s offer requires her not to choose her utility-maximizing response to *B*'s choice of *y'*, by making it she may expect an outcome *y'w* which affords her greater utility than the outcome *yx'* which she would otherwise expect. Note also that *B* would prefer *A* not to be in a position to make such an offer.

It will be evident that *A*'s conditional intention to choose a nonmaximizing *w* in response to *y'* raises precisely the same problem of rationality as her conditional intention to choose a nonmaximizing *x* in response to *y*—RETAL in response to ADVANT. In both cases she must form an intention to choose a course of action in itself nonmaximizing, as part of a policy intended to maximize her expected utility. I shall not address the problem of nonmaximizing offers in this paper, but an argument for the rationality of deterrent threats can easily be applied to the offers as well.

Before proceeding to that argument, let us relate our abstract treatment of deterrence to the particular issue of nuclear retaliation. In the terms in which we have posed that problem, the US corresponds to actor *A*, the SU to actor *B*. The policy of nuclear retaliation by the US corresponds to *x* or RETAL; the strike policy for the SU corresponds to *y* or ADVANT. Recall that "strike" and "retaliation" are shorthand for more complex policies; the core of a strike policy may be the *threat* to launch a nuclear strike should some initiative be resisted; the core of a retaliatory policy may be the refusal to acquiesce in such a threat—with, of course, the intention to retaliate should such refusal lead to a strike.

I suppose then that the US orders the possibilities: no-strike > strike & no-retaliation > strike & retaliation. The first preference is evident; the second preference follows from the assumption that the US wishes to minimize nuclear devastation, given that retaliation, as we have characterized it, increases its expectation of suffering such devastation. It is reasonable to assume that the SU orders the possibilities: strike & no-retaliation > no-strike > strike & retaliation. As I noted in the preceding paragraph, a strike policy may center on a threat; the SU's first preference need not indicate a passion for blood, but only a desire to get its way by resorting to whatever threat may be needed. The SU's second preference follows from the assumption that it too wishes to minimize being the victim of nuclear devastation.

These preference orderings satisfy the requirements for a deterrent situation. I suppose that they are a plausible schematic representation of the preferences of possible real-world counterparts of the US and the SU.

Thus our argument for the rationality of deterrent threats is not intended to be an inquiry into *merely* possible worlds. However, some of the points raised abstractly in this section should be borne in mind in any attempt to apply our argument. In particular, it is worth noting that the SU may suppose that the US has several possible responses to its no-strike policy, some of which, such as a unilateral US strike, might indeed be worse from its perspective than a strike policy coupled with US retaliation. Effective deterrence by the US may then require an offer sufficient to allay SU fears of possible unilateral US action in response to a no-strike policy. I shall not pursue this matter here, but it is essential to be aware that the components of an effective policy of nuclear deterrence are matters that require the most careful evaluation.

4. WHY DETERRENCE MAY BE RATIONAL

The key to understanding deterrence, or, for that matter, the key to understanding all forms of interaction, such as agreement, that require constraints on directly maximizing behavior, is that in interaction, the probability that an individual will be in a given situation or type of situation may be affected by the beliefs of others about what that individual would do in the situation. *B*'s willingness to put *A* in a situation, to face *A* with a choice, will be affected by his belief about how she will act in that situation, how she will choose. His belief about how she will act will be affected by his assessment of her intentions. In particular, if he knows that she is fully in control of what she does, he will, ceteris paribus, expect her to do what she conditionally intends to do should she be in that situation. Hence the probability of *A* being in a given situation, insofar as her being in that situation is determined by the actions of *B*, is affected by *A*'s prior intentions about what she will do in that situation.

It is of course true that if *A* is rational, then her intentions must be those that it is rational for her to hold. But neither *A* nor *B* can ascertain the rationality of her intentions merely by considering the actions to which various possible intentions might commit her, and their payoffs. If *B*'s beliefs about *A*'s intentions partially determine what situations she will be in, then *A*, in *forming* her intentions, must consider the situations she may expect to face given the possible intentions she might form, and the payoffs from those situations. It may be tempting to suppose that it is rational to form an intention if and only if it would be utility-maximizing to execute the intention. Instead we argue that it is rational to execute an intention if and only if it is utility-maximizing to form it.

Let us then examine the calculations of a rational actor choosing among possible intentions. I shall restrict our analysis to the simplest case, corresponding to our analysis of deterrent situations in the preceding section.

Suppose then that A must decide whether to adopt the intention to do x in a situation characterized by the performance of some action y by another actor B. Let $u(yx)$ be the utility she would expect were she to do x given y. Let x' be the alternative intention to x so that $u(yx')$ is the utility she would expect were she to act on x' given y. Let $u(y')$ be the utility she would expect were B not to do y. And let p_x be the probability that B will do y should A adopt the intention to do x given y, and $p_{x'}$ the probability that B will do y should A adopt the intention to do x' given y.

Then A's expected utility should she intend x is:

$$p_x u(yx) + (1 - p_x)u(y').$$

And her expected utility should she intend x' is:

$$p_{x'}u(yx') + (1 - p_{x'})u(y').$$

Our concern is with the rationality of a deterrent policy. Hence we suppose that A does not want to be faced with y, which corresponds to ADVANT, so that her utility $u(y')$ is greater than both $u(yx)$ and $u(yx')$. Furthermore, we suppose that doing x, which corresponds to RETAL, is not utility-maximizing for A, so that $u(yx')$ is greater than $u(yx)$. And finally, A must suppose that intending x should B do y reduces the probability of his doing y, so that $p_{x'}$ is greater than p_x.

Since A prefers facing y' to doing x' given y, and doing x' given y to doing x given y, there must be some lottery over facing y' and facing y with the intention of doing x, that A considers indifferent to the certainty of facing y with the intention of doing x'. Let p be the probability of facing y' in that lottery. Then we may express the utility of facing y with the intention of doing x', $u(yx')$, in terms of the utilities of facing y', $u(y')$, and of facing y with the intention of doing x, $u(yx)$:

$$u(yx') = pu(y') + (1 - p)u(yx).$$

Without loss of generality for our argument we may set $u(y') = 1$, and $u(yx) = 0$. Then:

$$u(yx') = p.$$

And so A's expected utility if she intends x given y is:

$$1 - p_x.$$

And her expected utility if she intends x' given y is:

$$p_{x'}p + (1 - p_{x'}).$$

Suppose that A maximizes her expected utility by forming the intention to do x should B do y, i.e., by forming the intention to RETAL should B ADVANT. Then it must be the case that:

$$(1 - p_x) > [p_{x'}p + (1 - p_{x'})].$$

Or equivalently:

$$[(p_{x'} - p_x)/p_{x'}] > p.$$

To interpret this condition, we note that avoiding y constitutes deterrent success, whereas facing y and doing x constitutes deterrent failure. Facing y and doing x' we may identify with nondeterrence. Then p is that probability of deterrent success, where the alternative is deterrent failure, that makes a deterrent policy indifferent to nondeterrence from the standpoint of the prospective deterrer. We may therefore call p the minimum required probability for deterrent success; it reflects the value of nondeterrence relative to deterrent success and failure. The expression $[p_{x'} - p_x]/p_x]$ is the proportionate decrease in the probability of being in the situation that the prospective deterrer would avoid, that is achieved by her policy of deterrence. Thus the condition states that, for a deterrent policy to be rational, the proportionate decrease that it effects in the probability of facing the undesired action, ADVANT, must be greater than the minimum required probability for deterrent success.

Consider a simple example. B, a university professor in Boston, is offered a position in Dallas. His wife, A, wishes to deter him from accepting the appointment, and so tells him that if he accepts it, she will leave him and remain in Boston, even though she would prefer to accompany him to Dallas. Then if A is indifferent between a lottery that would offer a 70 percent chance that B would stay in Boston and a 30 percent chance that he would go alone to Dallas, and the certainty that both would go to Dallas, .7 is the minimum required probability for deterrent success. If A supposes that there is a 50 percent chance that B will accept the appointment in Dallas if she will accompany him, but only a 10 percent chance that he will accept it if she won't, then the proportionate decrease effected by deterrence in the probability that he will accept the appointment is $(.5 - .1)/.5$, or .8. Since .8 is greater than .7, A indeed maximizes her expected utility by her adoption of a deterrent policy, requiring her to form the conditional intention not to accompany B should he accept an appointment in Dallas.

Consider now the application of our analysis to the policy of nuclear retaliation. Deterrent success for the US lies in not facing a strike policy by the SU – a policy that intends directly, or threatens and so intends conditionally, a nuclear strike. Deterrent failure lies in being faced with such a policy and being committed to a retaliatory response – to ignoring any threat by the SU and to responding to a nuclear strike by a counterstrike. Nondeterrence lies in facing a strike policy by the SU without being committed to a retaliatory response, and so it involves acceptance of the lesser evil between acquiescing in whatever initiative the SU takes and engaging in retaliation. Given these alternatives, we may suppose that, although deterrent success is of course preferred to nondeterrence, both are strongly preferred to deterrent failure. It may indeed be better to let the Reds have their way than to be among the nuclear dead. Thus a substantial decrease in the probability of facing a strike policy by the SU is required if the deterrent policy of nuclear retaliation is to maximize the expected utility of the US and so be rational to adopt.

I shall not try to estimate the extent of this decrease, or equivalently, the minimum required probability for deterrent success. This is a difficult empirical question. What is clear is that a merely ordinal ranking of preferences over possible outcomes does not afford sufficient information to assess the rationality of a deterrent policy, either in general or in the specific case of nuclear retaliation. An actor might prefer, and strongly prefer, to avoid facing a situation brought about by some other actor doing *y*, but the proportionate reduction in the probability of facing *y* that could be effected by a deterrent policy might not be worth the expected cost of facing it with the deterrent intention. The benefits of deterrent success must always be balanced against the costs of deterrent failure, and only the relevant probabilities of being in the undesirable situation, both with and without a policy of deterrence, together with an interval measure of utility in terms of which we may calculate the minimum required probability for deterrent success, enables us to calculate the balance of benefits and costs. Our argument shows that deterrrent policies in general, and nuclear retaliation in particular, may be utility-maximizing. It also shows that such policies may not be utility-maximizing. It may be extraordinarily difficult to determine, in a particular case, whether deterrence or nondeterrence is less disadvantageous.

But while I want to emphasize this cautionary note, I do not want to insist that my argument refutes the claim that deterrence is necessarily an irrational policy because carrying out the deterrent intention is not utility-maximizing. The argument for the irrationality of deterrence looks only to the costs of deterrent failure. Because there are such costs, it rejects the policy. My argument, on the other hand, relates the probability-weighted costs of deterrent failure to the probability-weighted benefits of deterrent success, in order to assess the rationality of forming the conditional, nonmaximizing intention which is the core of a deterrent policy. I claim that if it is rational to form this conditional, deterrent intention, then, should deterrence fail and the condition be realized, it is rational to act on it. The utility cost of acting on the deterrent intention enters, with appropriate probability-weighting, into determining whether it is rational to form the intention. But once this is decided, the cost of acting on the intention does not enter again into determining whether, if deterrence fails, it is rational to act on it. Acting on it is part of a deterrent policy, and if expected utility is maximized by forming the conditional, deterrent intention, then deterrence is a rational policy.

5. SOME OBJECTIONS ANSWERED

Let us turn to some possible objections to this argument. We may forestall one counterargument by noting that if one is able to achieve the same deterrent effect by pretending to form a conditional, nonmaximizing intention as by actually forming it, then such pretense would be rational. Even if pretense offers a lesser deterrent effect, its lesser possible costs may make it rational. But there is no reason to suppose that pretense must always have as great a net benefit as the actual formation of an intention. It must be judged on the same, utility-maximizing basis as the real thing.

An objector may insist that pretense can be rational because it does not commit one to nonmaximizing behavior, but that a genuine commitment to nonmaximization cannot be rational. If it is rational to form an intention that commits one to what, ceteris paribus, would not maximize one's utility, then the utility of forming the intention must affect the utility of carrying it out, increasing it so that execution is utility-maximizing. The US would, in the abstract, prefer not to engage in a nuclear exchange with the SU. Our objector admits this, but urges that, if a nuclear exchange arises from a rational policy of deterrence, then the US would prefer to maintain that policy and so prefer to engage in the exchange. On his view, preference for forming a conditional intention entails preference for executing it should the condition be met.

But what reason has he for claiming this, other than his insistence on a simple, and in my view simpleminded, account of the connection between utility-maximization and rationality?[4] I have shown that the adoption of an intention can be utility-maximizing even though acting on it would not be, at least considered in itself. Why then should we suppose that, because adoption is utility-maximizing, implementation magically becomes utility-maximizing? Why should we suppose that a preference for adopting or forming an intention must carry with it a preference for implementing or executing the intention? The two preferences are logically and actually quite distinct. We may grant that in most situations one prefers to adopt an intention because one would prefer to execute it. But my argument is intended to show that this connection does not hold between conditional intentions and their implementation in deterrent situations. I have shown why the connection does not hold—because adoption of the intention affects one's expected utilities by affecting the probability that the condition for implementation will be realized.

Our objector must surely take another and stronger tack. If he allows our argument about the rationality of adopting a nonmaximizing intention, then he must claim that it may be rational to adopt an intention even though it would be, and one knows that it would be, irrational to act on it should the condition for implementing it be realized. If our objector takes this tack, then he acknowledges the rationality of some deterrent policies, but nevertheless insists that these policies, although fully rational, involve the performance of irrational actions if certain conditions are satisfied. How then does his position differ from mine? I claim that deterrent policies may be rational, although they involve the performance of actions which, in themselves and apart from the context of deterrence, would be irrational.

And I claim that when deterrent policies are rational, then all of the actions they involve result from rational intentions, and so are themselves rational.[5] Surely he grants the substance of my argument, but expresses his agreement in a misleading and even paradoxical way, insisting that actions necessary to a rational policy may themselves be irrational. To assess an action as irrational is to claim that it should not be, or have been, performed. If our objector accepts deterrent policies, then he cannot consistently reject the actions they require, and so cannot claim that such actions should not be performed.

Suppose then that our objector confronts my position head on and rejects the rationality of deterrent policies. He insists that the execution of an intention must take precedence, rationally, over its adoption. He must insist that it is rational to form an intention if and only if one maximizes one's expected utility both in forming it and in executing it. If either condition fails, then formation of the intention is not rational.

This objector insists that the rationality of an action is always to be assessed *from now*, in the words of Bernard Williams.[6] The rationality of an action is to be assessed from the point at which the question, not of intending it, but of performing it, arises. And this is, I think, the heart of the matter. In taking this position the objector applies the utility-maximizing standard of rationality in the way generally approved by economists, decision-theorists, and game-theorists. But he, and they, are mistaken. The fully rational actor is not the one who assesses her actions *from now*, but rather the one who subjects the largest, rather than the smallest, segments of her activity to primary rational scrutiny, proceeding from policies to performances, letting assessment of the latter be ruled by assessment of the former.

A utility-maximizing policy may include non-utility-maximizing performances. Deterrence exemplifies this. The expected utility of a policy is the sum of the probability-weighted expected utilities of the performances it allows or requires. The apparent paradox, that a utility-maximizing policy may contain non-utility-maximizing performances, is resolved in the realization that altering the performances need not be independent of altering their probabilities. An assessment that begins and remains at the level of the performances neglects this crucial fact. Therefore, the actor who assesses the rationality of his actions only from now, from the point at which the question of performance arises, may expect a lesser overall utility than the actor who assesses the rationality of her actions in the context of policies, who adjusts performances so that the probability-weighted sum of their utilities is greatest.

Our objector will say that the policy-maximizer allows her choices to be ruled by the dead hand of the past, whereas he, the performance-maximizer, lives and chooses in the present. But our objector is mistaken. Unable to escape the burden of choice, the performance-maximizer must, choosing in the present, keep in mind that his attempt to minimize utility in the present performance is constrained by his future attempts to maximize utility on the occasion of each successive performance. He is ruled by the unborn, and perhaps never-to-be-born, hands of his possible futures. And his yoke is the worse. Maximization is the policy-maximizer's goal, but the performance-maximizer's fate.[7]

Before leaving our objector to that fate, let us note carefully that the reply to him does not insist that one should maximize in the long run rather than the short run. The would-be deterrer who fails to deter, and who must then make good on her threat in order to carry out her conditional intention, is not maximizing at all. Her reason for sticking to her guns is not to teach others by example, nor to improve her prospects for successful deterrence in the future, nor anything of the sort. Her reason is simply that the expected utility or payoff of her failed policy depended on her willingness to stick to her guns.

Let us suppose that each person or nation – each actor – knew (never mind how!) that but once in his life he would be in a situation in which, by convincing another actor that he would respond in a nonmaximizing way to a possible choice of the other, he could increase his expected utility by reducing the probability that the other would make that choice. Here, if the other is not deterred, carrying out the nonmaximizing response can, ex hypothesi, have no effect on the actor's credibility or on future deterrence. Yet he can hope to deter only if the other believes that he will, or at least may, make that nonmaximizing response. And adopting a genuine policy of deterrence may be the only way of bringing about that belief, or increasing its strength, in the other person. Even in this situation, a deterrent policy, committing one to a nonmaximizing choice should deterrence fail, may be utility-maximizing. Only those convinced of this can have a proper understanding, not only of deterrence, but of the whole range of situations, including most prominently generalized Prisoner's Dilemmas, in which policies that require nonmaximizing behavior are utility-maximizing, and so rational.[8] And what these policies effect is throughout the same – they alter the probabilities of an actor being in certain situations, facing certain choices. Only in understanding this do we begin to appreciate the true characteristics and complexity of utility-maximizing rationality.

6. THREAT-ENFORCEMENT AND THREAT-RESISTANCE

I have referred to the expression of a conditional intention to RETAL as a *threat*. The argument advanced for the rationality of a deterrent policy is indeed an argument for the rationality of threat-enforcement. If the expected gain from deterrence exceeds the expected cost of carrying out the deterrent threat, where each expectation is probability-weighted, and if no less costly means of deterrence is available, then the rational actor sincerely threatens and enforces her threat should it fail to deter.

Not all threats are properly deterrent. The kidnapper threatens the parents of his victim with the death of their child should they fail to pay; it would be perverse to say that he seeks to deter them from nonpayment. But I shall not attempt an analysis of threats here. My purpose in introducing the conception of threat is to broaden the perspective of our analysis so that it embraces both threatener and threatened, and in this perspective we shall find a new and problematic dimension in our argument.

If we think of nuclear retaliation as a policy of threat-enforcement, we must note that it is also a policy of threat-resistance. The US threatens nuclear retaliation to deter a strike by the SU. But a strike policy, as we have described it, may center on the issuance of a credible threat of nuclear attack should some initiative be opposed, and retaliation thus embraces resistance to such a threat. In the context of nuclear deterrence each party may be viewed both as threatener and threatened, as a potential threat-enforcer and threat-resister. Not all threat situations involve this symmetry, but the standpoints of threatener and threatened are themselves significantly parallel. For each must decide whether to adopt an intention – to enforce a threat or to resist a threat. The enforcer seeks to avoid that situation in which enforcement would be required; the resister seeks to prevent that situation in which resistance would be required. The argument previously stated may be adapted to show the rationale for both threat-enforcement and threat-resistance. Since taken together, enforcement and resistance make threat behavior unprofitable, the existence of parallel rationales may cast doubt on the rationality of any policy involving threats, and so on a policy of deterrence.

Let us consider briefly how the argument of section 4 applies to enforcement and resistance. Both the would-be threat-enforcer and threat-resister seek to reduce the probability of being in an undesirable situation (having one's threat ignored/facing a credible threat) by expressing a conditional intention to respond in a mutually costly way in that situation. The success of enforcement/resistance lies in avoiding the undesirable situation; enforcement/resistance failure lies in having to carry out one's conditional intention. The minimum required probability for enforcement/resistance success is defined as the probability of that success in the lottery between success and failure that the enforcer/resister considers indifferent to no-enforcement/no-resistance. A policy of threat-enforcement/threat-resistance is rational only if the proportionate decrease that it effects in the probability of having one's threat ignored/facing a credible threat is greater than the minimum required probability for enforcement/resistance success.

The parallel rationales that can be constructed for threat-enforcement and threat-resistance may seem to show the overall irrationality of threat behavior. If both enforcement and resistance are rational, then either the worst case prevails, in which a threat is issued, ignored, and executed; or the pre-threat situation prevails, no threat being issued since, if it were, it would be ignored and then executed. But although there is a deep irrationality in threat behavior, the parallel rationales do not themselves suffice to demonstrate it. For they show only that the structure of the argument for enforcement is the same as that for resistance. They do not show that, in a given situation, threat-enforcement and threat-resistance are equally rational or irrational.

We may illustrate this by our core example – nuclear deterrence. Suppose that the SU were to announce a policy of deterrence-resistance. It will carry out, or threaten, a nuclear strike if it considers that a retaliatory response would be costly to the US – if it believes that the maximizing US response would be acquiescence or submission.

As we noted in section 3, the SU prefers strike & no-retaliation to no-strike, and no-strike to strike & retaliation. A policy of deterrence-resistance is rational for the SU only if the proportionate decrease that it effects in the probability of a US policy of retaliation is greater than the minimum required probability for the success of deterrence-resistance. But this is the probability of strike & no-retaliation in that lottery between strike & no-retaliation and strike & retaliation that the SU finds indifferent to the certainty of no-strike. No-strike represents, in effect, acceptance of the status quo; we may plausibly suppose that the SU would require a very high probability of gain – of the US acquiescence entailed in strike & no-retaliation – and a correspondingly low probability of loss – of the nuclear exchange entailed in strike & retaliation – before it would be indifferent between such a lottery and the status quo. We may plausibly suppose that deterrence-resistance will not seem to the SU to be a utility-maximizing policy.

The US, as we also noted in section 3, prefers no-strike to strike & no-retaliation, and strike & no-retaliation to strike & retaliation. Thus, as we established in section 4, deterrence is a rational policy for the US only if the proportionate decrease that it effects in the probability of a strike policy by the SU is greater than the probability of no-strike in the lottery between no-strike and strike & retaliation that the US finds indifferent to the certainty of strike & no-retaliation. Although we have refrained from attempting to estimate this probability, except to suggest that it is likely to be high, yet we may note that strike & no-retaliation represents, not the status quo, but a real worsening of the situation of the US. Even though a nuclear exchange is a greater worsening, yet we may plausibly suppose that the US would not require a *very* high probability of maintaining the status quo implicit in no-strike, and a *very* low corresponding probability of loss through nuclear exchange, to be indifferent between such a lottery and the loss implicit in no-retaliation. Although any firm judgment must be beyond armchair competence, it may well be the case that nuclear retaliation is a rational policy for the US, although resistance to deterrence is not a rational policy for the SU.

Thus the parallel between the rationales for threat-enforcement and threat-resistance does not in itself show the irrationality of a policy of deterrence. However, even if threat behavior is rationally justifiable from the standpoint of a particular actor, there is a need for mutually agreed measures to remove the threat-inviting context. Fundamental to Hobbes's analysis of the state of nature is the need to exist through the acceptance of mutual constraints. The state of nations, and especially of nuclear powers, is our nearest analogue to the state of nature, and Hobbes's advice applies to it. The need to rely on deterrence is a sign of the presence of peril sufficient to justify an agreement removing or minimizing the need. This will be my final theme in this paper; even if deterrence not only may be, but is, a rational policy for the US, the nuclear status quo that demands deterrence is not a rational state of affairs.

7. WHY NUCLEAR RETALIATION MAY BE MORAL

Threat behavior is nonproductive, and indeed counterproductive, if we take its effects on all persons into account. This does not result directly from the intentions of the actors involved. The person who issues a threat seeks to increase her expectation of benefit, but only by reducing the expectation of the party threatened. The threat-enforcer's willingness to risk an unfavorable outcome lowers the prospects of the person threatened, and thus brings about a redistribution of benefits and costs. But a redistribution need not be a reduction of net benefit. The threat-resister simply seeks a restoration of the status quo; given a threat, his strategy is redistributive, but taken in a larger context, it is intended as a counter that renders threats ineffective. The threat-resister, through his willingness to risk an unfavorable outcome, seeks to restore his initial expectation of benefit, but not by *reducing* the pre-threat expectation of the prospective threatener. Again, there need be no reduction in net benefit.

However, if in an ideal world threat behavior might avoid mutual costs, yet in the real world we must expect that from time to time either a threat-enforcer or a threat-resister will be called upon to make good on a conditional nonmaximizing intention. And when this occurs, the result is sub-optimal. The payoff from a failed threat, or from failed threat-resistance, is less desirable to each party than either the payoff expected in the absence of any threat, or than the redistributed payoff resulting from a successful threat. Insofar as threat-behavior involves a real risk of such a sub-optimal result, it must be regarded as *ex ante* disadvantageous from the standpoint of any actor who is sufficiently uncertain about future prospects. Only someone who could expect to be especially favorably placed with respect to successful threatening would lack *ex ante* reason to agree to eschew threat behavior. Rational persons will therefore find the mutual avoidance of threat behavior to be an appropriate matter for agreement.

We should note here a contrast between threat situations and collective-goods situations. Where the possibility of providing collective goods is present, rational persons can expect to benefit from mutual agreement to ensure the optimal provision of these goods, even though such provision may require nonmaximizing behavior. For the outcome of individually maximizing behavior in such situations is typically sub-optimal; each party stands to gain from making and adhering to an optimizing agreement in comparison to the expected outcome of no-agreement. Here nonmaximizing behavior is set in a productive context. But in threat situations, the nonmaximizing behavior required to make the issuance of or resistance to threats rational is not productive. The parties to such behavior are not enabled to reach outcomes mutually preferable to those they would otherwise expect; instead, they are likely to reach outcomes mutually less preferable. Hence actors faced with the problem of providing collective goods have reason to enter into agreements calling for nonmaximizing behavior, whereas actors faced with the problem of threats have reason to enter into agreements calling for the renunciation of policies with nonmaximizing threat components. Faced with collective goods problems, rational actors will agree mutually to constrain their directly maximizing dispositions. Faced with threat problems, rational actors will agree mutually not to constrain their directly maximizing dispositions in ways that would make credible threats possible.

Deterrence, as a typical policy of threat-enforcement and threat-resistance, is itself clearly unproductive. But in considering the terms on which it should rationally be renounced, it is essential to recognize its role in stabilizing human interaction. For the threat implicit in nuclear deterrence is not a threat against social order, but rather a threat intended to maintain the conditions under which viable and fair social order is possible.

We may appeal here to a normative idea clearly formulated by John Rawls, that society is "a cooperative venture for mutual advantage."[10] This idea immediately suggests a baseline condition for social interaction: no person or other social actor is entitled to benefit at the expense or cost of another, where both benefit and cost are measured against a no-interaction baseline. That is, no actor is entitled to make himself or herself better off than could be expected in the absence of interaction, by policies or performances that render other actors worse off than they would expect to be in the absence of interaction. A refusal to accept or abide by this condition is an indication of an unwillingness to interact cooperatively with others – an unwillingness, in Hobbesian language, to seek peace and follow it.

Now, a policy that includes a willingness to resort to an initial nuclear strike, even if only in the event of a failed threat, is clearly ruled out by this condition. For the effect of such a policy is clearly to worsen the situation of the victim in a way that exceeds what he could expect in the absence of interaction. And the policy cannot itself be treated as defensive, as merely preventing the actor from having his own position worsened through interaction with the victim. An aggressive strike policy seeks to better the condition of its holder through measures that worsen the condition of those against whom it is directed. To resort to such a policy is to reject the prospect of cooperative interaction with others.

Nuclear retaliation, as a deterrent policy, is directed at protecting the retaliator from being victimized by any actor willing to engage in a first strike. It is, then, not to seek to redistribute benefits in a way more favorable to the would-be deterrer than could be expected in the absence of interaction, but rather to ensure that her situation is not worsened in terms of that baseline. It is directed at upholding, rather than subverting, the requirement that human society be a cooperative venture for mutual advantage.

In itself, of course, nothing could be less cooperative, less directed at mutual advantage, than the use of nuclear weapons. But a retaliatory, deterrent policy is directed at preventing such use – directed at maintaining those conditions in which societies may be brought to recognize the benefits of cooperation. A policy of nuclear deterrence clearly has failed if a nuclear exchange occurs. But the serious alternative to such a policy, in the absence of agreement to eschew all threat behavior, can only be the willingness to accept victimization, to suffer passively a nuclear strike or to acquiesce in whatever the potential striker demands as the price of its avoidance.

Morality, in my view, follows rationality. Practical rationality is concerned with the maximization of benefit; the primary requirements of morality are that in maximizing benefit, advantage must not be taken and need not be given.[11] Nuclear deterrence, despite its horrific character, is then a moral policy – a policy aimed at encouraging the conditions under which morally acceptable and rational interaction among nations may occur. If we agree that the idea of society as a cooperative venture for mutual advantage and the related proviso against benefiting through interaction that worsens the condition of others express a fundamental moral ideal, then the willingness to maintain those conditions under which this ideal may be realized and the refusal to acquiesce in measures that would subvert it must themselves be the objects of moral approval rather than censure.

Rational nations, recognizing the need to seek peace and follow it given the costs of war, can unilaterally renounce the first use of nuclear weapons and thereby end all strike policies. Rational nations can mutually agree to destroy their holdings of nuclear weapons, at least insofar as these weapons are directed against each other, and so can end all deterrent policies. Since the knowledge that brought nuclear weapons into being will not disappear, we cannot expect a world fully free of nuclear threats. We can only minimize a peril that cannot be exorcised. But to understand the conditions under which we may rationally agree to the mutual abandonment of deterrent and other threat policies, we must first understand the rationale of deterrent policies and the role of these policies in maintaining the conditions of acceptable international interaction. Hobbes conjoins two fundamental requirements in relating the law and the right of nature: "to seek Peace, and follow it," and "by all means we can, to defend our selves."[12] Hobbes understands that these requirements are mutually supportive; a correct understanding of nuclear deterrence supports his view.

NOTES

1 One who says "No" is Jonathan Schell, *The Fate of the Earth* (New York: Knopf, 1982), pp. 201-4.

2 Among these others are game-theorists who insist that strategic rationality demands perfect equilibria.

3 Thomas Hobbes, *Leviathan* (London, 1651), chap. 14.

4 If preference is necessarily *revealed* in behavior, then choosing a nuclear exchange *shows* that one prefers it to one's alternatives. Conceptually, we can (and many economists and game-theorists do) fit preference and choice so tightly together that nothing could count as non-utility-maximizing behavior. But this mode of conceptualization is a Procrustean bed for the treatment of such issues as the rationality of deterrence.

5 How his position may differ is made clear by David Lewis, "Devil's Bargains and the Real World," in this volume. I begin a rejoinder to Lewis in "Afterthoughts."

6 Bernard Williams, *Moral Luck* (Cambridge, England: Cambridge University Press, 1981), p. 35.

7 I expand on this point in "Afterthoughts."

8 I discuss this in "Reason and Maximization," *Canadian Journal of Philosophy* 4 (1975): 427-30. Matters are clarified in my forthcoming book, *Morals by Agreement*, Oxford University Press, chap. VI.

9 This is the import of Hobbes's second law of nature, *Leviathan*, chap. 14.

10 John Rawls, *A Theory of Justice* (Cambridge, Mass: Harvard University Press, 1971), p. 4.

11 Neither utilitarians nor Kantians will find this conception of morality to their taste. I cannot defend it here, but see *Morals by Agreement*.

12 *Leviathan*, chap. 14.

9

NUCLEAR DETERRENCE: SOME MORAL PERPLEXITIES

Gregory S. Kavka

Is it morally permissible for the United States to practice nuclear deterrence, given that doing so could eventuate in large-scale nuclear war, an unprecedented disaster for humanity?[1] This is a question not only of obvious moral (and political) importance, but also of great intellectual difficulty and complexity. I shall not attempt to answer it, but shall sort out and discuss some of the myriad perplexities that must be dealt with before an answer can be found. It is hoped that a potentially fruitful way of looking at the moral problem of nuclear deterrence will emerge from this discussion.

To get our minds churning on the subject, let us consider a fictional situation that parallels the nuclear balance of terror in certain key respects.[2] Hearing from a usually reliable source that a certain rival is out to get you, you begin to carry a gun when you go out. While you are so armed, an elevator you are riding in stops, apparently stuck, between floors. Looking up from your newspaper, you discover that the other occupants are a group of young children and your rival, who has noticed you and seems to be drawing a weapon. You simultaneously draw your gun and a standoff quickly ensues, with each of you pointing a gun at the other. You realize that firing could break out at any time and kill or injure the children as well as yourself and your rival. Yet you are afraid your rival will shoot you if you drop your gun, nor do you trust him to keep an agreement to drop guns simultaneously. In these circumstances, is it permissible for you to continue to point your gun at your rival? On the one hand, it appears clear that it is, since this reasonably seems necessary for self-defense. On the other hand, the act seems wrong because it seriously threatens the innocent youngsters with injury and death. Here we have a moral dilemma with no immediately evident solution.

Now, if we take you and your rival to be the governments and armed forces of the two superpowers,[3] and the youngsters to be the rest of the population of these countries (and other countries that would suffer in a nuclear war), our elevator case can serve as a model of the nuclear balance of terror. The two situations possess many of the same morally relevant features and pose somewhat similar moral dilemmas. In fact, I propose viewing the moral problem of nuclear deterrence as, like the elevator case, essentially involving a tension between threatening innocent people and doing what appears necessary for self-defense.

This tension is best brought out by noting that the following three propositions form an inconsistent triad, i.e., they cannot all three be true, though each pair of them is consistent.

(1) *Threat Principle:* It is impermissible to threaten and impose risks of death upon large numbers of innocent people.
(2) *National Defense Principle:* It is permissible for a nation to do whatever it reasonably believes is necessary for national self-defense.
(3) *Necessity Claim:* Practicing nuclear deterrence against the USSR in a way that involves threatening and imposing risks of death upon a large number of innocent Soviet civilians is necessary for the self-defense of the US, and is reasonably believed to be so by US leaders and citizens.

Two of these propositions are absolutist moral principles. The Threat Principle is prohibitive; it says acts of a certain sort are wrong in any circumstances. The National Defense Principle is permissive; it says acts of a particular kind are permissible in any circumstances. The Necessity Claim is an essentially factual[4] proposition that ascribes two properties to the practice of nuclear deterrence by the US. The first of these – that it threatens the innocent – renders the practice impermissible according to the Threat Principle. The second – that it is necessary for national defense – ensures, by the National Defense Principle, that the practice is permissible. Hence the inconsistency, which is disturbing in view of the fact that each of the three propositions has a considerable degree of initial plausibility.

How should this inconsistency be resolved? Which of the three propositions should we reject? Considering them in turn, I shall suggest that none of the propositions is acceptable as it stands. Each must be modified and revised. Identifying the weaknesses of these propositions, and the nature of the modifications needed to correct them, suggests further areas of injury. And while it does not provide a direct solution to the moral problem of deterrence, it does shed some definite light on what the problem really is.

I. THREATS TO THE INNOCENT

In practicing nuclear deterrence, the United States *threatens* Soviet civilians in two senses: we declare that we will kill them if their leaders behave in certain ways, and we actually put them under some risk of death. That is, nuclear deterrence normally involves a *declarative threat* together with *risk imposition*. It is this combination, directed against large numbers of innocents, which is morally prohibited under all circumstances by the Threat Principle.

Is such an absolutist prohibition plausible? To answer this I propose considering the two elements separately, focusing on the declarative threat first. Let us ask then what is normally wrong with threats, aside from the actual risks they impose on those to whom they are addressed. Four things come immediately to mind: threats may be counterproductive and encourage the wrongful conduct they attempt to deter, they may be effective in deterring permissible conduct (thus restricting the threatened party's rightful liberty), they may cause fear and anxiety, and their use may damage relations between the parties in question. Yet none of these seems to be the sort of consideration that would support an absolute prohibition. Further, there is little reason to suppose that declarative threats should not be permitted when these features are largely absent. Suppose, for example, that a declarative threat will very probably be effective, is aimed at deterring clearly impermissible conduct, does not cause devastating anxiety (compared to alternative courses of action open to the threatener) because people are used to living with it, and does not destroy relations between the parties because threats of this kind are considered a normal element in those relations. It is doubtful that a declarative threat of this sort is wrong simply because it is a threat. Yet is is arguable that the declarative threat involved in nuclear deterrence is just of this kind.

But perhaps it is the specific nature of the nuclear threat, rather than simply its being a threat, which ensures its wrongfulness. It has been frequently noted, for example, that the balance of terror holds each side's civilian population hostage to the good behavior of its government. And at least one writer has suggested that nuclear deterrence is wrong because hostage-taking is wrong.[5] But, if civilians are hostages to an adversary nation's nuclear weapons, they are hostages *in place*, who may go on with their normal activities without physical restriction. Hence, two of the usual objections to taking hostages do not apply: the violation of their personal integrity in seizing them, and the subsequent imposition of substantial limits on their liberty.[6] In view of this, it seems unlikely that nuclear deterrence must be wrong because, in a sense, it makes civilians hostages.

Does the *content* of the nuclear threat – to kill a large number of innocent people – render that threat impermissible under any circumstances? Suppose that we accept an absolute prohibition on killing the innocent and also accept the Wrongful Intentions Principle, which says that if an act is wrong, intending to perform it is also wrong. Since threats of nuclear retaliation (unless they are bluffs) involve the intention to kill innocent people, it follows that they are wrong.[7]

This reasoning is valid, but unsound. As I have argued elsewhere, the Wrongful Intentions Principle fails when applied to a conditional intention adopted solely to prevent the occurrence of the circumstances in which the intention would be acted upon.[8] Thus, for example, if I know I can prevent you from thrashing me only by sincerely threatening to retaliate against your beloved and innocent brother, it may not be wrong for me to do so. Since the intentions behind the threats of those who practice nuclear deterrence are presumably of this sort, these threats are not necessarily wrong.

I conclude that the present absolutist form of the Threat Principle cannot be supported on the basis of the declarative threat element. But, if we focus instead on the imposition of risks, we again find little reason to adopt an absolutist principle of this type.[9] For it is generally recognized that if we evaluate policies in terms of the risks involved, we must also consider and weigh up the benefits the policies bestow and the risks and benefits entailed by alternative policies. So our Threat Principle must assume some modified and nonabsolutist form such as:

(1') *Revised Threat Principle:* It is wrong to *disproportionately* threaten and impose risks of death upon large numbers of innocent people.

This revised principle requires that threats to the innocent not be excessively harmful or risky, compared to available alternatives. But how, in principle, are we to determine whether relevant harms and risks are proportionate or excessive? The most natural initial suggestion is to apply a utilitarian standard and ask whether a policy of nuclear deterrence promotes worldwide human welfare better than would its abandonment. However, casting the problem in these terms confronts us with yet another dilemma. For while we cannot reliably estimate the precise numerical probabilities, most of us would endorse the following ordinal judgment: it is considerably more likely that the Soviets would attack and/or dominate the world by blackmail, if the United States practices unilateral nuclear disarmament for a given period of time, than it is that continued United States nuclear deterrence (during the same period) would lead to large-scale nuclear war. If we believe this, then the choice we face, in utilitarian terms, is essentially between a smaller risk of a graver disaster for humanity (i.e., nuclear war), and a greater risk of a smaller disaster for humanity (i.e., Soviet attack and/or domination).[10]

Perhaps we could avoid this utilitarian dilemma by assessing risks in another way. In any case, evaluation of the prohibitory Threat Principle leads toward viewing the moral problem of deterrence as a problem of risk assessment under uncertainty. Does a similar view emerge if we approach the problem from the perspective of the permissive National Defense Principle?

II. NATIONAL DEFENSE

What is the moral basis on which we posit the existence of a right of national defense? For present purposes, I shall take it that such a right is derived from principles of individual self-defense in one of two ways. By analogy, with the reasoning being that a nation is like a person in morally significant respects, and therefore possesses a right of self-defense like that of a person. Or by composition, with the right of national defense consisting in an authorized government's exercising, in a coordinated fashion, the combined individual rights of self-defense of its citizens. In either case, we may assume that the right of national defense has the same limitations as the right of individual self-defense, unless there are specific differences between the situations of nations and individuals that either cancel or extend those limitations. Then we may use our knowledge of the individual right of self-defense to discover what limits, if any, govern the moral right of national defense.

Richard Wasserstrom, in his discussion of the morality of war, notes four restrictions on the individual legal right of self-defense: there must be an actual attack; the defender (unless on his own property) must have been unable safely to retreat; the force used must have been reasonably necessary; and the harm inflicted must be comparable to (or less than) that which would otherwise have been suffered by the defender.[11] Suppose that we agree that these are all limitations on the moral, as well as legal, right of individual self-defense. Are they also limits on the right of national defense?

With the exception of the use of force being reasonably necessary (a condition already reflected in the National Defense Principle), it is doubtful that they are. The other three limitations seem justified only because individuals generally can appeal to public authorities to protect themselves and vindicate their rights. Temporary retreat and acceptance of limited harm and/or risk to oneself are morally acceptable if actual and potential assailants can be punished and deterred through the legal system. But there is no effective system of international criminal law to punish and deter aggressor states. If nations retreat as far as possible, or wait until the other side attacks, they may gravely weaken their chances of defending themselves successfully, with no hope of having their losses restored. Further, if aggression is to be effectively deterred in the absence of an international police force to mete out punishments, successful defenders may have to inflict more than comparable harm on unsuccessful aggressors.[12] Hence, the legal limits on the right of individual self-defense do not point to any substantial limitations on the right of national defense, beyond those already contained in our National Defense Principle.

As Wasserstrom notes, nations do not die in the same sense as people do.[13] Does this imply any special restrictions on the right of national defense that might apply to nuclear deterrence? To answer this, we must first distinguish between two senses in which a nation can die. Its people can be physically annihilated (death$_1$), or the people can survive but lose their independence or have their basic institutions substantially and forcibly altered by outsiders (death$_2$). Now, it is doubtful that nuclear deterrence is the only way a nation can prevent its death$_1$. It is highly likely, for example, that either superpower could safeguard the lives of (at least almost all of) its citizens if it were willing to accept death$_2$ by simply surrendering to its rival.

However, consideration of the nature of the right of individual self-defense makes it plausible to suppose that nations have a strong right to defend themselves from death$_2$ as well as death$_1$. Suppose a gang goes around kidnapping people and then, without ever killing them, either (i) locks them up in secret prisons for life, or (ii) blinds them and amputates their limbs, or (iii) destroys their higher faculties by brain operations, or (iv) brainwashes them so they come to love what they previously hated and hate what they previously loved. Clearly whatever people are justified in doing to save themselves from murderers, they would be equally justified in doing to prevent being kidnapped by this gang. The implication of this is that the right of self-defense applies to the preservation of the central values of one's life as well as to biological survival. This suggests that a nation's right of self-defense applies to its central values (including its independence and the structure of its basic institutions), as well as the biological survival of its members – especially if, as seems likely, the central values of many of those members (and the survival of some of them) are inextricably bound up with the survival of the nation and its central values.[14] So even if nuclear deterrence were reasonably necessary only to protect our nation from death$_2$, it could still be sanctioned by a legitimate right of national defense.

We have yet, however, to consider the most important limit on the right of individual self-defense: restrictions on the risks or harms one may impose on other innocent parties in attempting to protect oneself. Suppose, for example, that mobsters credibly threaten to kill you unless you murder several innocent people. You may reasonably believe that doing these killings is necessary to save your life. It would be wrong, nonetheless, to do them. The same is true even in some cases in which the risk or harm you impose is decidedly less than the harm you are defending against. Thus, if you need a new kidney to survive, you have no right to kidnap an appropriate donor and have your surgeon friend transplant one of his kidneys into you.[15]

The lesson of the kidney case seems to be that one can, at most, actively impose substantially lesser risks or harms on other innocent people to protect oneself. Can this lesson be applied to national as well as individual self-defense? One might contend that it cannot be, appealing for support to the hallowed ought-implies-can principle. According to that principle, agents – including nations – can only be obligated to act in ways they are capable of acting. But, it may be suggested, nations are literally incapable of re-fraining from taking steps believed to be necessary for national defense, even if these impose horrible risks or harms on outside innocents. For any government that failed to undertake the requisite defensive actions (e.g., any government that abandoned nuclear deterrence) would be quickly ousted and replaced by a government willing to undertake them.

This argument that nations may permissibly do anything to protect themselves, because they can do no other, is interesting but unconvincing. In the first place, history shows that not all governments which fail to take available courses of action necessary for national defense fall when this be-comes apparent. Thus, Chamberlain's appeasement of Hitler led to his downfall, but Stalin's did not lead to his. This example suggests restricting the argument to *democratic nations*, where the people clearly have the power to replace unsatisfactory leaders.[16]

But there are further difficulties with the argument. If democratic gov-ernments are incapable, because of popular pressure, of refraining from necessary defensive actions, democratic *nations* are not. For the nation in-cludes the people, and if *they* allowed a government to forgo elements of defense to protect third parties, the government could do so. Hence, for the argument to establish that democratic *nations* are permitted to do whatever is necessary for defense, it must claim that the people, or an ef-fective majority of them, are collectively incapable of doing otherwise. But this would seem exceedingly difficult to establish, especially when – as in the case of nuclear deterrence – the acts thought necessary for defense themselves risk national and international destruction. No known princi-ple of individual or group psychology indicates that an effective majority of an independent nation's people *must* prefer to risk their own deaths and those of countless other innocents to losing their political independence. They certainly may so prefer, but the argument in question succeeds only if the opposite preference is impossible.

Finally, suppose it were true that democratic nations, at least, could do no other than defend themselves, even at the cost of imposing serious harms or risks on innocent others. Can we appropriately apply the ought-implies-can principle to conclude such nations act permissibly in imposing these harms and risks? Comparisons with the case of individuals suggests not. Neither law nor morality allows people to kill other innocents in self-defense. Even when there is genuine irresistible compulsion derived from self-preservative instincts, this at most excuses the killing of innocent others, or mitigates appropriate punishment;[17] it does not justify the killing. The same presumably holds true of the imposition of lesser but still serious harms (e.g., the theft of a kidney), and serious risks (e.g., tossing someone out of a crowded lifeboat when he or she has some reasonable chance of swimming to shore.) The "ought" in the moral rule "One ought not impose death, serious harms, or substantial risk thereof on innocent people" is apparently not strictly governed by the ought-implies-can principle. Hence an unlimited right of national defense would not follow even from a nation's incapacity to refrain from taking whatever measures seem necessary for defense.

Suppose then we accept the limit on the right of national defense suggested by the kidney case: nations, like individuals, can at most impose substantially lesser risks or harms on other innocent parties to protect themselves. We might be tempted to conclude that nuclear deterrence is impermissible because it imposes on innocent Soviet civilians risks as great as those from which it protects us. Before, however, we jump to that conclusion, we must look more closely at the concept of "innocence."

III. INNOCENCE AND IMMUNITY

As used in such claims as "Nuclear deterrence is wrong because it imposes risks on innocent people" and "It is wrong to kill innocent people," the notion of innocence has two components. Those people described as innocent are asserted to be innocent *of doing* (or bringing about) certain things, in the sense of lacking moral responsibility for them. Also, a certain moral status is ascribed to these people: that of being immune from deliberately imposed harm or risk. Thus, this use of the concept of innocence contains within itself a substantive moral doctrine.

(4) *Immunity Thesis:* Persons have moral immunity, and it is impermissible to deliberately impose significant harms or risks on them, unless they are themselves morally responsible for creating relevant harms or dangers.[18]

The intended concept of moral responsibility may be explained as follows. An agent is morally responsible for certain harms or risks when two conditions hold. First, certain moral flaws or shortcomings of the agent are expressed in his acts (or omissions) and make a significant causal contribution to the existence of those harms or risks. Second, the agent possesses the general psychological capacities necessary for being responsible for one's actions. Applying punishment only to those who are morally responsible in this sense seems sensible. It ensures that people are punished only for things over which they had some significant degree of control. And those punished can reasonably be said to merit punishment, because their moral flaws have produced identifiable harms or dangers. However, the concept of immunity has a use in some contexts in which punishment is not what is at issue. In particular, the question of an agent's moral immunity may arise in a dangerous situation, as one considers acting so as to redistribute risks among various parties.[19] Our intuitions about certain situations of this kind imply that the Immunity Thesis is not universally valid.

Imagine that a powerful man, whom I know to hate me and to be insane, rushes me with a knife. I can stop him either by shooting him or by shooting a third party who would fall in his path and delay him long enough for me to escape. It is clear that the former alternative is morally preferable, even though neither the lunatic nor the bystander is morally responsible for the danger to my life. Note also the standard belief that, in war, you are justified in shooting at enemy soldiers because they pose a threat to you, your comrades, and your country. An enemy soldier may not be morally responsible, in the sense described above, for the threat he poses. (He may reasonably believe that he is obligated to fight for his country, or he may have been coerced into fighting by threats of death.) Yet his lack of moral responsibility would not impose on you the obligation to treat him as you would a civilian bystander. Finally, consider an example involving nuclear deterrence. Compare deterring country Y from attack by threatening retaliation against its cities, with deterring it by threatening retaliation against the cities of uninvolved nation Z. Most of us believe that, questions of effectiveness aside, the latter practice is substantially more objectionable. Yet the vast majority of citizens of Y, as well as the citizens of Z, probably lack individual moral responsibility for the danger that Y creates.

The correct explanation of our reactions to these cases seems to be this. Our moral beliefs about dangerous situations are complex enough to take account of the fact that there are various kinds of connections an individual may have to a given danger, and that these may hold in various combinations and degrees. We regard the kind of connection set out in the usual conception of moral responsibility as sufficient to annul the agent's immunity. But other "looser" connections—creating danger out of madness or belonging to a group responsible for producing a harm—are also sometimes taken to weaken or annul that immunity.

It is not hard to understand why we thus subject the Immunity Thesis to qualification. The basic purpose of holding people liable for risks and harms is to protect people, by deterring and preventing dangerous and harmful acts. It is generally most efficient to control such acts by holding liable those morally responsible for them. Further, so doing gives people the opportunity to avoid liability by refraining from performing dangerous or harmful acts. In certain cases, however, control of harmful behavior is attained much more efficiently if looser conditions of liability are used. When the penalties are not severe, and the efficiencies are relatively large, we are not greatly bothered by such loosening of liability conditions. When penalties are more serious, such as imprisonment, death, or risk of serious injury, we generally believe that tight standards of liability should be employed. Thus, we are less inclined to accept vicarious liability in criminal than in civil law. However, when there is a significant present danger, and control of that danger *requires* loosening the conditions of liability, our inclination is to regard some loosenings as justified. This does not mean that we break down all distinctions. We still hold that the uninvolved bystander retains his immunity. What happens is that we shift more agents with intermediate degrees of connection to the danger out of the immune category (where the bystander resides), into the nonimmune category (where the deliberate wrongdoer resides), or into an intermediate "semi-immune" category.

Our justification for doing so in the case of collective action by an organized group is evident. In cases of cooperative action involving large numbers of people, it would be silly to require for liability that an individual's contribution to the group act be significant and flow from a flaw in the individual's character. When large groups act, individual members' contributions are typically indirect and too small to have substantial impact. Further, organizational decision procedures and group pressures can often funnel individually blameless inputs into an immoral group output. Hence, to require a significant causal contribution flowing from a character defect as a precondition of liability in such cases would be to let too many people (in some cases perhaps *everyone*) off the hook and largely lose the ability to influence group acts by deterrence. This is especially so when the group in question is a sovereign nation. For then, usually, outsiders can do little to punish key leaders who bear individual moral responsibility for the group's misbehavior, except by imposing military, economic, or political sanctions that affect the entire nation.

If we accept this limited defense of applying some notion of collective responsibility to citizens of nations, the argument against nuclear deterrence which was offered at the end of the last section fails. Soviet civilians typically lack full individual moral responsibility for the nuclear threat their government and military pose to us, but this does not render them fully immune to counterthreats from us. Like the mad attacker, they are partially responsible and hence partly liable. (As we are toward them; our mutual nuclear threats may even reciprocally justify each other.[20])

Taken together, considerations advanced in this section and the last suggest that a proper form of the National Defense Principle will be neither absolutely permissive nor absolutely prohibitory. It will not permit *anything* reasonably necessary for national defense, for there must be limits on what may be done to the innocent or partially innocent. But, as the adversary's civilian population lacks full immunity, it will not forbid imposing any substantial risks or harms on them. Perhaps the principle should read as follows:

(2′) *Revised National Defense Principle:* It is permissible for a nation to do whatever it reasonably believes is necessary for national self-defense, provided such measures do not impose disproportionate risks or harms on other parties.

The key term in this principle is "disproportionate." The appropriate criteria of proportionality take into account not only the relative sizes of the various risks and the risks that would be produced by alternative courses of action, but also the "degree" of innocence or immunity of the threatened parties. Considerations advanced in this section indicate that risks imposed on guilty parties count for much less than those imposed on the partially innocent (e.g., those only collectively responsible), which in turn count for less than those imposed on purely innocent bystanders. Reading backwards, we should also add this element to the interpretation of the term "disproportionately" in the Revised Threat Principle (1′).[21] This renders our two revised principles of one mind. Both forbid imposing disproportionate risks or harms on others, but allow all proportionate measures necessary for national defense.

We now see that the moral problem of deterrence is more complex, in at least one important way, than the utilitarian dilemma sketched at the end of section I. It involves assessing the degrees of responsibility and liability for military threats to others of the various parties and groups involved in the balance of terror and appropriately integrating this information into one's (otherwise) utilitarian analysis of risks and benefits.[22] The difficulty of this task may make us wish to avoid it. We could surely do so if nuclear deterrence were unnecessary for national defense, but is it?

IV. IS DETERRENCE NECESSARY?

Is threatening Soviet civilians with nuclear retaliation necessary for the defense of the US, given the Soviets' possession of a vast nuclear arsenal? At least one recent writer has answered "no" on the grounds that conventional arms alone would suffice to deter the Soviets from attack or successful nuclear blackmail,[23] but I shall make the usual assumption that this is wrong.[24] A recent proposal of President Reagan's suggests a different basis for answering our question in the negative.[25] Deterrence by threat of nuclear retaliation might be replaced by an effective technological defense against nuclear missiles, a system of lasers, missiles, and/or particle beams that would destroy enemy missiles before they have reached their targets. Critics of this proposal have claimed that such a system would be enormously expensive, would not work well enough, would itself be vulnerable to attack, could be counteracted by the other side's building more missiles, and might conceivably tempt the other side to strike first before the system was completed. They are probably right about much of this. But, unless such systems are perfect (i.e., 100 percent reliable) shields, there is yet another powerful strategic and moral reason against building them: they provide increased incentives for each side to select the other's cities instead of its missile bases as its primary targets.[26]

One side's possession of an effective defensive system makes the other side's missiles relatively less attractive targets—since they can probably be destroyed once fired, if necessary, they need not be attacked on the ground. This is starkly apparent in the simplest imaginary case in which each side has one missile, and one side has a defensive system providing a 90 percent probability of intercepting the other's missile if it is fired. If it lacked this defensive system, the side now possessing it would have to target the other side's missile as its own first-strike target. But now it may target the other's capital, relying on the defensive system to protect it against retaliation. Though the mathematics are more complicated, the same principle would seem to apply to cases involving more missiles.

What of the side that *lacks* a defensive system but faces an opponent with one? To ensure being able to inflict enough retaliatory damage to deter a first strike by its defended opponent, it will be forced to target virtually all its missiles on its opponent's population centers. In the case of *both* sides having effective, but imperfect, defensive systems, these two effects reinforce each other. The other side's missiles are rendered relatively less attractive as first-strike targets by one's own possession of a missile defense. And one's opponent's cities are rendered even more attractive as targets of retaliation. So the cumulative protective effect for civilians of both sides having 90 percent effective antimissile defensive systems would be *much less* than that provided by a 90 percent reduction of missiles on both sides (with defenses forgone). For the retargeting incentives with effective but imperfect defensive systems are such as to render population centers relatively more attractive as both first- and second-strike targets.

For this reason, as well as the others mentioned, I do not feel that technological defenses provide much hope of rendering nuclear deterrence entirely obsolete. It does not follow, however, that the answer to our question about whether threatening civilians with nuclear destruction is necessary for national defense is a simple "yes." For defense by deterrence is a matter of degree, or probability. Different nuclear policies may deter different possible moves by a nation's adversaries with various degrees of reliability. Whether a given nuclear policy is "necessary" for defense depends on what we seek to defend against and what probability of successful defense would satisfy us.

Nuclear deterrence policies vary along a number of dimensions. The one discussed above, targeting, has been frequently discussed in the literature. In particular, the issue of whether to target military bases and missiles, or cities, has been seen to have considerable moral, as well as strategic, significance.[27] I shall henceforth focus on a less noted and analyzed dimension, that of our willingness to retaliate if attacked with nuclear weapons.

Different imaginable policies reflect varying degrees of likely response, and willingness to respond, to nuclear attack. At one end of the spectrum is the construction of an *automatic retaliator* (such as the doomsday machine of *Dr. Strangelove*) that we could not turn off even if we wanted to, once we had been attacked. Convincing our adversaries that we had such a system in operation would provide maximum credibility of response to nuclear attack. Moving down the ladder of likely response, we might have a semi-automatic retaliatory system, a sincere and declared intention to retaliate, no announced policy about the use of our nuclear arsenal, or a bluff posture, i.e., a public policy of retaliation conjoined with a private determination by our leaders not to retaliate if the occasion should actually arise. Finally, at the end of the scale, is the least threatening posture possible short of dismantling our nuclear weapons–a public policy of *not retaliating* even if attacked.[28] To emphasize that deterrence is a matter of degree, and to trace some moral implications of this fact, let us look more closely at the two extremes along this dimension, the no-retaliation policy and the automatic retaliator.

Even a no-retaliation policy would probably have considerable deterrent value. The Soviets probably would not believe that we really did not now intend to retaliate and, if they did believe it, might with good reason fear that we would change our minds if actually attacked. In other words, there would probably be enough uncertainty about our response to provide us with a considerable degree of what McGeorge Bundy, in his contribution to this volume, calls "existential deterrence." Nonetheless, such a policy would probably make deterrence considerably less reliable than it is now. In any case, it would be a domestic political impossibility, for–regardless of its strategic or moral merits and demerits–it would require the government to spend billions on weapons it was pledged not to use under any circumstances.

The no-retaliation policy would mainly seem attractive to moralists who wish to retain an element of deterrence, but believe that *intending* to retaliate against civilians under any circumstances is impermissible. Earlier, I briefly summarized some reasons for rejecting this belief. It is worth noting, in addition, that a no-retaliation policy does not escape the main moral objection to the US practicing nuclear deterrence–that it imposes serious risks on many Soviet civilians. For, as just mentioned, a no-retaliation policy might well be abandoned in the heat of battle. Further, by decreasing the reliability of deterrence, such a policy might substantially raise the probability of Soviet nuclear attack. This could actually *increase* the net danger to Soviet civilians over that which they experience under present policies.[29]

What of the policy, on the other extreme, of building the automatic retaliator? Because of the dangers of mechanical breakdown and accidental war, and the problem of convincing an adversary that the system is non-recallable, it is doubtful that this would ever, *in practice*, be a morally permissible alternative. But suppose we put these problems aside, by stipulation, and imagined a mistake-proof and perfectly credible automatic retaliation system. Would there be any convincing moral objection to building such a system to obtain maximal deterrence?

Some writers have suggested that it is wrong to create circumstances one knows could lead uncontrollably to disaster.[30] In turning deterrence over to an auto-retaliator, we certainly would be doing this. But the principle that always forbids doing this is too strong. We cannot prohibit all acts that could uncontrollably lead to grave moral wrongs. If we applied this principle on a smaller scale, we would be much too restricted in our actions. We would not parole criminals, because this could lead to more serious crimes being committed. We could not give a political speech for disarmament, because this could cause a riot. More to the point, in the case of nuclear deterrence, any course of action we adopt *could* lead, in a way we could no longer control, to nuclear holocaust. If we built an auto-retaliator, a Soviet version of (fictional) General Jack Ripper could set it off. But it also could be, for all we know, that if we do not build it, the Soviets will eventually attack us. Choices of this sort must be evaluated in terms of how grave and how likely the various possible outcomes are, and what the alternatives are. We cannot proceed simply on the basis of what *could* happen.

There is also a positive argument that suggests it might be permissible, in principle, to build an auto-retaliator. Imagine that the US invents a radio device that 50 percent of the time is able to deflect Soviet ballistic missiles in flight and send them to pre-set targets. For purposes of deterrence, the US programs Soviet cities instead of the oceans as targets for the deflected missiles, and announces this openly. I think we would regard it as morally permissible to build and operate such a defensive system. (Just as we would regard it as permissible for you to use a bullet-deflecting shield against your rival in the elevator, if you had one, even if the deflected bullets might strike the children as well as your rival.) Yet the system seems like an auto-retaliator in virtually all morally relevant respects. The primary purpose of each system is deterrence,[31] and each could be built to preclude our side striking first. Both ensure the truth of the conditional statement, addressed to the Soviets, "If you attack us, your cities will be destroyed," and place control of the fate of both countries out of our hands and into that of our potential adversaries. There is this difference: in our latest scenario, the Soviets, if they attacked, would be destroyed by missiles they built themselves.[32] But is this a morally significant difference? It does not seem so. After all, nuclear deterrence as now practiced would be no less problematic if we were pointing captured (or purchased) Soviet missiles at the USSR. I conclude that, in principle, an ideal automatic nuclear retaliator might be permissible to build. Though I reemphasize that I am not thereby endorsing dangerous launch-on-warning strategies or other similar strategies in the circumstances we actually face.

Our analysis of the no-retaliation and automatic retaliation policies illustrates that there are a variety of different nuclear deterrence policies, each with their own advantages, dangers, and moral characteristics. This reinforces the main conclusion that emerged from our consideration of the Threat and National Defense principles: no absolutist principle – either permissive or prohibitory – is going to provide us with an easy and satisfactory solution to the moral problems posed by nuclear deterrence. Our approach to these problems must be more complex, beginning with the development of ways of assessing, under uncertainty, the dangers and advantages, for all humanity, of the various alternative nuclear deterrence policies.

V. THE SHAPE OF THE PROBLEM

I have argued that a utilitarian balancing of risks and benefits, rather than a rigid application of absolutist principles, should be the starting point of a moral evaluation of nuclear deterrence. But a starting point is only that. There are nonutilitarian dimensions to our problem as well, only some of which have been hinted at above, and all of which require careful attention. We need to know more about such issues as the role of collective responsibility in diluting civilian immunity, the relevance of the fact that the nuclear threats which superpowers impose on one another are reciprocal, and how a right of national defense is created out of individual rights of self-defense. To deal with the risks imposed by the balance of terror on nonnuclear nations and their citizens, special moral analysis of indirect risks and unintended side-effects is required. The moral significance of the *motives* of those who practice deterrence must also be considered; in particular, it is important to know which (if any) practitioners' motives must be purely defensive in order for a deterrent policy to be potentially morally permissible. Finally, there is the very special moral problem of how to take account of the risk of human extinction entailed by the practice of nuclear deterrence.[33]

In conclusion then, the unsolved utilitarian core of the moral problem of nuclear deterrence is itself surrounded by a number of complex and unresolved moral issues. As a result, we possess only one fairly obvious moral imperative concerning the balance of terror – that we should seek unceasingly to dissolve it through negotiations and mutual (eventually multilateral) disarmament.[34] The rest is a series of perplexities as stubborn and difficult as the plight of nervous armed rivals trapped together in a stalled elevator.[35]

NOTES

1 I focus on the morality of United States nuclear policies, but roughly the same analysis might apply to Soviet policies. Also, I only discuss the morality of nuclear deterrence, not the morality of actually waging nuclear war.

2 Adapted from James Mills's novel, *Report to the Commissioner* (New York: Pocket Books, 1973).

3 Perhaps others belong in this group as well. Cf. sec. II of this paper.

4 The question of whether the belief in question is reasonable might be regarded as normative, though not (directly) moral.

5 See Douglas Lackey, "Ethics and Nuclear Deterrence," in *Moral Problems*, edited by James Rachels, 2nd ed. (New York: Harper & Row, 1975), pp. 343–44.

6 This point is also made in Michael Walzer, *Just and Unjust Wars* (New York: Basic Books, 1977), p. 271.

7 According to Bryan Hehir's contribution to this volume, this argument still has considerable influence on Catholic thinking about the moral status of nuclear deterrence.

8 "Some Paradoxes of Deterrence," *Journal of Philosophy* 75 (June 1978): 285–302, sec. II. Compare, however, the rather different view expressed in David Gauthier's contribution to this volume.

9 If in (1), we read "threaten" purely in the risk imposition sense (ignoring the declarative element), the principle is obviously inadequate. For in some situations, every alternative may involve a risk of death for large numbers of innocents.

10 See my "Deterrence, Utility, and Rational Choice," *Theory and Decision* 12 (March 1980): 41–60.

11 Richard Wasserstrom, "On the Morality of War: A Preliminary Inquiry," in *War and Morality*, edited by Richard Wasserstrom (Belmont, Calif.: Wadsworth, 1970), p. 89.

12 See Locke's *Second Treatise of Government*, sec. 8.

13 Wasserstrom, "Morality of War," p. 90.

14 This presupposes that the values in question are not extremely evil. Nazi Germany, for example, had no right to survive as a Nazi state.

15 See Judith Jarvis Thomson, "A Defense of Abortion," *Philosophy & Public Affairs* 1 (Fall 1971): 47–66.

16 For an explanation of how a nation's people might lack the capacity to replace unsatisfactory leaders, see my "Rule by Fear," *Nous* 17 (November 1983): 601–20.

17 See, e.g., the report on the United States v. Holmes lifeboat case, in Philip Davis, ed., *Moral Duty and Legal Responsibility* (New York: Appleton-Century-Crofts, 1966), pp. 102–18.

18 The term "relevant" must be included because moral responsibility for one harm or danger does not render a person morally liable to just any harm or risk that might be imposed. There must be a rational connection between the two, such as the latter being (a) the recognized penalty for creating the former, or (b) a way of alleviating the former. A more precise specification of the Immunity Thesis would spell this out in more detail and would introduce qualifications to take account of justified paternalism and consent of the victim.

19 We may define a "dangerous situation" as one in which not everyone's life can be protected, i.e., in which any action (including inaction) will place (or leave) some people at significant risk of losing their lives.

20 Here two wrongs may make a right. See my "When Two Wrongs Make a Right: An Essay on Business Ethics," *Journal of Business Ethics* 2 (1983): 61–66. Note, however, that this approach does not deal with the nuclear risks – from fallout or off-target missiles – imposed by the superpowers on citizens of other countries. Analysis of this problem would involve consideration of the moral significance of alliances, and of the distinctions between intended and unintended effects of actions, and direct and indirect imposition of risks.

21 With the term "disproportionate" thus interpreted to take account of numbers, nature of the risks, alternatives, and degrees of innocence, we may reword and simplify the principle into the following. (1″) *Final Threat Principle:* It is wrong to disproportionately threaten and impose risks upon other people. The Necessity Claim must also be revised, so that Soviet civilians are described as "partly innocent."

22 One very crude way of doing it would be to choose very broad categories (e.g., military-government, civilians, populations of uninvolved neighboring nations that would be harmed in the event of nuclear war) and to assign to each a weighting-factor between zero (for the guilty or responsible) and one (for the purely innocent bystander), thought to represent the relative degree of immunity of members of the group. These weights would then be incorporated into one's utilitarian analysis.

23 Douglas Lackey, "Missiles and Morals: A Utilitarian Look at Nuclear Deterrence," *Philosophy & Public Affairs* 11 (Summer 1982): 189–231.

24 I reply to Lackey in "Doubts About Unilateral Nuclear Disarmament," *Philosophy & Public Affairs* 12 (Summer 1983): 255–60.

25 See "Current Policy No. 472," United States Department of State, Washington, DC, March 1983.

26 At current levels of offensive nuclear armaments, this may make little practical difference. For as George Quester indicated in his talk at the conference on which this volume is based, there are now enough weapons to cover all sensible targets. But the problems discussed below might become practical at some future time if defensive systems were conjoined with substantial negotiated reductions in offensive systems.

27 See, e.g., Robert Gessert and J. Bryan Hehir, *The New Nuclear Debate* (New York: Council on Religion and International Affairs, 1976); and Arthur Lee Burns, *Ethics and Deterrence* (London: Institute for Strategic Studies, 1969), Adelphi Paper 69.

28 In addition to discussing this policy in my seminars some years ago, I have recently seen it discussed in an unpublished paper by James Sterba.

29 That is, the probability of Soviet attack might increase more than the probability of United States retaliation to Soviet attack decreases. In that case, the probability of United States retaliation, which is the product of these two, would rise.

30 See, e.g., Walter Stein, "The Limits of Nuclear War: Is a Just Deterrence Strategy Possible," in *Peace, The Churches and the Bomb*, edited by James Finn (New York: Council on Religion and International Affairs, 1965), p. 83. Cf. Robert Nozick, *Anarchy, State, and Utopia* (New York: Basic Books, 1974), pp. 126–31.

31 Being only 50 percent effective, it could not physically protect our cities from destruction in an all-out Soviet attack. Hence, warding off an actual attack would probably be only a secondary purpose. Note that, due to its relative lack of defensive effectiveness and its capacity to punish an attacker with his own missiles, the deflector system would not provide its possessor with the retargeting incentives associated with the purely defensive system discussed earlier in this section.

32 They also *fire* the missiles themselves. But, in a sense, they also fire our missiles if they attack our auto-retaliator.

33 See, e.g., Jonathan Schell, *The Fate of the Earth* (New York: Avon Books, 1982), Part II; and Jefferson McMahan, "Nuclear Deterrence and Future Generations," in *Nuclear Weapons and the Future of Humanity*, edited by Avner Cohen and Steven Lee (Rowman and Allanheld, forthcoming).

34 Perhaps, as the National Conference of Catholic Bishops' Ad Hoc Committee on War and Peace suggests in "The Challenge of Peace: God's Promise and Our Response" (*Origins* 12 [October 28, 1982]: 316–17), the permissibility of our practicing nuclear deterrence is *conditional* on our obeying this moral imperative. Though the idea of conditional moral permissibility may sound a bit odd, it makes a good deal of sense when applied in contexts in which a significant danger or harm can be alleviated in the short run only by normally impermissible means, but may be alleviated over the long run by nonobjectionable means. In such contexts,

the permissibility of taking and continuing the short-run "objectionable" means is conditional upon pursuing the nonobjectionable means of solving the long-run problems. Thus, it is permissible for starving men to go on stealing bread only if they seek work, or government aid, or private aid, so as to eliminate the necessity of stealing. Similarly, if the social and economic costs to the local community of closing his polluting factory outweigh the health risks imposed by the pollution, a factory owner may keep his plant operating – but only so long as he pursues the available means of reducing or eliminating the pollution.

35 I wrote this paper while supported by a fellowship for independent study and research from the National Endowment for the Humanities. I thank the Endowment for its support.

10

DEVIL'S BARGAINS
AND THE REAL WORLD

David Lewis

The paradox of deterrence, in a nutshell, is as follows. Your best way to dissuade someone from doing harm may be to threaten retaliation if he does. And idle threats may not suffice. To succeed in deterring, you may have to form a genuine, effective conditional intention. You may have to do something that would indeed leave you disposed to retaliate if, despite your efforts, he does that thing which you sought to deter. It seems that forming the intention to retaliate would be the right thing to do if, all things considered, that was the best way to prevent the harm.

Yet it may also be, foreseeably, that should the occasion arise, it would serve no good purpose to retaliate. It would just inflict further, useless harm. Then it seems that retaliating would be the wrong thing to do. Thus it seems, incredibly, that it may be right to form the conditional intention, wrong to fulfill it. That is the paradox.

What to say? We might conclude, as Kenny and others have, that after all it is wrong to form the intention.[1] We might conclude, as Gauthier does, that after all it is right to fulfill the intention.[2] Either conclusion seems to fly in the face of powerful consequentialist arguments – and the stakes may be as high as you please. Or we might conclude, as Kavka has and as I do, that the truth is indeed remarkable: in such a case it is in truth right to form an intention that it would be wrong to fulfill.[3]

Battle is not squarely joined between Kenny, Gauthier, and Kavka. There are two different paradoxes, depending on what we mean when we speak of right and wrong. We might be speaking of instrumental rationality: of right and wrong ways to serve one's ends, whatever the moral quality of those ends may be. Then the paradox is that, seemingly, it may serve one's ends to form an intention that it would not serve one's ends to fulfill.

Or we might be speaking of morality: of good and evil ways to act or to be, whatever one's actual ends may be. Then the paradox is that, seemingly, it may be a good act to form an intention that it would be an evil act to fulfill; or that a good man might form an intention that it would take a wicked man to fulfill. Gauthier addresses the paradox about rationality; Kenny and Kavka mostly address the paradox about morality.

But it doesn't matter. Suppose that your ends are morally good ones, so that it would be morally right to pursue them in an instrumentally rational way. Suppose also that they are urgent enough that it would be morally wrong to pursue them in an instrumentally irrational way. This may be so – let the stakes be high. Then it doesn't matter whether we speak of right or wrong in an instrumental or in a moral sense. The two senses coincide, the two paradoxes coalesce.

Although I side with Kavka against Gauthier, I admire Gauthier's paper. Most of it is just right. In particular, I applaud the way that he distinguishes paradoxical cases of deterrence from all the other cases there might be. It is not to be thought that just any case of deterrence presents our twofold paradox.

It might be wrong for independent reasons to form the deterrent intention. For it might be too risky; it might be unlikely to succeed; it might carry other costs, e.g., in damaging the relationship between the parties. Or there might be better means of dissuasion available. It might be possible to deter without forming a conditional intention to retaliate: by pretending to have the intention, or by making retaliation automatic, or by creating fear not of intended retaliation but of uncontrolled rage, or simply by leaving it uncertain what might happen. It might be better not to use deterrence at all. If it is wrong to form the deterrent intention, for any of these reasons or any other, then our paradox does not arise.

Alternatively it might be right for independent reasons to fulfill the deterrent intention. Retaliation might not be retaliation pure and simple. It might serve some genuine end. Or it might at least seem to stand some chance of doing so. Or it might be foreseeable that retaliation would at least seem useful at the time. (Any of these things might be so by prearrangement, as when one stakes one's reputation in order to enhance the credibility of one's threat.) If it is right to fulfill the deterrent intention, for any of these reasons or any other, then again our paradox does not arise.

So much for agreement. I disagree with only one small part of Gauthier's paper. But it is the vital part, as he has said. (And vital for his views about many things besides deterrence.) What I reject is his "moving from the rationality of intention to the rationality of action, rather than vice versa." I move *neither* way. I insist on considering the two questions of rationality, or of morality, separately – each on its own merits.

In Section 5 of Gauthier's paper, several objectors come on stage one after another. The preliminary objector recommends the method of pretending to intend. He is misguided. By definition, the paradoxical case is one in which that method won't succeed. You don't make a paradox go away by talking about an unparadoxical case instead.

The first and third objectors both say that it is rational to form the deterrent intention only if it would maximize utility to retaliate, should the occasion arise. (The third objector says more besides, but he has already said too much to be true.) They are wrong: we have seen exactly how it might happen that it is rational to form the intention although it would not maximize utility to retaliate.

I am the second objector, the one who says that "it may be rational to adopt an intention even though it would be, and one knows that it would be, irrational to act on it"; I claim that it may be "rational to commit oneself to irrational behavior" (and also that it may be good to commit oneself to evil behavior). Gauthier claims that my position is no different from his own. Not so; I deny what he firmly asserts, that there may be actions which "in themselves and apart from the context of deterrence would be irrational, but which in that context result from rational intentions and so are rational." (Likewise I deny that there are actions which in themselves and apart from the context of deterrence would be evil, but which result from intentions it was good to adopt and so are good.)

When he is done saying that my view is the same as his own, Gauthier goes on to call it inconsistent. "If our objector accepts deterrent policies, then he cannot consistently reject the actions they require." Why not? I accept the policies as right, I reject the actions they (conditionally) require as wrong. My opposed judgments are consistent because I make them about different things. To form an intention today is one thing. To retaliate tomorrow is something else. If we have a genuine case of paradoxical deterrence, the first is right and the second is wrong.

Gauthier fears we are talking at cross-purposes, and so explains his meaning: "To assess an action as irrational is, in my view, to claim that it should not be . . . performed." Right; I *do* speak his language. What I claim about cases of paradoxical deterrence is that the action of forming the intention to retaliate should be performed, and that the action of retaliating should not be. The sad thing is that the action that should be performed might cause the one that shouldn't, if deterrence fails.

And that was all that Gauthier said against the second objector.[4] I rest my case.

* * *

It seems too quick. Perhaps we have asked the wrong question, and bypassed the heart of the paradox. (Henceforth, I shall have in mind mostly the paradox about morality.) We were asked to judge *actions*. And we were free to pass two opposed judgments because we found two different actions to judge. But there is only one *person* to perform the two actions. What shall we say if asked to judge not the two actions but the one person?

What if the nuclear deterrence practiced by the United States on behalf of all of us is paradoxical deterrence? Suppose it is. Then what are we to think of the men in the missile fields, in the cockpits, in the submarines? What are we to think of the Commander-in-Chief? These men, we suppose, have formed a conditional intention to do their part in retaliating if the country comes under attack. In forming that intention, they did the right thing: *ex hypothesi*, they did just what they had to do to protect their country in the best way possible. They are great patriots, and benefactors of us all. And now that they have formed the intention, they are ready to commit massacres whose like has never been seen. They are ready to inflict terrible devastation when they have no country left to defend, when what they do will accomplish nothing at all except vengeance. *Ex hypothesi*, that is what they even now (conditionally) intend to do. They are evil beyond imagining, fiends in human shape.

They are vengeful. Not because they formed the intention to retaliate; they had a better reason to form the intention, viz., that thereby they protected the country. But after they form it, then they have it; and to have such an intention as they now have – an intention to retaliate uselessly and dreadfully – is to be vengeful.

I myself would not despise them just for being vengeful, though I think many moralists would. For I think their vengefulness is part of a package deal. It is inseparable from their love of their country and their solidarity with their countrymen. Conceptually inseparable, I am inclined to think – could a man really be said to love his country if he were not at all disposed to make its enemies his own? Could he really be said to make them his enemies if he were not at all disposed to harm them? I doubt it. Be that as it may, surely the vengefulness and the solidarity are at least psychologically inseparable for people anything like ourselves. It seems artificial to try to take the package apart, despise part of it, and treasure the rest. And it seems repellent to despise the whole package. I cannot find it in my heart to reproach a fierce Afghan patriot who seeks to avenge his countrymen – I would sooner reproach the moralist who does reproach the Afghan – and I see no call to apply different standards to my own countrymen. True, the vengeful fall short of being utilitarian saints. They are not motivated entirely by impersonal benevolence. But, as philosophers increasingly perceive, the utilitarian saint himself is a repellent figure.[5] If it is the business of moral philosophy to sing his praises, moral philosophy only makes itself repellent. We should be less alienated from the things that real people really treasure. And these include the loyalties and affections from which vengefulness is inseparable.

(The Christians have a special objection to vengefulness. They say that vengeance is the Lord's; a vengeful man pridefully usurps the prerogative of his Superior. We atheists need not concern ourselves with that.)

But whatever may be said in (faint) praise of vengefulness falls far short of exonerating our retaliators, if indeed they would deliver massive nuclear retaliation to accomplish nothing but vengeance. Whatever might be said in favor of some vengefulness, we cannot condone theirs. For it is almost entirely off target. Only a small share of our vengeance would fall only on the enemy who had chosen to attack us, and on his loyal followers (if he has any). For the most part, it would fall on his powerless and disaffected slaves. By and large, these slaves obey him out of fear – like ourselves, they are subject to *his* deterrence – and do not accept him as acting on their behalf. However much can be said in favor of vengeance against our enemy, the slaves are not our enemy. They are our enemy's victims. And this goes for the slaves in Moscow as it does for the slaves in Warsaw and Prague.

(It would be otherwise if the Soviet Union were a popular democracy, as we are, full of citizens who by and large give allegiance to the regime and accept some responsibility – whether or not they are *causally* responsible – for its actions. Vengeance against such a population, whatever else could be said against it, would at least be on target. (Mostly. But of course there are still the infants.) That suggests a distressing conclusion. It *is* otherwise in the reverse direction. Must we conclude that those Soviet officers who stand ready to retaliate against us are in a better moral position, at least in this one way, than their American counterparts? As an American, I hope that isn't so. And I think it isn't, for reasons that will emerge before I finish.)

We are back to our question: what shall we think of one man who has done right and now stands ready to do wrong, who both does his best to protect his country and is prepared to massacre countless slaves, who is benefactor and fiend in one?

Well – I've just told you what to think. He is a man who does right and would do wrong. He is a strange mixture of good and evil. *That* is what to think of him. Isn't that enough? Why do we need a simple, unified, summary judgment?

If there were a last judgment, it would then be necessary to send the whole morally mixed man to Heaven or to Hell. *Then* there would be real need for one unified verdict. I would be very well content to leave the problem of the unified verdict to those who believe in a last judgment. And they would do well to leave it to the Judge.

(I am reminded of a problem put to me years ago by Philippa Foot: The Case of the Conscientious Nazi (or: Does Erring Conscience Excuse?).[6] The Nazi follows his conscience rigorously, resisting all temptation to do otherwise, and what his conscience tells him is to kill the Jews. What a steadfast sense of duty! What a vile notion of where his duty lies! Then what are we to think of him overall? I decline to think *anything* of him overall. I am prepared to recognize and admire and praise his genuine virtues, even when I meet them in the worst of company. (To some extent – his are not my favorite virtues.) I am no less prepared to detest his wicked and dangerous moral errors. But *is he a good man*? I leave this question to the Last Judge. Apart from Him, who needs it?)

Thus the paradox of deterrence in which persons are judged goes the way of the paradox in which actions are judged. Though we have only one person, that person has many moral aspects. We can still have the opposing judgments that seem called for, because we can still make them about different things.

It is even simpler if forming the intention to retaliate is what Kavka has called "self-corruption." That is: if we start with men who are good through and through, and they see that wickedly vengeful men are needed if their country is to be protected in the best way possible, and they volunteer for the tragic sacrifice of virtue, and they make themselves genuinely evil. Then the difference is one of time: first they are good, afterward evil. The question how they are, not at any time in particular, is another piece of nonsense for the Last Judge. But self-corruption is artificial. The more likely thing – if *any* tale of paradoxical deterrence can be called likely – is a deliberate slacking off in self-improvement, with good and evil mingled all along. Then we need simultaneous aspects, rather than successive temporal parts, as the different things to be judged differently. And we need separable aspects, not parts of a close-knit package deal. But if the evil in question is not just vengefulness, but wantonly off-target vengefulness, then I think we have separability enough.

* * *

I find it interesting to compare our paradox of deterrence with another paradoxical case: the Devil's bargain. It is a puzzle for Christians. They think that salvation of souls is of supreme importance, infinitely more valuable than life or pleasure or earthly love or knowledge or any others among the goods we usually cherish. Right; let's adapt a stock example to their new currency. The Devil offers you a bargain; you may give him your soul, and in return he will see to it that seven others are saved. Those seven would not otherwise have stood a very good chance. Here you have an opportunity to serve the very best purpose of all. Will you take it? What should we think of you if you do?

What a noble deed! You will have made the supreme sacrifice that others may live. You will have made the *really* supreme sacrifice – not just given up your earthly life. And you will have bought the seven a gift ever so much more precious than mere life itself. You will be a hero beyond compare.

You will be a damned soul. You will be a genuine damned soul, just like the others around you in the fire. Don't think you will suffer torture with a pure heart – the Devil will not be cheated. You will be despicable in the ways that any other damned soul is. You will be a hater of God. And that, so the Christians say, is the very worst thing that it is possible to be.[7] It seems, incredibly, that if you accept the Devil's bargain you will be each of two opposite things, wondrous hero and damned soul.

What to say? We might conclude that after all you will not be such a splendid hero, perhaps because an embargo against trading with the Devil takes precedence over the service of even the highest ends, or perhaps because you were meant to look after your own salvation rather than salvation generally. Or we might conclude that after all you will not really be a damned soul. *Ex hypothesi* you will be something exactly like one in intrinsic character, but perhaps damnation is a historical rather than an intrinsic property and your state will not be damnation when reached in the way that you reached it. Small comfort! Or we might conclude that, strange to say, you really will be both. In succession: first heroic, then damned.

Which conclusion should a Christian draw? None of them, I think. Instead, the Christian should insist that the case is completely bogus.[8] He should draw no conclusion about what you would be if *per impossibile* the Devil offered his bargain and you accepted it. It is preposterous to suppose that it is in the Devil's power to give or to deny salvation, to buy or sell souls. God offers salvation to all men, who accept or decline it of their own free will. The most the Devil can do is tempt us to damn ourselves.

* * *

I think the most important thing to say about the parallel case of paradoxical nuclear deterrence is exactly the same: the case is completely bogus. The paradox of deterrence is good fun for philosophers. But I think it has nothing to do with the nuclear deterrence that our country practices. It is good that Gauthier and Kavka have insisted that not just any case of deterrence is paradoxical, and good that they have declined to say that our nuclear deterrence is a paradoxical case. But such disclaimers do not go far enough. I am sorry to complain to the Center for Philosophy and Public Policy about their program for this conference, but I think this particular bit of philosophy contributes nothing but mischief to the discussion of public affairs. There is much that philosophers can indeed contribute to our understanding of issues about nuclear deterrence: for instance, to the topics of decision under extreme uncertainty, of incommensurable values, of complicity and innocence of civilians. But I wish we could leave the paradox of deterrence out of it. I am afraid that because paradoxical deterrence is philosophically fascinating, it will be much discussed; and because it is much discussed, it will be mistaken for reality. We don't need a bad reason to be discontented with our predicament and with our country's policies. After all, we have plenty of good reasons. And we don't need a picture of nuclear deterrence that implicitly slanders many decent patriots in the American armed forces and in the White House.

In his contribution to this volume, McGeorge Bundy has a lot to say about our vast ignorance of what would happen in a nuclear war and afterward.[9] It is a vivid awareness of this ignorance, on all sides, that is our great safeguard against nuclear adventures when the time seems as opportune as it ever will be. All that is right. And I add that the ignorance would diminish very little if the war had actually begun.

That is why our nuclear deterrence is not paradoxical. It might indeed be true, if deterrence failed, that our retaliation would serve no good purpose, would accomplish nothing but dreadful and off-target vengeance. It might also be false. What is preposterous, no less preposterous than it would be to think the Devil could grant salvation, is to imagine that anyone could *know* that there was nothing left but vengeance. It is perfectly all right if our retaliators do not intend to inflict useless and off-target vengeance. For the choice whether to deliver that vengeance is not a choice they could ever knowingly face. Whatever happened, the real choice before them would be a harder one.

Imagine the situation of the Commander-in-Chief (de jure or de facto), if deterrence had failed and there had been a large nuclear attack. How much would he know? He would know that there had been many nuclear explosions. He would probably know roughly where some of them had been. He would know something about how much was gone; less, about how much was left. It would be hard for him to know the yield of the explosions, their exact location with respect to vulnerable populations and weapons, which were groundbursts and which airbursts. Perhaps he would know what sort of attack the enemy *could* deliver; but he should not take it for granted that they had done their worst. He should put no faith in scenarios of "wargasm" that flourish mainly because they make for a good read. Neither should he be taken in by circular reasoning to the effect that nuclear war would have to be fought in the most mad and fiendish way possible, because those who fought it would be mad fiends, as is shown by the mad and fiendish way they would fight. Neither should he put his faith in the opposite scenarios of "surgical war." He might indeed have his a priori scenarios for nuclear war—even as you and I do—but he ought to put little trust in any of them.

Even if, *per impossibile*, he knew exactly what attack had been delivered, he would still not know how much would be left when its effects had run their course. He would probably not know which way the winds were blowing, or where there had been fog. And he would not know whether to believe all the prophecies that indirect effects – economic disruption, disabling despair, anarchy, plague – would prove more lethal than the blast and fire and fallout. He might have his opinions on the question – even as you and I do – but he ought to know that such opinions are sheer speculation. In short, he would be far from knowing whether or not he had a country left to protect.

He would be far from knowing what would best protect his country, if it still exists. Maybe surrender would be best. But maybe it would be best to destroy the enemy's unfired strategic nuclear weapons – *some* would be unfired, who knows how many. Maybe an attempt at tit-for-tat retaliation would offer the best hope of stopping the war before all was lost. Maybe it would be useful to destroy the weapons and the resources that could give the enemy command over the affairs of the postwar world. A nuclear counterattack would not be *known* to be useless. It might indeed be useless; or it might serve a good purpose. It might even be the only way to save the country. The duty of the Commander-in-Chief is to protect his country, in war no less than in peace. He would have to consider whether some sort of counterattack might be the best way to disarm the enemy, to stop the war, or to give the country some chance of surviving the years ahead. It might well be so. But there could be no certainty that a counterattack would accomplish these things. And it would be risky: it might elicit a further attack that could have been avoided. And it would massacre vast numbers of the enemy's slaves, who are our fellow-victims; there would be no telling how many. And it would devastate a great part of the earth. And if our country were doomed already, the counterattack and its dreadful harm would be all in vain. The decision whether to launch a counterattack, or what sort of counterattack to launch, would be a hard one indeed. It would be a terrible decision under extreme uncertainty, with extremely high stakes and incommensurable values. I say that it might well be right to launch the counterattack: instrumentally rational and morally right, all things considered. As right, that is, as any choice could be in so desperate and tragic a predicament.[10]

Likewise for the men in the missile fields, in the cockpits, and in the submarines. They too would know what vital purposes a counterattack might serve, if all was not yet lost; and they too would know the harms and risks that it would bring. They would know even less than the Commander-in-Chief about the attack that had taken place. But they would know that their orders come from someone whose aims are much the same as theirs, who is probably somewhat better informed than they are, and whose orders afford their only hope of coordinated action. I say that it would be right for them to obey orders to fire: instrumentally rational and morally right, all things considered. As right, that is, as any choice could be in so desperate and tragic a predicament.

(Also, they have sworn obedience, at least if the Commander-in-Chief from whom they have their orders is so de jure. I do not at all mean to set aside reasons of honor as morally weightless, but I do think that they fade into insignificance when the stakes get high enough. Consequentialism is all wrong as everyday ethics, right as a limiting case. So I rest my argument on the consequential reasons why it would be right to obey.)

Suppose that our retaliators intend to launch a counterattack if and only if it would be right to do so; and that they intend to launch only the right sort of counterattack. Then what they conditionally intend to do if deterrence fails is no more than what it would be right for them to do. Then our nuclear deterrence is not paradoxical. Nor can they be reproached for intending to retaliate, if they intend to do no more than would be right. They are right so to intend, and they would be right to fulfill their intentions. I think that this is the actual case: that our retaliators rightly intend to do no more than would be right. I certainly hope that this is so.

But suppose it is not so. Suppose instead that our retaliators intend to launch a counterattack whether or not it would be right, or that they intend to launch more of a counterattack than could possibly be right. They would be wicked in so intending, even if they became wicked or remained wicked for admirable reasons, and even if there was much good mixed in with their wickedness. They would also be a danger to mankind, and we ought to remove them from their posts at once. But our nuclear deterrence *still* would not be paradoxical. For on this supposition, I say that it was wrong for them ever to form such intentions. They would have been mistaken when they thought it beneficial to implant wicked intentions in themselves. There is no paradox if they have wrongly formed an intention that it would be wrong to fulfill.

Their intentions would be wrong to form not because they would be wrong to fulfill, but because they present a needless danger. Here I rely on a premise of fact: that no such intentions are needed to provide deterrence. The intention to launch a counterattack only if, and only to the extent that, it is right provides deterrence galore. We don't need "assured destruction." The sort of counterattack that might serve good purpose would be a dreadful retaliation as well. If that is our only threat, maybe we threaten less-than-assured less-than-destruction, but our threat remains fearsome. Take an extreme case: suppose we attacked nothing but the enemy's unfired strategic nuclear weapons (plus a lot of empty holes, unless we had better information than seems likely) and suppose we attacked those in the very most "surgical" way. We would still destroy much more than the weapons, for the enemy has by no means cooperated in the separation of targets. And would he not fear to lose the weapons, even if he stood to lose nothing else? He would probably think he had need of them, no less after he had provoked our anger than before.

Anyway, we can threaten worse retaliation than we really intend. For he cannot know just what we do intend, and he cannot know that we would not do worse when angered than we intend beforehand. Again I join Bundy in praise of uncertainty, and in insisting that the owners of an arsenal like ours just do not have any problem in looking scary.

Thirty-five years ago, our nuclear threat was puny by present standards. Yet we thought it a convincing deterrent, and I dare say we were right. In those days, we deterred Stalin himself. Are his successors bolder desperadoes than he? To be sure, the *balance* of threats has changed since then; and advocates of a larger arsenal do claim that an uneven balance is what deters, rather than the size of our threat; but why should that be so?

No; our enemies are cowards. Their cautious adventures scare *us* — because we too are cowards, well and truly deterred, and a good thing too — but they really do not act like people whom it is difficult to deter.

* * *

Kavka and Kenny have suggested that although the deterrent threat to launch a counterattack if, and to the extent that, it was right is not itself paradoxical, yet paradoxical deterrence must lurk in the background.[11] Whatever we might do on the lower rungs of the ladder of nuclear escalation, doesn't it remain true that we intend to respond to an all-out countervalue salvo with a like salvo of our own? And wouldn't that be useless off-target vengeance? And isn't it this ultimate threat that affords our only slim hope of staying on the lower rungs?

I don't think so. I agree that an all-out retaliatory salvo could be nothing but vengeance. It could not possibly be right. But I hope and believe that we intend no such thing. If we did receive an all-out salvo, we could not recognize it as such. Our counterattack might in fact be nothing but useless and off-target venegance on behalf of the doomed, but we would nevertheless launch it in the hope that it would serve a purpose, and we might well be right to do so.

And if I am wrong, and we do intend to deliver a useless all-out salvo if worst comes to worst, then there is still no paradox. It is wrong to form or retain such an intention, unless that intention is needed for deterrence. I say that our deterrence, even if it is deterrence of escalation during nuclear war, needs no such intention. In the very worst case as in other cases, the counterattack thought to serve a good purpose would be retaliation enough, and the threat of it would afford deterrence enough.

I said that I hope and believe we do not intend to respond to even the worst nuclear attack by launching an all-out salvo, a counterattack that would be good for nothing but off-target vengeance. – But do we not have plans for just such salvos? – We do: our war plan calls them "massive attack options."[12] But do not infer our intentions from our plans. I suppose that our planmakers are told that it is not for them to set national policy, and that it is better to have too many options than too few; and obligingly they churn out all sorts of plans. These include some very frightening plans that it would be wrong to carry out, no matter what had happened. It is no waste of effort if they produce plans that no one ever intends to follow. For one thing, the making of many plans contributes to our own understanding of nuclear warfare.[13] Further, the plans themselves are part of our deterrent – after all, they do not come bearing the label "will not be followed no matter what." They are no secret, except in their details. If a scholar in Canberra can write about our massive attack options in the unclassified article I cited, surely the enemy is no less well informed. And if you and I find these plans frightening, even doubting as we should that anyone intends to carry them out, surely the enemy finds them no less frightening.

*   *   *

I find myself in unwelcome company. I seem to be agreeing with the views of the war-fighters. I say, as they do, that nuclear retaliation might serve a useful purpose, might accomplish something better than vengeance. I say, as they do, that the right retaliation would be a counterattack meant to accomplish something useful. I say, as they do, that such retaliation is the only sort we ought to intend. I say, as they do, that if it is our policy to deliver useless vengeance, then our policy is immoral and our retaliators are wicked.

It is true that I have taken a leaf from the war-fighters' book. But it is a loose-leaf book, and I insist that I have left most of it behind. Their position is founded on confidence: confidence in certain remarkably optimistic scenarios for nuclear war. Mine is founded rather on skepticism: even-handed skepticism, directed against optimistic and pessimistic scenarios alike. They say that victory is possible.[14] (Provided, of course, that their views about strategy and procurement gain acceptance.) I would not go so far as to speak of "victory," but I do take an interest in outcomes that would be noticeably better than total destruction. I would not go so far as to say that such outcomes are "possible" (except in the philosophers' sense, in which it is also possible that pigs have wings); but I do say that we cannot have much confidence that they are not possible, wherefore it might well be right to try for them even by means of a nuclear counterattack.

It's not that they go in for optimisim generally, whereas I am a general skeptic. They are optimistic about success in nuclear war, something of which we have next to no experience; they are skeptical about success in deterrence, something of which we have a great deal of experience. With me it's the other way around.

They say that deterrence is difficult, so that one main reason to intend only useful retaliation is that otherwise our threats will be incredible and the enemy will not be deterred. I say that deterrence is easy, given an arsenal like ours and an enemy like ours. Credibility is not a worry. At least, not if we limit the scope of our nuclear deterrence; and probably not even if we extend it beyond (what I would take to be) prudent limits. My reason for intending only useful retaliation has nothing to do with credibility. My reason is that if deterrence failed, it would be better not to do a lot of useless harm.

Bundy has suggested that debates about how to fight a nuclear war are not what they seem to be; really, they are debates about criteria for the procurement of weapons.[15] Often so, I'm sure; but not in my case. I have been talking about how we ought to intend to use whatever weapons we might have. What I have said is consistent with a wide range of positions on questions of procurement. Not with all conceivable positions – it is possible to favor weapons that are no good for anything except useless vengeance, it is possible to favor skimping on command and control – but with all that stand any serious chance of adoption by an American government, and with more besides. It is otherwise with the war-fighters. Their position is indeed part of a case for procurement. They have higher hopes and more confidence than I about what a counterattack could accomplish, if only the weapons were right. Therefore it is more important to them than it is to me that the weapons should be right.

NOTES

1 Anthony Kenny, "Counterforce and Countervalue," in *Nuclear Weapons and Christian Conscience*, edited by Walter Stein (London: The Merlin Press, 1965).

2 David Gauthier, "Deterrence, Maximization, and Rationality," in this volume. My quotations come from the preliminary version of the paper which Gauthier gave at the Maryland conference on "Nuclear Deterrence: Moral and Political Issues," at which the papers in this volume were first presented. Not all of these quotations appear in his final version.

3 Gregory S. Kavka, "Some Paradoxes of Deterrence," *Journal of Philosophy* 75 (1978): 285–302; see also Kavka, "Nuclear Deterrence: Some Moral Perplexities," in this volume.

4 There is something else to be said on Gauthier's side, however, as follows. What is it to "implant an intention" in yourself? It's not enough just to mutter "I shall . . . " in the right tone of voice! An intention seems to be some sort of compound of belief and desire concerning your own future actions. To implant an intention, you would have to implant something that would motivate you to fulfill it. But then this something would be a desire that would make it instrumentally rational to fulfill the intention. So if it were instrumentally rational to implant the intention, and if you *did* implant it, then it would be instrumentally rational to fulfill it. (Of course, this argument concerns only the paradox about rationality, not the paradox about

morality.) I reply thus. If you implant the intention by implanting a desire that fails to cohere rationally with the rest of your desires, then fulfilling the intention is instrumentally rational only in a minimal sense: it does fulfill a desire you have, but it cannot be said to serve your system of desires taken as a whole. For related discussion of the difficulty of implanting an intention that would not cohere with your other desires, see Gregory S. Kavka, "The Toxin Puzzle," *Analysis* 43 (1983): 33–36.

5 See Susan Wolf, "Moral Saints," *Journal of Philosophy* 79 (1982): 419–39.

6 A related question, whether to say that a murderer who boldly faces danger in order to commit his vicious crime has acted courageously, comes in for discussion in Philippa Foot, "Virtues and Vices," in her *Virtues and Vices and Other Essays in Moral Philosophy* (Berkeley and Los Angeles: University of California Press, 1978).

7 Not I; I only take it as a hypothesis of the case. My own opinion is rather that of Mill and McTaggart: see John Stuart Mill, *An Examination of Sir William Hamilton's Philosophy* (London: Longmans, Green, Reader, & Dyer, 1865), chap. VII; and J. M. E. McTaggart, *Some Dogmas of Religion* (London: Edward Arnold & Co., 1906), secs. 174–77.

8 At this point I have consulted some who are more expert than I about Christian thought; I am grateful to Robert M. Adams, Mark Johnston, and Ewart Lewis. Adams notes a complication. The case of an *honest* Devil's bargain is bogus, but the case of a fraudulent one is not. Then the thing for a Christian to say resembles our first conclusion. The man who accepts the fraudulent bargain is reprehensible. He was gullible; what's worse, he lacked faith, because he was ready to suspect God of allowing the Devil to buy and sell souls.

9 McGeorge Bundy, "Existential Deterrence and Its Consequences," in this volume.

10 I do not mean that it is "objectively" right to launch a counterattack: that is, that doing so would in fact produce the best consequences. Maybe so, but I don't know it. In fact, it is my main point that such things cannot be known. Rather, I mean that it might well be "subjectively" right: that it might well be the best gamble, taking account of the full range of uncertainty about what had already happened and about what actions would produce what outcomes. To understand the distinction, imagine that an epidemic is raging and you have inadvertently locked the entire supply of antitoxin in a safe and lost the combination. The subjectively right thing to do might well be to hunt up a skilled safecracker, even if finding him would take a week you can ill afford. That would be objectively wrong. The objectively right thing to do would be to dial 44-0223-65979 straightway, for that is the unknown combination that would in fact open the safe. The objective wrongness of going off to find a safecracker is no reason – or it is merely an "objective reason" – not to do it. Throughout this paper, I have been speaking always of subjective, never of objective, rightness. But take care: subjective rightness is only one department of reason and morality. What you do may be the best gamble, given your beliefs; it may in that sense be rational and right; but it may in a broader (but still subjective) sense be irrational and wrong, if the beliefs on which your actions are premised are themselves irrational given your evidence.

11 Kavka, in discussion; Kenny, "Counterforce and Countervalue."

12 Desmond Ball, "U.S. Strategic Forces: How Would They Be Used?" *International Security* 7 (1983): 31–60.

13 And thereby makes a welcome contribution to our self-deterrence; as witness the tale of McNamara's unsettling briefing at SAC headquarters, told in Gregg Herken, "The Nuclear Gnostics," in this volume.

14 Colin S. Gray and Keith Payne, "Victory Is Possible," *Foreign Policy* 39 (1980): 14–27.

15 Bundy, "Existential Deterrence."

11

RESPONSES TO THE PARADOX OF DETERRENCE

Deterrent Intentions and Retaliatory Actions
Gregory S. Kavka

An intention to perform an action at a later time may have two sorts of effects. It may produce the act itself and physical acts performed by the agent as a means to, or preparations for, the act. These acts, and their effects, I shall call the *direct effects* of the intention. An intention may also produce effects independent of its actually being carried out, since the existence of the intention itself, when perceived, may lead other agents to act in various ways – to praise or punish the intender; to deter, prevent, or encourage the intended action; and so on. I shall call such acts, and their effects, *autonomous* effects of the intention.

Usually the direct effects of an intention are more important than its autonomous effects. But this is not always the case. In particular, there are cases in which the expected direct effects of an intention are undesirable (from the agent's point of view), but the expected autonomous effects are so desirable as to render the total package of effects desirable.[1] Intentions such as these may be labeled *problematic*, because they seem desirable to have, but not to carry out (once their autonomous effects have been produced). An important class of problematic intentions consists of what I have elsewhere dubbed *deterrent intentions*.[2] These are conditional intentions whose form is represented by the schema "If A does X, which I do not want, I shall do retaliatory act Y, which neither of us wants."[3] The point of such an intention is to bring about the desirable autonomous effect of deterring A's doing X, thus preventing the occasion for the performance of the undesired retaliatory act (the main direct effect) from arising.

Are deterrent intentions, and the retaliatory acts which they are the (conditional) intentions to perform, rational? More generally, are problematic intentions and their target actions rational? David Gauthier, in his contribution to this volume, suggests they are. He, as do I, rejects the view that the relevant intention is irrational because its target act would be irrational. Instead, he turns this view around and says that the target act is rational because the intention to perform it is. Thus, he and the supporters of the view we both reject share the assumption that the rationality of a deterrent intention and of its retaliatory target act must stand or fall together. I (and David Lewis) reject this assumption in favor of a more complicated view of the matter. The act of forming a deterrent (or, more generally, a problematic) intention is rational because of its desirable effects,[4] but performing the target action is not rational, because of its undesirable effects.[5] The intention itself, or the state of having it, has a more ambiguous status. It is rational in that it is the outcome of the rational act of forming it, and it is irrational in that it is itself the intention to perform an irrational action.[6]

The desire to avoid this apparently ambiguous, even paradoxical, conclusion might drive us back to Gauthier's position. But the price we would pay is heavy. It seems to me that some of whatever initial plausibility attaches to Gauthier's view is based on a simple but natural mistake. We are used to thinking of deterrence operating in repeatable contexts – like that of criminal punishment – where one's future credibility and ability to deter depends heavily upon one's willingness to carry out one's retaliatory threats once deterrence has failed in the case at hand. Habituated to thinking in this way, we may find it easy to suppose retaliatory actions following failed deterrence rational, as Gauthier suggests, in problematic situations as well. But the difference between the two cases is crucial for rationality. The long-range deterrent effects which may render retaliation rational in the repeatable context are, by definition, either absent or outweighed in the problematic deterrent situation. Thus, the case for the rationality of retaliation in such situations rests entirely on the contested assumption that the rationality of the intention and of its target act must be evaluated together.

Here is an argument against that assumption. Consider a hypothetical situation involving a problematic intention of a different kind – an unconditional intention with a desired autonomous effect other than deterrence.[7] You are offered a million dollars to be paid tomorrow morning, if at midnight tonight you intend to drink a vial of toxin tomorrow afternoon that will make you very sick for a day. If you believe the offer and believe that the offerers can really tell whether, at midnight, you have the requisite intention, you would clearly have a good reason (in fact, a million good reasons) to form that intention. Suppose that you do so and bank the money the next morning – cashing in the desired autonomous effect of your intention. Would it then be rational for you to carry out your intention and drink the toxin? Surely not. If not, we have a divergence between the rationality of forming a problematic intention and the rationality of carrying it out. And the assumption shared by Gauthier and our common opponents is shattered.[8] Seeing no valid reason to suppose that the assumption still holds in the special case of problematic *deterrent* intentions, I stand by my original view despite Gauthier's challenge.

Gauthier's reluctance to sever the evaluation of intentions and the evaluation of their target actions does, however, reflect a valid point. There are conceptual ties between rational intention and action. In particular, the intentions of a perfectly rational agent must be in accordance with her reasons for action. Hence, she will be *unable* to intend (what she views as) undesirable retaliation, even if she regards so intending as rational and valuable. To come to possess the desired deterrent intention, she must either alter her beliefs and values so she no longer views retaliation as undesirable, or make herself less rational.[9]

Some may find this too paradoxical a result to stomach. I regard it, instead, as revealing something deep and interesting about deterrent intentions. In any case, accepting this odd-sounding conclusion is surely preferable to the alternatives of (1) ignoring the autonomous effects of deterrent intentions, or (2) endorsing the rationality of drinking the toxin after pocketing the million.

What is the relevance, for nuclear deterrence, of these abstract ruminations about deterrent intentions and retaliatory actions? David Lewis says there is little or none, since in the most likely nuclear war scenarios the potential retaliating agents would never be in a position to know that retaliation would have undesirable effects on the whole. I *partly* agree with him. In an earlier paper, I noted that the paradoxes of deterrence arise only in *special deterrent situations*, which are a subclass of the situations involving problematic deterrent intentions. And the nuclear war scenario I used to illustrate such a situation was the highly unlikely one of a massive first strike obliterating one's homeland and confronting the surviving potential retaliators (in submarines, airborne command centers, or underground shelters) with the decision whether to obliterate the attacking nation in retaliation.[10] Nonetheless, it seems to me highly likely that parts of our contingency nuclear war plans do involve obliteration-type retaliation against the Soviets. (This belief is reinforced by George Quester's remarks to the effect that the US has weapons assigned to cover virtually every conceivable military *and industrial* target in the USSR – with the obliteration of Soviet society the predictable result of a high percentage of these targets being hit.[11]) If this is so, and we identify national intentions with official war plans conjoined with the means for carrying them out, then our nation has the conditional intention to obliterate Soviet society should certain contingencies arise. Hence the paradoxes concerning problematic deterrent intentions do apply to some, though not all, of our nuclear weapons policies and should be noted and understood by those concerned about the rationality and morality of these policies.

There is, however, a further problem here. The paradoxes of deterrence involve agents' *intentions*, and it is rather unclear what constitutes having an intention when the agent is a nation rather than an individual. Declared national policies, even when backed by plans and capacities to put them into effect, need not constitute genuine national intentions, since they may be mere postures that the country's leaders do not intend to carry out if the occasion should arise. Are we then to identify national intentions with those of the nation's citizens, or its political leaders, or some other elite group? But there are likely to be contrary intentions within and among each of these various groups. Further, it is doubtful that even *all* group members sharing the intention to do their part in a joint undertaking is always sufficient to constitute a group intention. For even if the physical means of carrying out the intention are available, and each fully intends to do his best, it may be apparent that things are not sufficiently organized to get the job done. Thus, for example, there may be enough shelters to protect all, and each may be committed to doing his part to get himself and others into shelters in the event of attack. But if it is patently obvious to most that there are not sufficient workable organizational and operational plans to get people into shelters, so that chaos would be the likely actual result of attack, the nation could hardly be said to genuinely intend to protect itself and its citizens by means of shelters, if attacked. So even unanimous individual intentions plus physical capability need not add up to a group intention.

On the other hand, there may conceivably be a group intention to do X even if *no* individual member of the group intends to do (his part of) X. Suppose each member of a society secretly opposes the official policy of nuclear retaliation, but wrongly believes that all others favor that policy. Each intends not to do his part in retaliating, should the occasion arise. But it is predictable that enough would do their parts, if the occasion arose, because of the pressure of the perceived expectations of their comrades, and the (perhaps true!) belief that if one did not act (e.g., did not press the button firing the missile), someone else surely would.[12] In this case, it would seem appropriate to ascribe the intention to retaliate to the nation, though none of its members at present share that intention.

Even if we could develop appropriate criteria for ascribing intentions to nations and other groups, we would still have to carefully consider whether the *same* principles of moral and rational appraisal apply to individual and group intentions. In the meantime, we may have to settle for tentative and limited conclusions about the rationality and morality of nuclear deterrence. Among these conclusions is the observation that some of our deterrent policies may well involve us in rational and moral paradoxes. Nor can these paradoxes truly be avoided by stretching the extension of the term "rational," or by ignoring the implications of the wide scope of our plans for possible nuclear retaliation.[13]

Afterthoughts
David Gauthier

As a preliminary point, let me note that I do not deny that it may be rational to adopt an intention but not act on it. But when this is so, conditions must change from those envisaged in adopting the intention. What I do deny is that it can be rational to adopt an intention and then rational to abandon it should the very conditions envisaged in adopting it come to pass. That one adopted the intention in the hope that those conditions would not come to pass does not affect the argument. If it is rational for me to adopt an intention to do x in circumstances c, and if c come about, and if nothing relevant to the adoption of the intention is changed save what must be changed with the coming about of c (such as my hope of avoiding c), then it is rational for me to carry out x.

I state in Chapter 8, sec. 5, that "to assess an action as irrational is to claim that it should not be, or have been, performed." This is too strong, but only in the failure to distinguish rationality of choice from rationality of manner. I may act in an irrational manner–refusing to reflect or deliberate, carried away by passion. Although it is usually the case that one should not so act, it need not be. It may be that if I act in a rational manner– consider alternatives, deliberate about them, keep passion in its place–I shall choose irrationally. I may be the type of person whose native hue of resolution is always sicklied o'er with the pale cast of thought. Knowing this, I may realize that in some circumstances, if I deliberate, I shall hesitate and be lost. I may then, quite rationally, seek to ensure that I act in an irrational manner.

If an objector were to claim that to act on a nonmaximizing intention is to act in an irrational *manner*, then, although I should dispute the appropriateness of assimilating such behavior to failing to deliberate or being overcome by passion, I should not find myself fundamentally in disagreement as long as he allowed that it could be rational so to act, and that in some circumstances one should so act, and one chose rationally in so acting.

None of this touches the objection raised by David Lewis.[14] For he embraces a position I failed to consider. I took the objector who claims that a rational policy may involve irrational actions to be nevertheless endorsing the actions as part of the policy. This is not Lewis's view. He endorses the policy as rational and rejects the actions as irrational. Yes, he says, it is rational to form a conditional, nonmaximizing intention. But no, he says, it is not rational to act on that intention should the condition be met. Both rationally and morally, the formation of the intention is right; both rationally and morally, the execution of the intention given the condition is wrong. Forming the intention is one thing; carrying it out is another; because they are different things, opposed judgments about them are consistent.

And what are we to think of those who both form and execute, or are willing to execute, such intentions? Lewis is very clear: "They are great patriots and benefactors of us all" in forming the intentions; "They are evil beyond imagining, fiends in human shape" in being ready to carry them out. Only a last judgment would, in Lewis's view, create the need for a unified verdict.

Lewis seems committed to a schizophrenic view of rationality and morality. But suppose I accept it. Suppose that I think it would be wrong, irrational (we may leave morality to one side here), to act on the intention to RETAL, given ADVANT. Suppose that I am a rational actor, considering now what to do should I find myself faced with ADVANT. If I know, as Lewis supposes that I do, that it would be irrational for me to RETAL given ADVANT, then is it *possible* for me to form the intention to RETAL? It seems clear to me that it is not possible. If Lewis were to say that it *would* be rational for me to form the intention to RETAL, if I *could*, then I could understand, although not accept, his position. But I find that I do not understand it.

Forming an intention and carrying it out are indeed separate actions. But we may not then infer that a rational or moral assessment of one is entirely separate from an assessment of the other. I suppose that any such assessment proceeds from the standpoint of an actor who, given a basis for action in his preferences and beliefs, relates the possible actions that may contribute to the satisfaction of his preferences to a principle that provides that, if he chooses only actions conforming to the principle, he may expect a utility greater than if he chooses on any other basis. Overall utility maximization is his objective.

If his principle selects those actions that maximize his expected utility, then he will not always find that he may expect a greater overall utility than if he were to choose on some other basis. Use of such a principle may affect his opportunities unfavorably. This has been the core of my argument. His maximizing choices then stand in the way of his maximizing goal. The choices fail to express the unified concern that characterizes an individual, that distinguishes him from a mere aggregation. If utilitarianism fails to take individuals seriously by uniting their separate concerns into a single whole, performance-maximization also fails to take individuals seriously by dividing their unified concerns into disparate parts.

NOTES

1 Desirable relative to available alternatives, that is. (And, of course, desirable from the agent's current viewpoint.)

2 See my "Some Paradoxes of Deterrence," *Journal of Philosophy* 75 (June 1978): 290.

3 Not all deterrent intentions are problematic, since Y may be too much worse than X, given the likelihood of successful deterrence via possession of the intention. Here, however, I shall be concerned with the subclass of deterrent intentions that are also problematic.

4 This claim must be qualified in a way that I did not explicitly qualify it in "Some Paradoxes." The possibly negative expected effects of forming the intention (e.g., undesirable changes in the agent's character) must be weighed in the balance with the expected direct effects and the expected autonomous effects. Only if the latter are good enough to outweigh both of the former together is the act of forming the intention rational.

5 See "Some Paradoxes," pp. 288–91.

6 See "Some Paradoxes," p. 293.

7 This situation is described and discussed in more detail in my "The Toxin Puzzle," *Analysis* 43 (January 1983): 33–36.

8 In "Afterthoughts," this volume, Gauthier allows that "it may be rational to adopt an intention but not act on it. But when this is so, conditions must change from those envisaged in adopting the intention." Note, however, that in the toxin case, conditions have *not* changed in this manner.

9 See "Some Paradoxes," secs. III–IV. Note that, in the course of this process, the initially irrational target act may *become rational*, relative to the agent's (revised) beliefs and values.

10 "Some Paradoxes," pp. 286–87.

11 Quester made these remarks at the conference on "Nuclear Deterrence: Moral and Political Issues," which was the origin of this volume. On this point, see also Desmond Ball, "U.S. Strategic Forces: How Would They Be Used?" *International Security* 7, no. 3 (Winter 1982–83): 31–60.

12 For further analysis of situations having this odd structure, see my "Rule by Fear," *Nous* 17 (November 1983): 601–20.

13 This paper was written while I was supported by a fellowship for independent study and research from the National Endowment for the Humanities. I thank the Endowment for its support.

14 In this and the ensuing paragraphs I refer to and quote from Lewis's arguments in "Devil's Bargains and the Real World," this volume.

INDEX

NOTES ON CONTRIBUTORS

McGeorge Bundy was National Security Advisor to President Kennedy during the Vietnam War and later served as President of the Ford Foundation. Currently Professor of History at New York University, he coauthored the influential recent article "Nuclear Weapons and the Atlantic Alliance" (*Foreign Affairs*, Spring 1982).

David Gauthier, Professor of Philosophy at the University of Pittsburgh, is well known for his work using the concepts of game theory and decision analysis in moral and political philosophy. His many publications include *The Logic of Leviathan* and *Practical Reasoning*.

William Greider was formerly *Washington Post* Assistant Managing Editor for National News and is currently National Editor of *Rolling Stone*. He is perhaps best known for his 1981 article, "The Education of David Stockman," which appeared in the *Atlantic*.

J. Bryan Hehir is Director of the Office of International Justice and Peace of the U.S. Catholic Conference, where he played an instrumental role in drafting the U.S. bishops' pastoral letter on nuclear deterrence. He is the recent recipient of a MacArthur fellowship.

Gregg Herken is Associate Professor of History at Yale University. He is the author of *The Winning Weapon: The Atomic Bomb in the Cold War* and numerous articles on nuclear diplomacy.

Gregory S. Kavka is Associate Professor of Philosophy at the University of California at Irvine. His publications include several articles on philosophical problems of deterrence theory, among these, "Some Paradoxes of Deterrence" (*Journal of Philosophy*) and "Deterrence, Utility, and Rational Choice" (*Theory and Decision*).

Christopher M. Lehman is Special Assistant to the President for National Security Affairs at the National Security Council. He is the author of several works on strategic policy and defense issues.

David Lewis, Professor of Philosophy at Princeton University, is well known among philosophers for his work in decision analysis and conflict theory. These topics are discussed in several articles and in his book, *Convention: A Philosophical Study.*

George H. Quester is Professor and Chairman in the Department of Government and Politics at the University of Maryland. His books on deterrence include *Deterrence Before Hiroshima, Nuclear Diplomacy: The First Twenty-Five Years,* and *Offense and Defense in the International System.*

George Sher, Associate Professor of Philosophy at the University of Vermont, has written widely on ethics and social and political philosophy.